THE INTIMATE CRITIQUE

THE INTIMATE CRITIQUE

Autobiographical Literary

Criticism

*

Edited by

Diane P. Freedman,

Olivia Frey, &

Frances Murphy Zauhar

Duke University Press

Durham and London

1993

© 1993 Duke University Press
All rights reserved
Printed in the United States of America
on acid-free paper ∞
Typeset in Perpetua by Keystone Typesetting, Inc.
Library of Congress Cataloging-in-Publication Data
The intimate critique : autobiographical literary criticism / edited
by Diane P. Freedman, Olivia Frey, and Frances Murphy Zauhar.
Includes bibliographical references.
ISBN 0-8223-1285-9.—ISBN 0-8223-1292-1 (pbk.)
1. American literature—History and criticism—Theory, etc.
2. English literature—History and criticism—Theory, etc.
3. Reader-response criticism. 4. Authors and readers. 5. Critics—
Biography. 6. Autobiography. I. Freedman, Diane P. II. Frey,
Olivia. III. Zauhar, Frances Murphy.
PS25.I57   1993
810.9—dc20   92-28049 CIP
Second printing, 1995

CONTENTS

ACKNOWLEDG-

MENTS

We have received much help from our contributors as we have put together this book, and we are grateful to them. But there are others whose voices are not directly represented in this book, whom we also want to thank. Frances especially wants to thank Nancy Chadburn, Anne-Marie Gronhovd, Lisa Heldke, and Colette Hyman, her colleagues at Gustavus Adolphus college, who listened to her essay and provided helpful feedback as well as vital emotional support and good humor. Diane thanks Skidmore College for the faculty research grants which in part supported this project. She also thanks an assortment of faculty and present and former graduate students at the University of Washington for listening to her self-assertions and critical confessions. Olivia thanks Jane Tompkins and Linda Hunter, who always had words of encouragement, and her feminist colleagues at St. Olaf College. We all thank Reynolds Smith, who believed in the project from the first. Finally, we thank the hundreds of women who have attended our conference sessions and also the Midwest Modern Language Association, which accepted our proposals for sessions when other organizations were skeptical. Those who made our conference sessions possible, writers not included in this anthology, and an even larger number of other readers and writers have supported our work by sharing it, by doing it. We hope that the work of this book can likewise support theirs.

The following have appeared in other books or journals. Grateful acknowledgment is made to the publishers and authors for permission to reprint them here.

"Breaking Silence: *The Woman Warrior*," by Shirley Nelson Garner, appered in *Hurricane Alice* (Fall–Winter 1983–84).

"What's in a Name?" by Henry Louis Gates, Jr., appeared in *Dissent* 35–36 (1988–89).

"Somebody Must Say These Things: An Essay for My Mother," by Melody Graulich, appeared in *Women's Studies Quarterly* 13 nos. 3&4 (Fall–Winter 1985).

"Me and My Shadow," by Jane Tompkins, appeared in *Gender and Theory: Dialogues on Feminist Criticism,* edited by Linda Kauffman (New York: Basil Blackwell, 1989). Parts of the essay were reprinted from *New Literary History* 19 no. 1 (1987).

"Beyond Literary Darwinism: Women's Voices and Critical Discourse," by Olivia Frey, appeared in *College English* 52 no. 5 (September 1990).

"Border Crossing as Method and Motif in Contemporary American Writing, or, How Freud Helped Me Case the Joint," by Diane P. Freedman, is excerpted from Diane P. Freedman, *An Alchemy of Genres: Cross-Genre Writing by American Feminist Poet-Critics* (Charlottesville: University Press of Virginia, 1992).

INTRODUCTION

Women want to invent new types of criticism, alternate forms of cooperation . . .
less compulsive, aggressive, lonely, competitive; more communal, caring, and
integrated with love and politics.—Carol Ascher, Louise DeSalvo, Sara Ruddick, *Between Women*

The Intimate Critique: Autobiographical Literary Criticism was conceived in the
fall of 1988 when we submitted a proposal to the MLA for a session on
what we then called "interactive discourse." Although MLA rejected the
proposal, we convened the panel, renamed "Masculine and Feminine
Modes of Literary Criticism," at the Midwest/Modern Language Association Convention in St. Louis. Even before the last member of our large
audience left the room, we determined to edit together an anthology of
personal criticism and propose another session to the MLA entitled "In
Our Own Voices: Feminist Forms of Literary Criticism."
   Like our contemporaries and the scores of scholars and researchers
who had come before us, we had been trained in graduate school in the
methods of "objective criticism." Obviously and increasingly, however,
not everyone has embraced a discourse we have come to see as pseudo-
objective, impersonal, and adversarial, a discourse Jane Tompkins likens
to a "straitjacket" and that Cheryl Torsney has called "comfortless." We
ourselves had long experimented with alternative forms—Diane with
poetic amalgams and Olivia and Frances with personal stories in scholarly
writings. Elsewhere, composition theorist William Zeiger laments that

"with overpowering frequency, college composition classes today teach the writing of an essay which conforms to the scientific model of thesis and support" and urges us to adopt other forms and other ways of knowing about literature. In a 1988 *College English* essay, Chris Anderson wishes that more scholars wrote "essays," the old belles lettres—personal, eccentric, exploratory. More recently, Peter Elbow asks us to take a "larger view of human discourse," urging us to help our students leave behind a uniform, "author-evacuated" prose with its "rubber-gloved" quality of voice (145) in favor of "a kind of polyphony—an awareness of and pleasure in the various competing voices that make up their own" (153).

The selections in this volume are rich in a range of personal and passionate voices. As feminists, composition theorists, poststructuralists, African-Americanists, reader-response critics, and/or poet-critics, the writers and editors of this volume have resisted the formal distance and conventional hierarchies of what has been termed by Thomas J. Farrell and others the "male" mode of rhetoric, "the predominant mode of formal academic discourse" (Farrell 920). In Farrell's schema the "male" mode is logical, controlled, framed, and contained (910); it presents the thesis/conclusion at the beginning of an article (920) and supports a need for closure. The "female" mode, on the other hand, may appear open-ended, generative, and process-oriented (910). Further, as in the autobiographical-critical essays here, the female mode "seems at times to obfuscate the boundary between the self of the author and the subject of the discourse, as well as between the self and the audience, whereas the male mode tends to accentuate such boundaries" (910).

As Farrell, and we, concede, however, it is not surprising to find many women who write and speak in the school-inculcated male mode, nor is it impossible to find men (our contributors, for example) who write and speak in the female mode (909). Thus, to paraphrase Helene Cixous's disclaimer in "Reaching a Point of Wheat," "every time [we] say 'masculine' or 'feminine,' or 'man' or 'woman' [or 'male' or 'female'], please use as many quotation marks as you need to avoid taking these terms too literally" (1). We see such terms as socially constructed but helpful labels for distinguishing the formality, linearity, and abstractions of conventional academic discourse from alternative models. Our bibliography lists essays by Mary K. DeShazer, Pamela Annas, and others who similarly refer to these gender-inflected modes.

In putting this volume together, we encouraged writing that challenged argument as the preferred mode for discussion, questioned the importance of the objective and impersonal, and, rather than aiming for a

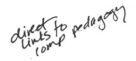

seamless, finished "product," characteristically made direct reference to the process by which it was accomplished. We sent out calls for papers to journals and departments around the country, encouraging contributors to write in nontraditional forms: personal, narrative, mixed-genre, interactive, associative, relational, subjective, and/or feminist. "In other words," we said, "write the essay about the literature you love in the way you would write it if you were not worrying about publishing it in a mainstream academic journal."

Thus began a passionate correspondence among us that extended to a web of passionate correspondence with would-be contributors. It was like no other scholarly or research project of ours. With each manuscript, contributors sent long personal letters thanking us for creating space for writing that had never before had a home. Writers talked about the publication histories of the pieces, relating their often frustrating attempts to be heard. Each letter was a sigh of relief.

In their essays, letters, or excerpts our contributors frequently contextualize their efforts by describing their compositional shapes and motivations. In describing her essay, Brenda Daly observes, "It not only avoids argumentation, . . . it also resists the possible loss of voice (my own)." Writing on Rachel Brownstein, Blanche Gelfant, and others, Frances Murphy Zauhar herself emulates each writer's commitment to being "a totally engaged, emotionally involved reader." Gail Griffin welcomes this collection because, as she wrote in a letter,

> I've found myself progressively alienated from the lit crit game by precisely those obstacles of discourse convention you cite [in the call for submissions], as well as a few others. And yet the critical reading of literature has, if anything, become a more significant part of my intellectual life. The problem, as I've seen it, is that I can never envisage a 'venue' for criticism as I genuinely prefer to write it.

This anthology provides just such a venue for writers whose essays refuse to separate impetus and content, their lives and their words.

Part I, "Muse-ings on Genre, Autobiography, Narrative: Formative Strategies" challenges, in what the essays say and how they say it, the conventions of traditional literary critical discourse. Diane P. Freedman's "Border Crossing as Method and Motif" is an appropriate entrée into the volume. With the discovery of a text of Freud's writings in her father's library, including a footnote by the editor exclaiming over the Nazi holocaust threatening Freud and his family, Freedman realizes "that every book, every reading, is laced and surrounded with circumstances worth considering, border crossings within the text as well as its edges." Freedman works the image of border crossing throughout as a metaphor for alternative feminist forms as well as her own literal writing "at the edges of desks and days."

Jane Tompkins's "Me and My Shadow" was first published in *New Literary History* in 1987. Several writers, including Tompkins, had been invited by the editors to respond to Ellen Messer Davidow's "The Philosophical Bases of Feminist Literary Criticisms," which explores what feminists' "posture" should be "toward the dominant male intellectual traditions" (65). Tompkins's title, a takeoff on the popular song, introduces the metaphor that expresses her doubled perspective (then) about her adoption of the male literary and rhetorical traditions. The longer version reprinted here suggests that it may not only be dangerous for women to adopt male-inflected rhetoric, because of what must be "left behind," but that decontextualized, depersonalized theory "may be one of the patriarchal gestures that women *and* men ought to avoid."

Olivia Frey's "Beyond Literary Darwinism," first published in *College English* in 1990, responds to the example of Tompkins's essay by recognizing, after examining every essay published in *PMLA* from 1975–88 as well as a scattering of other journals, that too much traditional criticism is adversarial, a kind of literary survival of the fittest. As a result of her essay—and of this anthology, in fact—Frey would like to see the profession "open up" and provide writers with "more freedom to write about literature in alternative forms and to be rewarded for it: the dissertation topics supported, the articles published; the writers hired, tenured, promoted."

In her essay "'Everyday Use': My Sojourn at Parchman Farm," Cheryl Torsney also echoes Tompkins's sentiments by acknowledging that although she risks being accused of lacking professionalism and/or rigor because she does not begin with "the requisite prefatory litany of past adventures in criticism," she nonetheless maintains that "reading and writing and teaching with real conviction necessitate personal engagement with the text."

Susan Koppelman asks "why the letter form isn't sufficient?" as literary criticism. She "prefers reading letters to reading essays," writing, "I like the special feeling of being addressed that letters give me—either I am being addressed or I am eavesdropping on a personal communication." Too many essays "are like pre-packaged diet foods—no schmaltz, no seasoning, no garnish, no taste." She asks, "Is it the patriarchy that teaches that discussion of literature has to take . . . impersonal form . . . that emotional-after-the-fact form?"

Too often criticism (or the eminent practitioners themselves) renders students and even women colleagues as "objectified as a statue, as silent as a text," according to rhetorician Linda Robertson's account, in "Social Circles: Being a Report on J. Hillis Miller's Campus Visitation," of the visit of a famous critic-theorist to her campus.

It may be stories we need, not theory, Victoria Ekanger implies in "Touchstones and Bedrocks: Learning the Stories We Need." Ekanger talks about stories—the opposite of silences "unnatural and oppressive"—and speaks of her mother and grandmother. According to Ekanger's perspective, the story is not a temporary diversion from the serious work of our lives or our teaching. The story is a model of knowing, a means of defining and shaping our present realities and future possibilities.

Part II, "Critical Confessions," features stories of personal and professional silencing and repression. Frances Murphy Zauhar recounts her learning that a professional response to literature was supposed to differ from a reader or lover's response to literature. Zauhar echoes the protests of others in this section: "We might write in strong words about our subject, we might even be enchanting in the arguments we make, but if we are personal, intimate, if we try to create for our readers, or between our readers and ourselves, the affiliation we feel with the texts most important to us—we will be emoting, we will not be working, we will not be writing criticism." Reading Blanche Gelfant, Rachel Brownstein, and Judith Fetterley restored for Zauhar the intricate tie between the personal and professional, the personal and theoretical.

Shirley Nelson Garner understands the significance of Kingston's breaking silence in *The Woman Warrior* through the broken silences in her own life—her office door full of revealing sexist quotations, the secrets her mother tells after Shirley divorces of a great-great-grandmother's illegitimate children. Garner proclaims, "Not being ashamed to tell the story means not being ashamed of the woman and the self." Both Kingston and Garner have learned that while there may be costs of breaking silence—censure, lost jobs—the cost of keeping silent is greater.

In "Different Silences," Traise Yamamoto, articulating the paradoxes of speech and silence, describes other things "besides fear and frustration" that keep her silent: "If you grow up Japanese American, you grow up with the intense insider/outsider mentality that the Isseis brought from a country where therapy is still not widely practiced." For her, "Silence is a part of speaking; silence is also habit, protection." And yet, being forced into speech, particularly by outside expectations about the sound of one's ethnic or gendered voice, can be as silencing as silence. Silence can be more beautiful, more articulate than speech, like "the soundless sound of one hand clapping." Yamamoto thus complicates the notions of speech and silence that other essays implicitly or explicitly explore here.

In "What's in a Name?" Henry Louis Gates, Jr., uses the changes in African-American nomenclature in the United States and in his own life to sketch the evolution of the African-American literary scholar. He suggests that renaming, a version of the African-American practice of "signifying," is crucial not only for self-affirmation but for the definition of an aesthetic true to the complicated varieties of black experience over time.

In "Poetry and the Age: 'A Girl in a Library' to Randall Jarrell," Sandra M. Brown reads a former era of literary critical practice through the poetry of Randall Jarrell and her memories of the way in which it had been taught to her and the way she now introduces it to her students. Brown judges Jarrell's importance to be his writing well about women, "without obvious misogyny," and yet she describes her realization that Jarrell didn't acknowledge those things about which "the girl in the library"—someone like herself or her students—might be thinking. While still in some ways indebted to Jarrell, Brown narrates her own transformation, that of her generation of civil-rights and feminist activists, and, most recently, the transformation of the students in her class into poets whose poems are woven into Brown's meditation.

"Not until my father's funeral in 1976," Brenda Daly writes, "when I wrote 'I am my father's daughter' in the funeral register, could I begin to write." The intimate readerly and writerly tie she has had with the prolific writer Joyce Carol Oates has helped liberate Daly from her father's sexual abuse of her sister and mother as well as her own subsequent parallel professional "abuse." Daly's professional abuse resulted in the silencing and distortion of her voice, the trivialization of her work. "Even now I feel that my testimony [on the topic of paternal rape] will be discredited, that it will 'taint' my authority (which must remain lofty and theoretical to be 'important.')"

Like other contributors, Melody Graulich's meditation begins with a personal rather than a literary experience, a description of violence against women akin to Daly's. She tells the story of her grandfather beating her grandmother "not simply to establish my relationship to my subject but because the engagement between critic and subject and how it shapes both reader and text *is* my subject." Graulich traces her reading of

Mari Sandoz's *Old Jules* and other stories of the Old West to dramatize the process of her former identification with her grandfather and idealization of his rugged life in the Badlands. Graulich admits that until she learned that "Somebody Must Say These Things" (her essay's title), she herself had removed her mother's secrets, her grandfather's legacy of violence, her personal story from her published essays, thus rendering her "foremothers invisible and thoughtlessly [covering] up the real costs of abuse of women."

In "The Scarlet Brewer and the Voice of the Colonized," Shirley Geok-Lin Lim recounts her growing up in Malacca and her momentous introduction to R. F. Brewer's *The Art of Versification and the Technicalities of Poetry,* a book which served to demystify the British literary canon she encountered early. The "mysterious English poetry of the British imperialists was laid bare for me in [Brewer's] revolutionary red book as the bones of craft. . . . The simple naming of craft as craft unweighted the imperialism in English poetry and sent it floating deliriously within my grasp." Geok-Lin Lim extends her own discovery and method to other postcolonial writers such as Soyinka, Achebe, Head, and Mukherjee, all of whom have transformed English to serve their own agendas.

Similarly using a central image—this time, "Dividing Fences," which is also the title of her essay—Carol Taylor dramatizes the difficulty of crossing racial, professional, and rhetorical boundaries erected by tradition. As a folklorist, Taylor collects the oral histories of forgotten peoples, establishing epistemic authority of the marginalized and defying still other boundaries. She writes, "Knowledge of the unwritten legacy my foremothers and fathers left in folktales, folksongs, family stories, proverbs, and superstitions can provide that historical link with the past so needed to make us whole."

Like oral stories of marginalized people, the diary has long lacked epistemic authority, according to feminist scholars. In "What do Women *Really* Mean? Thoughts on Women's Diaries and Lives," Suzanne Bunkers writes of women students who are as likely to throw their journals in the trash as to keep them: " 'I just never thought they were worth anything' is a common sentiment, expressed with a curious blend of embarrassment and pride, by many of these women." Bunkers goes on to trace her interest in diaries, from her own journal writing that produced forty-five volumes over twenty-one years to her research into the diaries of midwestern women. She presents this essay as an ongoing attempt to "name and understand the ways in which [her] own presuppositions, biases and hidden agendas might influence the ways in which [she] reads and interprets nineteenth-century women's diaries and journals" as well as attempting to write in a form reflective of the texts under study.

Part III, "Autobiographical Literary Criticism," contains increasingly self-revelatory examples of this border-crossing genre. The essays are studies of literature through studies of relevant personal experiences. The writers know the literature through themselves and know themselves through the literature.

In "Between the Medusa and the Abyss: Reading *Jane Eyre,* Reading Myself," Ellen Brown notes that when she started writing her essay exploring her relation to the text and character of Jane Eyre over time she knew she would be writing in several voices—her adolescent self, her older self, herself as student, as teacher, as daughter, granddaughter, sister, her personal self, and her professional self. What she did not know was that speaking in her own voice(s) meant being silent so that other voices could speak through her.

In "Rereading *Middlemarch, Rereading Myself,*" Peter Carlton repudiates the shame-based academic interpreter, the Casaubon in himself. Seeking to leave behind "the kind of literary criticism that aspired to objectivity, validity, and inclusiveness" and through which he "strove to *master* and *control* the literary text," Carlton imagines a professional conference where the goals and practices of this anthology would be enacted, a conference where "we talked with each other as much about ourselves as about literature," or "about how reading this poem or that novel had . . . served for us an occasion of grief, or outrage, or joy."

Like Carlton, in her essay "The Crippling of the Third World: Shiva Naipaul's Heritage," Rosanne Kanhai-Brunton insists "we need to avoid a discourse that assigns a 'master' position and instead to discover the insecurity of a group that devises desperate machinations of oppression." Speaking of such a prominent scholar as Gayatri Spivak, she asks: "Trained in the western academy, is her own turning toward the East itself a Eurocentric desire? Can she un-learn her own privileged discourse so that she can be heard by people that are not within the academy?" Borrowing the motif of the cripple and the traveler from Naipaul's "Unfinished Journey," Brunton asserts that by trading texts like those of T. S. Eliot, with their imagery of "cripples," for a West Indian text by Derek Walcott, for example, she and her readers can take the necessary first steps against the academic power structure which cripples and dominates.

Stories, Gail Griffin reminds us, are subversive, coded, like the Negro spirituals that seemed to express resignation, but which in fact inscribed liberation and strategies for escape. Griffin retells Penelope's story, an epic of endurance in its own right usually overshadowed by Odysseus's story. The web that Penelope weaves is Griffin's metaphor for the work that women do, work too often trivialized, overlooked, undone. The endless necessity and subversive power of recreation and revision pay homage to all the work, the fiction and letters, written and lost, the domestic chores never finished.

Dolan Hubbard sees in his own work and the African-American texts he loves the wonderful fact that "writing is fighting," that the fist that fights can also hold a pen that writes. To Hubbard, Frederick Douglass's *Narrative* provides an excellent model for a critical essay proud of its capacity to defend, unashamed of its no longer suppressed rage. Hubbard's own essay, like the classroom it describes, is a scene of uplift, anger, and societal and historical critique offered by Douglass, Washington, Malcolm X, and Richard Wright, writers whose work thus serves Hubbard and his students the way the *Columbian Orator* served Douglass.

In "Catherine Trotter Cockburn and Me: A Duography," Kendall acknowledges that one's reading is always a kind of projection, a longing to hear one's own voice, admitting that Catherine Trotter Cockburn's story, "in the context of my own life's questions, obsesses me." Such a need for a model or double lead Kendall to discover and further document the late-seventeenth-century playwright's lesbianism in her life and art. Just as the scholar-critic has newly illuminated the playwright's life, the playwright offers the scholar an enriched identity. Kendall thus concludes, "I have taken Catherine Trotter Cockburn into myself and merged with her; like an ex-lover, she fuses with my present and gives shape to my ever-mobile identity, which can always use a little help."

Through a variety of textual perspectives, including the fiction of Jamaica Kincaid and of Jessamyn West, theoretical comments by Freud and Jane Gallop, telephone conversations, and interior monologues, Dana Beckelman explores the anxiety and sense of loss engendered when one loses or thinks of losing one's daughter, mother, or grandmother. Such a fear of loss, Beckelman—in an essay entitled "In Between Abject and Object: The Mourning Sickness of the Expectant Mother (or) Three Movements of the Blues in B Minor"—calls "the mourning sickness of the expectant mother."

Julia Balén, in "*La Ronde* of Children and Mothers," blends the voices of Roland Barthes, Julia Kristeva, Alice Jardine, and Dorothy Dinnerstein with a back-to-the-body discourse of her experiences birthing, nursing, and nurturing her son—and her writing. She calls her approach "a dance, *un ronde,* with Roland Barthes's *Plaisir du Texte,* that explores post-modern problems of language and literature from a motherly point of view." As the mother-writer locates herself in her bodily self, among so many voices and visions, our volume closes with yet another vivid movement toward a politics of location, a literary criticism of personal, political, and critical self-revelation.

Autobiographical literary criticism occurs in the intersections of feminism, poststructuralism, black and ethnic literary theories, composition theory, reader-response theory, and poetry, answering the anti-essentialist "gender-skepticism"[1] of postfeminism by its capacity to express and construct multiple locations. Autobiographical literary criticism eschews what writer and activist Lillian Smith calls the "deadly sameness of abstraction," a sameness which, Adrienne Rich reminds us, "allows no differences among places, times, cultures, conditions, movements" (Rich 221). To Rich, "Theory—the seeing of patterns, showing the forest as well as the trees—theory can be a dew that rises from the earth and collects in the rain cloud and returns to earth over and over. But if it doesn't smell of the earth, it isn't good for the earth" (213–14). While not essentializing, the writers in this volume assume the categories of gender, race, class, and ability are among matrices that influence their reading, knowing, and writing. Rather than fixed and separate, these categories are open and tangled, identifying and initiating conversations about the localcs of thought and language.

We deeply hope that the variety of voices and locations presented here will call forth more voices out of the void.

Notes

1. See Susan Bordo, "Feminism, Postmodernism, and Gender-Scepticism."

References

Anderson, Chris. "Hearsay Evidence and Second-Class Citizenship." *College English* 50 (1988): 300–308.

Bordo, Susan. "Feminism, Postmodernism, and Gender-Skepticism." *Feminism/Postmodernism*. Ed. Linda Nicholson. New York and London: Routledge, 1990. 133–56.

Cixous, Hélène. "Reaching a Point of Wheat, Or, Portrait of the Artist as a Maturing Woman." *New Literary History* 19.1 (Fall 1987): 1–22.

Elbow, Peter. "Reflections on Academic Discourse: How It Relates to Freshmen and Colleagues." *College English* 53.2 (February 1991): 135–55.

Farrell, Thomas J. "The Male and Female Modes of Rhetoric." *College English* 40.8 (April 1979): 909–21.

Rich, Adrienne. "Notes Towards a Politics of Location." *Blood, Bread, and Poetry: Selected Prose, 1979–1985.* New York: Norton, 1986. 210–31.

PART I

Muse-ings on Genre,

Autobiography, Narrative:

Formative Strategies

*

*I refuse to be bound by any one literary tone,
just as I refuse to be bound by any one literary
genre. Or I refuse to be bound because I don't
feel that one genre does everything I want.
And so my voices are wide and wild and sometimes varied. And in the real world this
makes it hard for me to be catalogued by
publishers, critics, readers. It means I feel
the continuous pressure to shout, continual
uncertainty that my voice may not be heard,
because it does not run smoothly into any
single, clear channel.*
——*Michelene Wandor, "Voices are Wild"*

Border Crossing as

Method and Motif in

Contemporary American

Writing, or, How Freud

Helped Me Case the Joint

*

Diane P. Freedman

Throughout women's lives, the self is defined through social relationships; issues of fusion and merger of the self with others are significant, and ego and body boundaries remain flexible.—Judith Kegan Gardiner, "On Female Identity and Writing by Women"

When a graduate student in English, I became fascinated by post-Freudian theories like those informing Judith Kegan Gardiner's essay. As a writer-critic, I could identify with Gardiner's notion that for women there is a "continual crossing of self and other."[1] Because of this ego crossing or merging, Gardiner goes on, "women's writing may blur public and private and defy completion"; it resists tidy alignment with a single genre or realm of discourse. For women, borders—of ego, genre, discipline, geography—are made to be crossed (for warring men, too, though their deadly border wars that simply reaffirm and rearrange dividing lines among nations are not what most women writers seek). Many contemporary women writers want an intimacy with their readers and subjects as well as with themselves, for, as Susan Griffin puts it, "separated from our authentic cries we become weak imitations of who it is we think we should be" (249). In a series of self-disclosures like Griffin's, increasing numbers of feminist poet-critics explicitly announce their commitment to forms which transgress conventions and so better facilitate communion with self and others. This metadiscursivity is another way in which women writers cross borders, loop the inside to the outside.

Many of these writers find border crossing a simultaneously risky and empowering metaphor or compositional mode. Perhaps the works best exemplifying the crossover and even cross-fire mode are those by writers who have had literal, geographic borders to cross, those writers exiled from both home and dominant, white, heterosexist, bourgeois culture. So Gloria Anzaldúa, in *Borderlands/La Frontera: The New Mestiza,* a text foregrounding border crossing as the chief mode of her life and language, asserts she will face and overlap the borders of her many selves, countries, and cultures in her writing: "I will no longer be made to feel ashamed of existing. I will have my voice: Indian, Spanish, White. I will have my serpent's tongue—my woman's voice, my sexual voice, my poet's voice. I will overcome the tradition of silence." Yet there are those not so often or obviously marginalized as a Chicana lesbian feminist writer from the working class who nonetheless feel themselves to be in the "Borderlands," where, as Anzaldúa describes it, "Being a writer feels very much like being a Chicana, or being queer—a lot of squirming, coming up against all sorts of walls. Or its opposite: nothing defined or definite, a boundless, floating state of limbo; . . . [and yet] living in a state of psychic unrest, in a Borderland, is what makes poets write and artists create" (72–73).

Many of us whose essays are assembled here feel ourselves in a kind of borderland, too often caught in the cross fire between cold, competitive, critical writing on the one hand and personal, even confessional, creative responses to literature and life on the other. We're caught between our families and our work, facing the pressures of publishing or perishing, choosing between traditional scholarship and feminism. Or we find ourselves faced with no such choices at all, scarcely being listened to, asked to quit griping and turn in our poetic licenses or quit this heady scene.

On the other side, we do have allies, even in surprising places. As Jane Gallop, who crosses disciplinary borders in her writing to join psychoanalysis with literary criticism, feminism, and poststructuralism, tells us, "[Freud] too worked at the juncture of the autobiographical and the theoretical, inventing a science by interpreting his own dreams and personal history in connection with his work with others. . . . Willy-nilly, he stumbled into a realm of knowledge where science is not clearly separated from poetry" (5–6). And it is that Jewish writer-analyst Freud, I recently realized, who helped me route my way away from tidy generic and critical borders or boundaries. As I read and was inspired by the liberatory aesthetics of American poet-critics Gallop, Anzaldúa, Adrienne Rich, Louise Bernikow, Susan Griffin, Marge Piercy, Maxine Hong Kingston, Judy

Grahn, Mary Daly, and so many others, Freud—and my father's home library—came to mind.

When as a sophomore English major I learned that several of my professors considered Freud's and other psychoanalysts' writing relevant to the study of literature, I looked around at my father's collection for a book of Freud's work. I knew my father had once intended to become a psychiatrist and had earned an M.A. in psychology; moreover, he had an extensive collection of books, most stamped with the little man (Mercury) that is the logo of the Random House "Modern Library." The text I found, *The Basic Writings of Sigmund Freud,* translated, edited, and introduced by Dr. A. A. Brill, fascinated me, and my father said I could keep it for my own. I have it to this day, though I have not read much beyond Brill's introduction, having taken most of my Freud in smaller, paperback doses doctored by other editors and translators. But what fascinated me about this edition was the final footnote to Brill's introduction: "Alas! As these pages are going to the printer we have been startled by the terrible news that the Nazi holocaust has suddenly encircled Vienna and that Professor Freud and his family are virtual prisoners in the hands of civilization's greatest scourge" (32).

This footnote or epilogue showed me that a book's "borders"—its packaging, format, and the contexts in which it is read and published— are inseparable from its more apparent content. Not only was an author more a part of the text than I had imagined, but so were its editors and readers. Brill alerted me to the fact that every book, every reading, is laced and surrounded with circumstances worth considering, border crossings within the text as well as at its edges. (It wasn't until later that I saw the sustained and sophisticated use of border imagery foregrounded in works by ethnic-American women, about which I speak more in the book-length study from which this essay derives.)[2]

Brill's entire introduction expresses, even without its final alarum and news brief, such personal and dramatic concern for the safekeeping of Freud's works that I was shocked, since such voicings, such extratextual paraphernalia were not a concern of the New Criticism practiced in the literature seminars of my day. The introduction forced me to be an active reader newly attentive to the many forces behind a published text. I was intrigued by Brill's personal relationships with Freud and Jung as well as with the notion that Nazism threatened all readers of the Random House *Basic Writings* along with "Professor Freud." I was amazed by the intrusion of the "real" world into the written. I might never read another book immune to the circumstances of its production and my reception. For all I could not comprehend the bulk of the translated Freud, I nonetheless could be both moved and amused by Dr. Brill's old-fashioned cry, "Alas!"

Knowing little about Freud at the time, I had no idea whether he escaped the Nazi occupation unharmed or died in fear or violence. World War II became suddenly real to me, while Freud's life became novelistic: he, his translators, and I traversed the borders of fiction and fact, story and data. I felt invaded by the text as my personal circumstances seemed suddenly written into it. Brill couldn't resist the simultaneous melodrama and authenticity of an exclamatory footnote; I couldn't resist it either. The text expanded to include for me the mysterious fact of my father the doctor almost becoming a psychiatrist; my own desire for father Freud's book from my father's large library of male-tattooed texts; my being a woman with a Jewish surname long after the Nazi reign and Freud's death from natural causes; and, finally, my written record of all this here. We were language lovers all—writer, translator, reader. Philology brought us into countries occupied by one another. Footnotes and margin notes suddenly confettied and confounded the tome.

Like my father, however, I am not a psychoanalyst, so I stop this story, whose full psychological significance is likely beyond me, here. I can say, however, that in the footnote (or this preamble) lies the beginning of my fascination with texts on the border, authors in war zones, the imagery of edges, cross fire, crosshatching. Yet I wanted my own library, one of recent writers whose experiences were closer to my own, one with no more little men embossing the book covers. Perhaps even more to the point, I needed to tell my own story, and now I am. As Barbara Christian, quoting Marcelle Thiébaux, writes in *Black Feminist Criticism*, "The only possible library for a woman is one invented by herself, writing herself or her own discourse into it" (x).

When I began to write poems, I found it necessary to express what I considered the end points of my identity: the Russian Jew and the Ukrainian Catholic. Part of what disturbed me about the Freudian footnote was that I was a Jew terrified of Nazism—and yet, I was not a Jew. I felt awed and guilty as I read about Freud's danger: I was not a Jew in danger; I didn't know enough about World War II; I felt *ineligible* to learn even my own family's history. I wrote poems informed by these twin senses of uncertainty and guilt and learned that my identity was not in fact neatly suspended between two poles or end points. Instead, like the identities of the contemporary feminist writers whose border-crossing works originally inspired this essay,[3] my identity oscillates among sometimes fogged-in points of reference, multiple angles of vision—and confusion. Like other contemporary women poet-critics, I find I oscillate between poetry and prose as well. I seek prose to relieve the gnomic anxiety of poetry, poetry to override the seeming clarity and control of prose. Prose has tidy borders on the page, poetry a tidal edge—no clear edge at all.

Yet though poetry may "speak the language of wildness and danger," it is also, according to Susan Griffin, "a secret way through which we can restore authenticity to ourselves" (245). This alternating of prose with poetry keeps me from sticking too blandly to a critical discourse I find constricting, helps me find my true subject and subjectivity, as the Lacanians say. And that subjectivity is inevitably crosshatched, multiple.

poetry + prose.

I thus cross and examine (or cross-examine) the borders, edges, limits, overlaps of my ethnic and religious identities in my poems "The Performance" and "The Way the Gravestones Align." Like Adrienne Rich, I grew up technically neither Jew nor Gentile and yet temperamentally, genealogically, both. Under Conservative or Orthodox Jewish law, Rich and I are not Jewish because our mothers are not. We also did not qualify under Reformed Jewish law because although one parent was Jewish, we were not raised as Jews.[4] And I'm not considered Catholic because my father is not, although my having been baptized may complicate things.

While Rich had a largely Christian social life and even attended for five years an Episcopalian church where she was baptized and confirmed, I had a largely Jewish social life in my Long Island, New York, hometown of Jericho, but I was sent neither to temple nor church and was kept fairly ignorant of both religions, their rituals, their politics. I did learn that my mother's church had been a Ukrainian Catholic one, itself a cross between the Greek and Russian Orthodox churches, though the services in her hometown, Shamokin, Pennsylvania, were in either Latin or Ukrainian. When I was about eight, I found a rosary in her bedroom, and I asked her whether she still believed in Jesus; she said yes. And then, about the time I was twelve and beginning to attend my school friends' bar or bat mitzvahs, my mother told me I had been baptized as an infant and that I had godparents somewhere in Pennsylvania. My younger sisters and brother had not been similarly baptized, and I never saw my godparents. I was left in limbo, which alternately relieved me (I did not have to learn Hebrew like my complaining friends, nor did I have to devote Sundays to dressing up and quieting down) and left me painfully without faith—in anything:

The Performance

You go over the parts of your costume:
black tights, black slippers, tunic,
a black cross on a black string.

You play a nun, a barmaid, a singer
all rolled into one.
You've washed the tights, your cap,
and your feet,
but you're not sure about
this part.

The curtain is black. The stage will be dark.
They'll film you
with eely black film.

In the dressing room, before the show,
the cast has forgotten roses
for the director.
She has penned notes.
In yours, black squiggles say: "Hold onto your
cross!" She doesn't want your arms to bounce up and
down when you sing.

You can do nothing right.
You've left your husband.
You forgot about gift-giving.
When you get whacked in the ass by the
bartender on stage, you don't react.
You never had any faith.
You never knew your lines.

You try to pray.

I had gotten too many mixed messages about how best to perform, not
only as an actor in an ambiguous role, but as wife, daughter, woman,
Christian, Jew. Perhaps, as Gloria Anzaldúa confesses she sometimes feels,
"I have so internalized the borderland conflict that . . . I feel one cancels
out the other, and [I am] zero, nothing, no one" (63). I have been at a cold
and uncomfortable cross/roads:

The Way the Gravestones Align:
Ithaca, NY/Shamokin, PA

When it snows, the churchyard in Ithaca
is as clean as a salt crystal.
The pastor heaves the church-big door,
and I cover my head with a red wool hat.

Sunday makes me angry;
I wear red instead of veiling myself.
I never go to church; my mother married a Jew.

But once with my grandmother and in a purple coat,
I went to a Ukrainian service in Shamokin—
where my uncle as a child fell off the only bicycle
and broke his arm, so my mother was forbidden to try.

Since in Shamokin lavender is for
ladies' death clothes, I remember
I had to beg my mother for that coat.
My cousin and I dozed as the nuns spoke.

> (Today the churchyard in Ithaca is cold,
> and all the crosswalks are empty.)

The graveyard in Shamokin is
the highest point in town, higher
than the stripped coal hills:
old women tighten *babushkas* and hope to be buried
in warm weather, deep, with all the people there.

It was hard, that December, seeing
my lilac-clad *Baba* in the middle of a box,
feeling forced to kiss the cross, wear black,
and pray, as snow furred the ground
and made slippery our vows and wheels.

Since writing this poem and reading accounts of others "split at the root," to borrow Adrienne Rich's repeated image, I am more at home with my collective past, feeling generally enriched by my double heritage, my connection with other Americans of mixed heritage, my connection to "old country" Russia.[5] I have felt a mild but lingering guilt about not identifying equally with my parents' different heritages, this milder guilt replacing the unease I'd felt earlier about not knowing my past, of having it kept a secret from me. But I have also found strength in resisting what may be the coercive aspects of each heritage: I always caricatured my relatives on my mother's side as people who said "be good" and those on my father's side as those who said "do well." I suppose I feel I've done mostly the latter by becoming a poet-scholar, following in the tradition of my Jewish great-great-grandfather. In Russia, just before the turn of the century, he published books of Jewish philosophy and history in which four

[handwritten margin note: and all of us are hybrids.]

different speakers argue in poetry throughout (his original form contains six words per line, six lines per stanza). In America many of my Jewish relatives were great students, if not writers; my own father, a physician, recited Blake and Keats to me when as a child I watched him shave. It is easy to see how I became enamored of his library, including his *Oxford Book of English Verse*—and yet I am adverse to writing formal verse myself.

In contrast, many of my Catholic relatives today, none of them scholars, work in factories or service positions. My maternal grandmother, a wonderful gardener, seamstress, and cook, never learned to read either Ukrainian or English; my grandfather the coalminer wasn't much of a reader or writer, though my mother tells me he was extremely gentle, a pacifist. Herself a college-educated nurse, my mother read my siblings and me Bible stories in our youth. Though she confided to me her own love for flashlight-reading Shakespeare (over the objections of her mother, who wanted her early in bed), my mother rarely if ever read us poems or plays. Yet the enduring details of her family members' lives—my aunt still lives in the house where she and my mother were born—held me too. I learned from them the pleasures of personal history and continuity in the face of my perceived conflicts and discontinuities. I grew proud of both my heritages, envious of *Baba*'s enduring faith, her girlhood in the Ukrainian countryside, and her house in the Pennsylvania hills (Long Island is flat, our house on a dull, suburban grid), if more comfortable with the Jewish intellectual tradition and the reading and writing it has led me to do.

Obviously, borders, narrow lines, can provide the form and context of composition and not merely a central image. I have often had to write in small pockets of time at the borders of other tasks. I have written (and read) in installments, in ribbons or borders, margin notes. Adrienne Rich has graphically described her own writing in the margins, as it were:

> For ten years I was reading in fierce snatches, scribbling in notebooks, writing poetry in fragments. . . . In the late fifties I was able to write, for the first time, directly about experiencing myself as a woman. The poem was jotted in fragments during children's naps, brief hours in the library, or at 3:00 a.m. after rising with a wakeful child. I despaired of doing any continuous work at this time. Yet I began to feel that my fragments and scraps had a common consciousness. ("When We Dead Awaken: Writing as Re-Vision," 44)

Even without the pressures of childcare, I find I have a strategy, even an aesthetic, in keeping with any woman who, for whatever reasons, feels herself a borderline artist. I expend much energy over the small: the small lyric poem, the pun, the alliterative line. Like Hester Prynne, I embroider my A's and days, make do with what little I have or perceive I have. Then, in an effort to make the small things into a whole, I pull texts out of previous texts, my own or others, and so lengthen my links, my woman's web of extended identity and identification. I think of the little stitches creating Emily Dickinson's fascicles, the packets of poems secretly and slyly composed. I think of Dickinson's written image of her stitches—the dashes following, and thereby extending, her short lines. Because of Hester's gift as a seamstress, the townspeople of *The Scarlet Letter* soon believed the letter that is the novel's title stood for "Able" instead of the intended "Adultress." The move from daily ability to art—or to a sense that those fragmented daily acts in fact are art—is what recent women writers often accomplish, but not to valorize some notion of high art over low. We mean instead to authorize our own anthologies, to celebrate an aesthetic of the many or the split making a creative collectivity, explore an aesthetic of familiarity, invitation, emulation, relation—not of postmodern alienation, numbness, surface, coolness.[6] Rather than some postmodern expression of perpetual alienation and decenteredness, this writing resembling a crazy-quilt gestures toward the kind of women's community a quilting bee recalls, the kind of community that helped Hester learn to read herself differently. And I write this as part of a community of creative critics refusing to be co-opted by the usual critical conventions of impersonality coupled with one-upmanship and the linear "logic" that keeps the poetic and personal from the professional and theoretical.

Of *Borderlands,* Anzaldúa writes, "This book, then, speaks of my existence . . . and with my almost instinctive urge to communicate, to speak, to write about life on the borders, life in the shadows" (Preface). If the Freudian footnote taught me how to read, Anzaldúa (and other creative critics like her) have taught me how to write. While I know that my words come from spiritual, cultural, racial, sexual, and class identities that widely differ from her own, I nonetheless cross and ally myself with Anzaldúa in her perceptions about writing. We must write out of that psychically unrestful juncture—a juncture dangerous for tenure, publication, and promotion—of the personal and the theoretical, in the realm where knowledge is not separated from poetry, where borders of self and other and one genre or language and another collide.

Notes

1. Perhaps this further explains the well-meaning but often wrongheaded tendency of (white) feminists like myself to confuse our individual experiences with that of (an)-

other. At times, co-(r)responding with (an)other may be appropriate; at others, it suggests an act of appropriation or even colonization.

2. See "Border Crossing as Method and Motif in Contemporary Feminist Writing" in my book, *An Alchemy of Genres: Cross-Genre Writing by American Feminist Poet-Critics* (Charlottesville: University Press of Virginia, 1992).

3. I was going to write, "which are the 'true' subject of my study," only to realize there are in fact several subjects and subjectivities crosshatching here. A combination of Freud's work and that of those "strange bedfellows" Barthes and Rich authorized Gallop's "own push out of objective, scholarly discourse into something more embodied" (11). In this essay, Freud/my reading of the Freudian text and now Gallop (along with Rich, Anzaldúa, Griffin, Christian, and Gardiner) similarly authorize my pushing at the (seeming) borders of books, genres, self, and (these) others to blend "theory and intimacy," analysis and poetry, autobiography and literary criticism.

4. Rich is now an affiliated or self-identified Jew; she married a Jew, raised her four sons as Jews, and writes and speaks out of an ever-sharper Jewish identity. See *Blood, Bread, and Poetry* and her most recent books of poems.

5. Rich uses the phrase "split at the root" in an early poem entitled "Readings of History" (in *Snapshots of a Daughter-in-Law*), in an essay entitled "Split at the Root: An Essay on Jewish Identity" (in *Blood, Bread, and Poetry*), and in a still more recent long poem, "Sources" (*Sources* and *Your Native Land, Your Life*).

6. Todd Gitlin in a *New York Times Book Review* so characterizes the postmodern in art and literature.

References

Anzaldúa, Gloria. *Borderlands/La Frontera: The New Mestiza.* San Francisco: Spinsters/aunt lute, 1987.

Brill, A. A. Introduction. *The Basic Writings of Sigmund Freud.* New York: Random, 1938. 3–32.

Christian, Barbara. *Black Feminist Criticism.* New York: Pergamon, 1985.

Gardiner, Judith Kegan. "On Female Identity and Writing by Women." *Writing and Sexual Difference.* Ed. Elizabeth Abel. Chicago: University of Chicago Press, 1982. 177–91.

Gallop, Jane. *Thinking through the Body.* New York: Columbia University Press, 1988.

Gitlin, Todd. "Hip-Deep in Post-Modernism." *New York Times Book Review.* Nov. 16, 1988: 1+.

Griffin, Susan. *Made from this Earth.* New York: Harper, 1982.

Rich, Adrienne. "Split at the Root: An Essay on Jewish Identity." *Blood, Bread, and Poetry: Selected Prose 1979–1985.* New York: Norton, 1986. 100–123.

———. *Sources.* Woodside, Calif.: Heyeck, 1983. Reprinted in *Your Native Land, Your Life.* New York: Norton, 1986. 3–27.

———. " 'When We Dead Awaken': Writing as Re-Vision." *On Lies, Secrets, and Silence: Selected Prose 1966–1978.* New York: Norton, 1979. 33–49.

———. "Readings of History." *Snapshots of a Daughter-in-Law.* New York: Norton, 1967. 36–40.

Me and

My Shadow

*

Jane Tompkins

I wrote this essay in answer to Ellen Messer-Davidow's "The Philosophical Bases of Feminist Literary Criticisms" which appeared in the Fall 1987 issue of *New Literary History* along with several replies, including a shorter version of this one. As if it weren't distraction enough that my essay depends on someone else's, I want, before you've even read it, to defend it from an accusation. Believing that my reply, which turns its back on theory, constituted a return to the "rhetoric of presence," to an "earlier, naive, untheoretical feminism," someone, whom I'll call the unfriendly reader, complained that I was making the "old patriarchal gesture of representation" whose effect had been to marginalize women, thus "reinforcing the very stereotypes women and minorities have fought so hard to overcome." I want to reply to this objection because I think it is mistaken and because it reproduces exactly the way I used to feel about feminist criticism when it first appeared in the late 1960s.

I wanted nothing to do with it. It was embarrassing to see women, with whom one was necessarily identified, insisting in print on the differences between men's and women's experience, focusing obsessively on women authors, women characters, women's issues. How pathetic, I thought, to have to call attention to yourself in that way. And in such bad taste. It was the worst kind of special pleading, an admission of weakness so blatant it made me ashamed. What I felt then, and what I think my unfriendly reader feels now, is a version of what women who are new to feminism often feel: that if we don't call attention to ourselves *as* women, but just shut up about it and do our work, no one will notice the difference and everything will be OK.

Women who adopt this line are, understandably, afraid. Afraid of being confused with the weaker sex, the sex that goes around whining and talking about itself in an unseemly way, that can't or won't do what the big boys do ("tough it out") and so won't ever be allowed to play in the big boys' games. I am sympathetic with this position. Not long ago, as organizer of an MLA session entitled "Professional Politics: Women and the Institution," I urged a large roomful of women to "get theory" because I thought that doing theory would admit us to the big leagues and enable us at the same time to argue a feminist case in the most un-impeachable terms—those that men had supplied. I busily took my own advice, which was good as far as it went. But I now see that there has been a price for this, at least there has been for me; it is the subject of my reply to Ellen. I now tend to think that theory itself, <u>at least as it is usually practiced</u>, may be one of the patriarchal gestures women *and* men ought to avoid.

There are two voices inside me answering, answering to, Ellen's essay. One is the voice of a critic who wants to correct a mistake in the essay's view of epistemology. The other is the voice of a person who wants to write about her feelings (I have wanted to do this for a long time but have felt too embarrassed). This person feels it is wrong to criticize the essay philosophically and even beside the point: because a critique of the kind the critic has in mind only insulates academic discourse further from the issues that make feminism matter. That make *her* matter. The critic, meanwhile, believes such feelings, and the attitudes that inform them, are soft-minded, self-indulgent, and unprofessional.

These beings exist separately but not apart. One writes for professional journals, the other in diaries, late at night. One uses words like "context" and "intelligibility," likes to win arguments, see her name in print, and give graduate students hardheaded advice. The other has hardly ever been heard from. She had a short story published once in a university library magazine, but her works exist chiefly in notebooks and manila folders labeled "Journal" and "Private." This person talks on the telephone a lot to her friends, has seen psychiatrists, likes cappuccino, worries about the state of her soul. Her father is ill right now, and one of her friends recently committed suicide.

The dichotomy drawn here is false—and not false. I mean in reality there's no split. It's the same person who feels and who discourses about epistemology. The problem is that you can't talk about your private life in the course of doing your professional work. You have to pretend that epistemology, or whatever you're writing about, has nothing to do with your life, that it's more exalted, more important, because it (supposedly) *transcends* the merely personal. Well, I'm tired of the conventions that keep discussions of epistemology, or James Joyce, segregated from meditations on what is happening outside my window or inside my heart. The public-private dichotomy, which is to say, the public-private *hierarchy, is a* founding condition of female oppression. I say to hell with it. The reason I feel embarrassed at my own attempts to speak personally in a professional context is that I have been conditioned to feel that way. That's all there is to it.

I think people are scared to talk about themselves, that they haven't got the guts to do it. I think readers want to know about each other. Sometimes, when a writer introduces some personal bit of story into an essay, I can hardly contain my pleasure. I love writers who write about their own experience. I feel I'm being nourished by them, that I'm being allowed to enter into a personal relationship with them. That I can match my own experience up with theirs, feel cousin to them, and say, yes, that's how it is.

> When he casts his leaves forth upon the wind [said Hawthorne], the author addresses, not the many who will fling aside his volume, or never take it up, but the few who will understand him. . . . As if the printed book, thrown at large on the wide world, were certain to find out the divided segment of the writer's own nature, and complete his circle of existence by bringing him into communion with it. . . . And so as thoughts are frozen and utterance, benumbed unless the speaker stand in some true relation with this audience— it may be pardonable to imagine that a friend, a kind and apprehensive, though not the closest friend, is listening to our talk. (Nathaniel Hawthorne, "The Custom-House," *The Scarlet Letter*, 5–6)

Hawthorne's sensitivity to the relationship that writing implies is rare in academic prose, even when the subject would seem to make awareness of the reader inevitable. Alison Jaggar gave a lecture recently that crystallized the problem. Western epistemology, she argued, is shaped by the belief that emotion should be excluded from the process of attaining knowledge. Because women in our culture are not simply encouraged but *required* to be the bearers of emotion, which men are culturally conditioned to repress, an epistemology which excludes emotions from the process of attaining knowledge radically undercuts women's epistemic authority. The idea that the conventions defining legitimate sources of knowledge overlapped with the conventions defining appropriate gender behavior (male) came to me as a blinding insight. I saw that I had been socialized from birth to feel and act in ways that automatically excluded me from participating in the culture's most valued activities. No wonder I felt so uncomfortable in the postures academic prose forced me to assume; it was like wearing men's jeans.

Ellen Messer-Davidow's essay participates—as Jaggar's lecture and my précis of it did—in the conventions of Western rationalism. It adopts the impersonal, technical vocabulary of the epistemic ideology it seeks to dislocate. The political problem posed by my need to reply to the essay is this: to adhere to the conventions is to uphold a male standard of rationality that militates against women's being recognized as culturally legitimate sources of knowledge. To break with the convention is to risk not being heard at all.

exactly

This is how I would reply to Ellen's essay if I were to do it in the professionally sanctioned way.

The essay provides feminist critics with an overarching framework for thinking about what they do, both in relation to mainstream criticism and in relation to feminist work in other fields. It allows the reader to see women's studies as a whole, furnishing useful categories for organizing a confusing and miscellaneous array of materials. It also provides excellent summaries of a wide variety of books and essays that readers might not otherwise encounter. The enterprise is carried out without pointed attacks on other theorists, without creating a cumbersome new vocabulary, without exhibitionistic displays of intellect or esoteric learning. Its practical aim—to define a field within which debate can take place—is fulfilled by *New Literary History*'s decision to publish it, and to do so in a format which includes replies.

(Very nice, Jane. You sound so reasonable and generous. But, as anybody can tell you, this is just the obligatory pat on the back before the stab in the entrails.)

The difficulty with the essay from a philosophical, as opposed to a practical, point of view is that the theory it offers as a basis for future work stems from a confused notion of what an epistemology is. The author says: "An epistemology . . . consists of assumptions that knowers make about the entities and processes in a domain of study, the relations that obtain among them, and the proper methods for investigating them" (p. 87). I want to quarrel with this definition. Epistemology, strictly speaking, is a *theory* about the origins and nature of knowledge. As such, it is a set of ideas explicitly held and consciously elaborated, and thus belongs to the practice of a subcategory of philosophy called epistemology. The fact that there is a branch of philosophy given over to the study of what knowledge is and how it is acquired is important, because it means that such theories are generated not in relation to this or that "domain of study" but in relation to one another: that is, within the context of already existing epistemological theories. They are rarely based upon a study of the practices of investigators within a particular field.

An epistemology does not consist of "assumptions that knowers make" in a particular field; it is a theory about how knowledge is acquired which makes sense, chiefly, in relation to other such theories. What Messer-Davidow offers as the "epistemology" of traditional literary critics is not *their* epistemology, if in fact they have one, but her description of what she assumes their assumptions are, a description which may or may not be correct. Moreover, if literary critics should indeed elaborate a theory of how they got their beliefs, that theory would have no privileged position in relation to their actual assumptions. It would simply be another theory.) This distinction—between actual assumptions and an observer's description of them (even when one is observing one's own practice)—is crucial because it points to an all-important fact about the relation of epistemology to what really gets done in a given domain of study, namely this: that epistemology, a theory about how one gets one's knowledge, in no way determines the particular knowledge that one has.

This fact is important because Messer-Davidow assumes that if we change our epistemology, our practice as critics will change, too. Specifically, she wants us to give up the subject-object theory, in which "knowledge is an abstract representation of objective existence," for a theory which says that what counts as knowledge is a function of situation and perspective. She believes that it follows from this latter theory that knowledge will become more equitable, more self-aware, and more humane.

I disagree. Knowing that my knowledge is perspectival, language-based, culturally constructed, or what have you, does not change in the slightest the things I believe to be true. All that it changes is what I think about how we get knowledge. The insight that my ideas are all products of the situation I occupy in the world applies to all of my ideas equally (including the idea that knowledge is culturally based) and to all of everybody else's ideas as well. So where does this get us? Right back to where we were before, mainly. I still believe what I believe and, if you differ with me, think that you are wrong. If I want to change your mind I still have to persuade you that I am right by using evidence, reasons, chains of inference, citations of authority, analogies, illustrations, and so on. Believing that what I believe comes from my being in a particular cultural framework does not change my relation to my beliefs. I still believe them just as much as if I thought they came from God, or the laws of nature, or my autonomous self.

Here endeth the epistle.

But while I think Ellen is wrong in thinking that a change of epistemology can mean a change in the kinds of things we think, I am in sympathy with the ends she has in view. This sympathy prompts me to say that my professionally correct reply is not on target. Because the target, the goal, rather, is not to be fighting over these questions, trying to beat the other person down. (What the goal is, it is harder to say.) Intellectual debate, if it were in the right spirit, would be wonderful. But I don't know how to be in the right spirit, exactly, can't make points without sounding rather superior and smug. Most of all, I don't know how to enter the debate without leaving everything else behind—the birds outside my window, my grief over Janice, just myself as a person sitting here in stockinged feet, a little bit chilly because the windows are open, and thinking about going to the bathroom. But not going yet.

I find that when I try to write in my "other" voice, I am immediately critical of it. It wobbles, vacillates back and forth, is neither this nor that. The voice in which I write about epistemology is familiar, I know how it ought to sound. This voice, though, I hardly know. I don't even know if it has anything to say. But if I never write in it, it never will. So I have to try. (That is why, you see, this doesn't sound too good. It isn't a practiced performance, it hasn't got a surface. I'm asking you to bear with me while I try, hoping that this, what I write, will express something you yourself have felt or will help you find a part of yourself that you would like to express.)

The thing I want to say is that I've been hiding a part of myself for a long time. I've known it was there, but I couldn't listen because there was no place for this person in literary criticism. The criticism I would like to write would always take off from personal experience. Would always be in some way a chronicle of my hours and days. Would speak in a voice which can talk about everything, would reach out to a reader like me and touch me where I want to be touched. Susan Griffin's voice in "The Way of All Ideology." I want to speak in what Ursula LeGuin, at the Bryn Mawr College commencement in 1986, called the "mother tongue." This is LeGuin speaking:

> The dialect of the father tongue that you and I learned best in college . . . only lectures. . . . Many believe this dialect—the expository and particularly scientific discourse—is the *highest* form of language, the true language, of which all other uses of words are primitive vestiges. . . . And it is indeed a High Language. . . . Newton's *Principia* was written in it in Latin . . . and Kant wrote German in it, and Marx, Darwin, Freud, Boas, Foucault, all the great scientists and social thinkers wrote it. It is the language of thought that seeks objectivity.
>
> . . . The essential gesture of the father tongue is not reasoning, but distancing—making a gap, a space, between the subject or self and the object or other. . . . Everywhere now everybody speaks [this] language in laboratories and government buildings and head-quarters and offices of business. . . . The father tongue is spoken from above. It goes one way. No answer is expected, or heard.
>
> . . . The mother tongue, spoken or written, expects an answer. It is conversation, a word the root of which means "turning together." The mother tongue is language not as mere communication, but as relation, relationship. It connects. . . . Its power is not in dividing but in binding. . . . We all know it by heart. John have you got your umbrella I think it's going to rain. Can you come play with me? If I told you once I told you a hundred times. . . . O what am I going to do? . . . Pass the soy sauce please. Oh, shit. . . . You look like what the cat dragged in. (3–4)

Much of what I'm saying elaborates or circles around these quotes from LeGuin. I find that having released myself from the duty to say things I'm not interested in, in a language I resist, I feel free to entertain other people's voices. Quoting them becomes a pleasure of appreciation rather than the obligatory giving of credit, because when I write in a voice that is not struggling to be heard through the screen of a forced language, I no longer feel that it is not I who am speaking, and so there is more room for what others have said.

One sentence in Ellen's essay stuck out for me the first time I read it and the second and the third: "In time we can build a synchronous account of our subject matters as we glissade among them and turn upon ourselves" (p. 79).

What attracted me to the sentence was the "glissade." Fluidity, flexi-bility, versatility, mobility. Moving from one thing to another without embarrassment. It is a tenet of feminist rhetoric that the personal is political, but who in the academy acts on this where language is con-cerned? We all speak the father tongue, which is impersonal, while decry-ing the fathers' ideas. All of what I have written so far is in a kind of watered-down expository prose. Not much imagery. No description of concrete things. Only that one word, "glissade."

> Like black swallows swooping and gliding
> in a flurry of entangled loops and curves

Two lines of a poem I memorized in high school are what the word "glissade" called to mind. Turning upon ourselves. Turning, weaving, bending, unbending, moving in loops and curves.

I don't believe we can ever turn upon ourselves in the sense Ellen intends. You can't get behind the thing that casts the shadow. *You* cast the shadow. As soon as you turn, the shadow falls in another place. Is still your shadow. You have not got "behind" yourself. That is why self-consciousness is not the way to make ourselves better than we are.

Just me and my shadow, walkin' down the avenue.

It is a beautiful day here in North Carolina. The first day that is both cool and sunny all summer. After a terrible summer, first drought, then heat-wave, then torrential rain, trees down, flooding. Now, finally, beauti-ful weather. A tree outside my window just brushed by red, with one fully red leaf. (This is what I want you to see. A person sitting in stockinged feet looking out of her window—a floor to ceiling rectangle filled with green, with one red leaf. The season poised, sunny and chill, ready to rush down the incline into autumn. But perfect, and still. Not going yet.)

My response to this essay is not a response to something Ellen Messer-Davidow has written; it is a response to something within myself. As I reread the opening pages I feel myself being squeezed into a straitjacket; I wriggle, I will not go in. As I read the list "subject matters, methods of reasoning, and epistemology," the words will not go down. They belong to a debate whose susurrus hardly reaches my ears.

The liberation Ellen promises from the straitjacket of a subject-object epistemology is one I experienced some time ago. Mine didn't take the form she outlines, but it was close enough. I discovered, or thought I discovered, that the poststructuralist way of understanding language and knowledge enabled me to say what I wanted about the world. It enabled me to do this because it pointed out that the world I knew was a construct of ways of thinking about it and, as such, had no privileged claim on the truth. Truth in fact would always be just such a construction, and so one could offer another, competing, description and thus help to change the world that was.

The catch was that anything I might say or imagine was itself the product of an already existing discourse. Not something "I" had made up but a way of constructing things I had absorbed from the intellectual surround. Poststructuralism's proposition about the constructed nature of things held good, but that did not mean that the world could be changed by an act of will. For, as we are looking at this or that phenomenon and re-seeing it, re-thinking it, the rest of the world, that part of it from which we do the seeing, is still there, in place, real, irrefragable as a whole, and making visible what we see, though changed by it, too.

This little lecture pretends to something I no longer want to claim. The pretense is in the tone and level of the language, not in what it says about poststructuralism. The claim being made by the language is analogous to what Barthes calls the "reality effect" of historical writing, whose real message is not that this or that happened but that reality exists. So the claim of this language I've been using (and am using right now) lies in its implicit deification of the speaker. Let's call it the "authority effect." I cannot describe the pretense except to talk about what it ignores: the human frailty of the speaker, his body, his emotions, his history; the moment of intercourse with the reader—acknowledgment of the other person's presence, feelings, needs. This "authoritative" language speaks as though the other person weren't there. Or perhaps more accurately, it doesn't bother to imagine who, as Hawthorne said, is listening to our talk.

How can we speak personally to one another and yet not be self-centered? How can we be part of the great world and yet remain loyal to ourselves?

It seems to me that I am trying to write out of my experience without acknowledging any discontinuity between this and the subject matter of the profession I work in—and at the same time find that I no longer want to write about that subject matter, as it appears in Ellen's essay. I am, on the one hand, demanding a connection between literary theory and my own life and asserting, on the other, that there is no connection.

But here is a connection. I learned what epistemology I know from my husband. I think of it as more his game than mine. It's a game I enjoy playing but which I no longer need or want to play. I want to declare my independence of it, of him. (Part of what is going on here has to do with a need I have to make sure I'm not being absorbed in someone else's personality.) What I am breaking away from is both my conformity to the conventions of a male professional practice and my intellectual dependence on my husband. How can I talk about such things in public? How can I *not*.

Looking for something to read this morning, I took three books down from my literary theory shelf, in order to prove a point. The first book was Félix Guattari's *Molecular Revolution*. I find it difficult to read, and therefore have read very little of it, but according to a student who is a disciple of Deleuze and Guattari, "molecular revolution" has to do with getting away from ideology and enacting revolution within daily life. It is specific, not programmed—that is, it does not have a "method," nor "steps," and is neither psychoanalytic nor Marxist, although its discourse seems shaped by those discourses, antithetically. From this kind of revolution, said I to myself, disingenuously, one would expect some recognition of the personal. A revolution that started with daily life would have to begin, or at least would have sometimes to reside, at home. So I open at a section entitled "Towards a New Vocabulary," looking for something in the mother tongue, and this is what I find:

> The distinction I am proposing between machine and structure is based solely on the way we use the words; we may consider that we are merely dealing with a 'written device' of the kind one has to invent for dealing with a mathematical problem, or with an axiom that may have to be reconsidered at a particular stage of development, or again with the kind of machine we shall be talking about here.
>
> I want therefore to make it clear that I am putting into parentheses the fact that, in reality, a machine is inseparable from its structural articulations and conversely, that each contingent structure is dominated (and this is what I want to demonstrate) by a system of machines, or at the very least by one logic machine. (111)

At this point, I start to skip, reading only the first sentence of each paragraph.

> "We may say of structure that it positions its elements . . ."
> "The agent of action, whose definition here does not extend beyond this principle of reciprocal determination . . ."
> "The machine, on the other hand remains essentially remote . . ."
> "The history of technology is dated . . ."

"Yesterday's machine, today's and tomorrow's, are not related in their structural determinations . . ."

I find this language incredibly alienating. In fact, the paragraph after the one I stopped at begins: "The individual's relation to the machine has been described by sociologists following Friedmann as one of fundamental alienation." I will return to this essay some day and read it. I sense that it will have something interesting to say. But the effort is too great now. What strikes me now is the incredibly distancing effect of this language. It is totally abstract and impersonal. Though the author uses the first person ("The distinction I am proposing," "I want therefore to make it clear"), it quickly became clear to me that he had no interest whatsoever in the personal, or in concrete situations as I understand them—a specific person, at a specific machine, somewhere in time and space, with something on his/her mind, real noises, smells, aches and pains. He has no interest in his own experience of machines or in explaining why he is writing about them, what they mean to him personally. I take down the next book: *Poetry and Repression* by Harold Bloom.

This book should contain some reference to the self, to the author's self, to ourselves, to how people feel, to how the author feels, since its subject is psychological: repression. I open the book at page 1 and read:

> Jacques Derrida asks a central question in his essay on "Freud and the Scene of Writing": "What is a text, and what must the psyche be if it can be represented by a text?" My narrow concern with poetry prompts the contrary question: "What is a psyche, and what must a text be if it can be represented by a psyche?" Both Derrida's question and my own require exploration of three terms: "psyche," "text," "represented."
>
> "Psyche" is ultimately from the Indo-European root. . . . (1)

—and I stop reading.

The subject of poetry and repression will involve the asking and answering of questions about "a text"—a generalized, nonparticular object that has been the subject of endless discussion for the past twenty years—and about an equally disembodied "psyche" in relation to the thing called "a text"—not, to my mind or rather in view of my desires, a very promising relation in which to consider it. Answering these questions, moreover, will "require" (on whose part, I wonder?) the "exploration" of "three terms." Before we get to the things themselves—psyches, texts—we shall have to spend a lot of time looking at them *as words*. With the beginning of the next paragraph, we get down to the etymology of "psyche." With my agenda, I get off the bus here.

But first I look through the book. Bloom is arguing against canonical readings (of some very canonical poems) and for readings that are not exactly personal, but in which the drama of a self is constantly being played out on a cosmic stage—lots of references to God, kingdom, Paradise, the fall, the eternal—a biblical stage on which, apparently, only men are players (God, Freud, Christ, Nietzsche, and the poets). It is a drama that, although I can see how gripping Bloom can make it, will pall for me because it isn't *my* drama.

Book number three, Michel Foucault's *History of Sexuality,* is more promising. Section One is entitled "We 'other Victorians.'" So Foucault is acknowledging his and our implication in the object of the study. This book will in some way be about "ourselves," which is what I want. It begins:

> For a long time, the story goes, we supported a Victorian regime, and we continue to be dominated by it even today. Thus the image of the imperial prude is emblazoned on our restrained, mute, and hypocritical sexuality. (3)

Who, exactly, are "we"? Foucault is using the convention in which the author establishes common ground with his reader by using the first person plural—a presumptuous, though usually successful, move. Presumptuous because it presumes that we are really like him, and successful because, especially when an author is famous, and even when he isn't, "our" instinct (I criticize the practice and engage in it too) is to want to cooperate, to be included in the circle the author is drawing so cosily around "us." It is chummy, this "we." It feels good, for a little while, until it starts to feel coercive, until "we" are subscribing to things that "I" don't believe.

There is no specific reference to the author's self, no attempt to specify himself. It continues:

At the beginning of the seventeenth century . . .

I know now where we are going. We are going to history. "At the beginning of the seventeenth century a certain frankness was still common, it would seem." Generalizations about the past, though pleasantly qualified ("a certain frankness," "it would seem"), are nevertheless disappointingly magisterial. Things continue in a generalizing vein—"It was a time of direct gestures, shameless discourse, and open transgressions." It's not so much that I don't believe him as that I am uncomfortable with the level or the mode of discourse. It is everything that, I thought, Foucault was trying to get away from in *The Archaeology of Knowledge*. The primacy of the subject as the point of view from which history could be written, the bland assumption of authority, the taking over of time, of substance, of event, the imperialism of description from a unified perspective. Even though the subject matter interests me—sex, hypocrisy, whether or not our view of Victorianism and of ourselves in relation to it is correct—I am not eager to read on. The point of view is discouraging. It will march along giving orders, barking out commands. I'm not willing to go along for the march, not even on Foucault's say-so (I am, or have been, an extravagant admirer of his).

So I turn to "my" books. To the women's section of my shelves. I take down, unerringly, an anthology called *The Powers of Desire* edited by Christine Stansell, Ann Snitow, and Sharon Thompson. I turn, almost as unerringly, to an essay by Jessica Benjamin entitled "Master and Slave: The Fantasy of Erotic Domination," and begin to read:

> This essay is concerned with the violence of erotic domination. It is about the strange union of rationality and violence that is made in the secret heart of our culture and sometimes enacted in the body. This union has inspired some of the holiest imagery of religious transcendence and now comes to light at the porno newsstands, where women are regularly depicted in the bonds of love. But the slave of love is not always a woman, not always a heterosexual; the fantasy of erotic domination permeates all sexual imagery in our culture. (281)

I am completely hooked, I am going to read this essay from beginning to end and proceed to do so. It gets better, much better, as it goes along. In fact, it gets so good, I find myself putting it down and straying from it because the subject is *so* close to home, and therefore so threatening, that I need relief from it, little breathers, before I can go on. I underline vigorously and often. Think of people I should give it to to read (my husband, this colleague, that colleague).

But wait a minute. There is no personal reference here. The author deals, like Foucault, in generalities. In even bigger ones than his: hers aren't limited to the seventeenth century or the Victorian era. She generalizes about religion, rationality, violence. Why am I not turned off by this as I was in Foucault's case? Why don't I reject this as a grand drama in the style of Bloom? Why don't I bridle at the abstractions as I did when reading Guattari? Well?

The answer is, I see the abstractions as concrete and the issues as personal. They are already personal for me without being personal*ized* because they concern things I've been thinking about for some time, struggling with, trying to figure out for myself. I don't need the author to identify her own involvement, I don't need her to concretize, because these things are already personal and concrete for me. The erotic is already eroticized.

Probably, when Guattari picks up an article whose first sentence has the words "machine," "structure," and "determination," he cathects it immediately. Great stuff. Juicy, terrific. The same would go for Bloom on encountering multiple references to Nietzsche, representation, God the father, and the Sublime. But isn't erotic domination, as a subject, surer to arouse strong feeling than systems of machines or the psyche that can be represented as a text? Clearly, the answer depends on the readership. The people at the convenience store where I stop to get gas and buy milk would find all these passages equally baffling. Though they *might* have uneasy stirrings when they read Jessica Benjamin. "Erotic domination," especially when coupled with "porno newsstands," does call some feelings into play almost no matter who you are in this culture.

But I will concede the point. What is personal is completely a function of what is perceived as personal. And what is perceived as personal by men, or rather, what is gripping, significant, "juicy," is different from what is felt to be that way by women. For what we are really talking about is not the personal as such, what we are talking about is what is important, answers one's needs, strikes one as immediately *interesting*. For women, the personal is such a category.

In literary criticism, we have moved from the New Criticism, which was antipersonal and declared the personal off-limits at every turn—the intentional fallacy, the affective fallacy—to structuralism, which does away with the self altogether—at least as something unique and important to consider—to deconstruction, which subsumes everything in language and makes the self non-self-consistent, ungraspable, a floating signifier, and finally to new historicism which re-institutes the discourse of the object—"In the seventeenth century"—with occasional side glances at how the author's "situatedness" affects his writing.

The female subject par excellence, which is her self and her experiences, has once more been elided by literary criticism.

The question is, why did this happen? One might have imagined a different outcome. The 1960s paves the way for a new personalism in literary discourse by opening literary discussion up to politics, to psychology, to the "reader," to the effects of style. What happened to deflect criticism into the impersonal labyrinths of "language," "discourse," "system," "network," and now, with Guattari, "machine"?

I met Ellen Messer-Davidow last summer at the School of Criticism and Theory where she was the undoubted leader of the women who were there. She organized them, led them (I might as well say us, since, although I was on the faculty as a visiting lecturer, she led me, too). At the end of the summer we put on a symposium, a kind of teach-in on feminist criticism and theory, of which none was being offered that summer. I thought it really worked. Some people, eager to advertise their intellectual superiority, murmured disappointment at the "level" of discussion (code for, "my mind is finer and more rigorous than yours"). One person who spoke out at the closing session said he felt bulldozed: a more honest and useful response. The point is that Ellen's leadership affected the experience of everyone at the School that summer. What she offered was not an intellectual performance calculated to draw attention to the quality of her mind, but a sustained effort of practical courage that changed the situation we were in. I think that the kind of thing Ellen did should be included in our concept of criticism: analysis that is not an end in itself but pressure brought to bear on a situation.

Now it's time to talk about something that's central to everything I've been saying so far, although it doesn't *show,* as we used to say about the slips we used to wear. If I had to bet on it, I would say that Ellen Messer-Davidow was motivated last summer, and probably in her essay, by anger (forgive me, Ellen, if I am wrong), anger at her, our, exclusion from what was being studied at the School, our exclusion from the discourse of "Western man." I interpret her behavior this way because anger is what fuels my engagement with feminist issues; an absolute fury that has never even been tapped, relatively speaking. It's time to talk about this now, because it's so central, at least for me. I hate men for the way they treat women, and pretending that women aren't there is one of the ways I hate most.

Last night I saw a movie called *Gunfight at the OK Corral,* starring Burt Lancaster and Kirk Douglas. The movie is patently about the love-relationship between the characters these men play—Wyatt Earp and Doc Holliday. The women in the movie are merely pawns that serve in various ways to reflect the characters of the men and to advance the story of their relationship to one another. There is a particularly humiliating part, played by Jo Van Fleet, the part of Doc Holliday's mistress—Kate

Fisher—whom he treats abominably (everybody in the movie acknowledges this, it's not just me saying so). This woman is degraded over and over again. She is a whore, she is a drunkard, she is a clinging woman, she betrays the life of Wyatt Earp in order to get Doc Holliday back, she is *no longer young* (perhaps this is her chief sin). And her words are always in vain, they are chaff, less than nothing, another sign of her degradation.

Now Doc Holliday is a similarly degraded character. He used to be a dentist and is now a gambler who lives to get other people's money away from them; he is a drunk, and he abuses the woman who loves him. But his weaknesses, in the perspective of the movie, are glamorous. He is irresistible, charming, seductive, handsome, witty, commanding; it's no wonder Wyatt Earp falls for him, who wouldn't? The degradation doesn't stick to Kirk Douglas; it is all absorbed by his female counterpart, the "slut," Jo Van Fleet. We are embarrassed every time she appears on the screen, because every time, she is humiliated further.

What enrages me is the way women are used as extensions of men, mirrors of men, devices for showing men off, devices for helping men get what they want. They are never there in their own right, or rarely. The world of the Western contains no women.

Sometimes I think *the world* contains no women.

Why am I so angry?

My anger is partly the result of having been an only child who caved in to authority very early on. As a result I've built up a huge storehouse of hatred and resentment against people in authority over me (mostly male). Hatred and resentment and attraction.

Why should poor men be made the object of this old pent-up anger? (Old anger is the best anger, the meanest, the truest, the most intense. Old anger is pure because it's been dislocated from its source for so long, has had the chance to ferment, to feed on itself for so many years, so that it is nothing but anger. All cause, all relation to the outside world, long since sloughed off, withered away. The rage I feel inside me now is the distillation of forty-six years. It has had a long time to simmer, to harden, to become adamantine, a black slab that glows in the dark.)

Are all feminists fueled by such rage? Is the molten lava of millennia of hatred boiling below the surface of every essay, every book, every syllabus, every newsletter, every little magazine? I imagine that I can open the front of my stomach like a door, reach in, and pluck from memory the rooted sorrow, pull it out, root and branch. But where, or rather, who, would I be then? I am attached to this rage. It is a source of identity for me. It is a motivator, an explainer, a justifier, a no-need-to-say-more greeter at the door. If I were to eradicate this anger somehow, what would I do? Volunteer work all day long?

A therapist once suggested to me that I blamed on sexism a lot of stuff that really had to do with my own childhood. Her view was basically the one articulated in Alice Miller's *The Drama of the Gifted Child,* in which the good child has been made to develop a false self by parents who cathect the child narcissistically. My therapist meant that if I worked out some of my problems—as she understood them, on a psychological level—my feminist rage would subside.

Maybe it would, but that wouldn't touch the issue of female oppression. Here is what Miller says about this:

> Political action can be fed by the unconscious anger of children who have been . . . misused, imprisoned, exploited, cramped, and drilled. . . . If, however, disillusionment and the resultant mourning can be lived through . . . , then social and political disengagement do not usually follow, but the patient's actions are freed from the compulsion to repeat. (101)

According to Miller's theory, the critical voice inside me, the voice I noticed butting in, belittling, doubting, being wise, is "the contemptuous introject."—the introjection of authorities who manipulated me, without necessarily meaning to. I think that if you can come to terms with your "contemptuous introjects," learn to forgive and understand them, your anger will go away.

But if you're not angry, can you still act? Will you still care enough to write the letters, make the phone calls, attend the meetings? You need to find another center within yourself from which to act. A center of outgoing, outflowing, giving feelings. Love instead of anger. I'm embarrassed to say words like these because I've been taught they are mushy and sentimental and smack of cheap popular psychology. I've been taught to look down on people who read M. Scott Peck and Leo Buscaglia and Harold Kushner, because they're people who haven't very much education and because they're mostly women. Or if not women, then people who take responsibility for learning how to deal with their feelings, who take responsibility for marriages that are going bad, for children who are in trouble, for friends who need help, for themselves. The disdain for popular psychology and for words like "love" and "giving" is part of the police action that academic intellectuals wage ceaselessly against feeling, against women, against what is personal. The ridiculing of the "touchy-feely," of the "Mickey Mouse," of the sentimental (often associated with teaching that takes students' concerns into account), belongs to the tradition Alison Jaggar rightly characterized as founding knowledge in the denial of emotion. It is looking down on women, with whom feelings are associated, and on the activities with which women are identified: mother, nurse, teacher, social worker, volunteer.

So for a while I can't talk about epistemology. I can't deal with the philosophical bases of feminist literary criticisms. I can't strap myself psychically into an apparatus that will produce the right gestures when I begin to move. I have to deal with the trashing of emotion and with my anger against it.

This one time I've taken off the straitjacket, and it feels so good.

References

Benjamin, Jessica. "Master and Slave: The Fantasy of Erotic Domination." *The Powers of Desire: The Politics of Sexuality*. Ed. Ann Snitow, Christine Stansell, and Sharon Thompson. New York: Monthly Review Press, 1983. 280–89.

Bloom, Harold. *Poetry and Repression: Revision from Blake to Stevens*. New Haven, Conn.: Yale University Press, 1976.

Foucault, Michel. *The History of Sexuality, Volume 1: An Introduction*. Trans. Robert Hurley. New York: Vintage Books, 1980. Copyright 1978 by Random House. [Originally published in French as *La Volonté de Savoir*. Paris: Editions Gallimard, 1976.]

Griffin, Susan. "The Way of All Ideology." *Made from the Earth: An Anthology of Writings*. New York: Harper and Row, 1982. 161–82.

Guattari, Félix. *Molecular Revolution: Psychiatry and Politics*. Trans. Rosemary Sheed, intro. David Cooper. New York: Penguin Books, 1984. [First published as *Psychanalyse et transversalité* (1972), and *La Révolution moléculaire* (1977).]

Hawthorne, Nathaniel. *The Scarlet Letter and Other Tales of the Puritans*. Ed. with an intro. and notes by Harry Levin. Boston, Mass.: Houghton Mifflin, 1960–61.

LeGuin, Ursula. "The Mother Tongue." *Bryn Mawr Alumnae Bulletin* (Summer 1986): 3–4.

Miller, Alice. *The Drama of the Gifted Child*. New York: Basic Books, 1983.

Beyond

Literary Darwinism:

Women's Voices and

Critical Discourse

*

Olivia Frey

In an unusual and important essay in *New Literary History* entitled "Me and My Shadow," Jane Tompkins breaks with the conventions of our literary professional community, at least for a moment. She writes, "There are two voices inside me. . . . One is the voice of a critic who wants to correct a mistake. . . . The other is the voice of a person who wants to write about her feelings. (I have wanted to do this for a long time but have felt too embarrassed.)" (169). Ostensibly, Tompkins's essay is a response to Ellen Messer-Davidow's "The Philosophical Bases of Feminist Literary Criticisms," but it becomes more than this. At least by implication, it is also a critique of the way that we write literary criticism. The essay becomes an opportunity for Tompkins to throw off the conventions of our discipline, constraints that she likens to a "straitjacket," and to write in a way that seems more "natural" to her. She writes that she has felt "uncomfortable in the postures academic prose forced me to assume; it is like wearing men's jeans" (170).

"Me and My Shadow" is by no means *ecriture feminine,* although I would describe it as revolutionary. It is Tompkins's brave experiment in writing literary criticism in her own personal voice. Like many feminist writers these days, she is struggling to find "(m)other tongues," a new feminist language that is not derivative of male language, a new language that is accessible, concrete, real, an embodiment of the feminine.

With her essay, Tompkins raises several important issues that those of us in the community of literary scholars cannot ignore. Although we can count numerous powerful works by feminist literary critics; although we have Rachel Blau DuPlessis and "For the Etruscans"—personal, angry, evocative, sensual, not easily categorized as either prose, poem, or song; although we have Diane P. Freedman's *An Alchemy of Genres* in her personal feminist voice, weaving her poetry throughout her prose as she describes other women writers, like Gloria Anzaldúa, breaking through the boundaries of literary critical form; although we have these writers in our hands, the profession by and large values conventions of literary critical discourse that may not fit the values, the perceptual frameworks, and the ways of writing of many women in English departments across the country. These women are me and you. Some are famous, more are not. Some of us have families and companions; some of us live alone. Some of us are women of color. Some of us are white middle class. Most of us want to write. Many of us want to have our work published. We also yearn to take the risks that Jane Tompkins or Rachel Blau DuPlessis does. But we play it safe. Otherwise our writing might not be published.

Many of the day-to-day activities of the profession seem unbiased. The president of the Modern Language Association is a woman. Feminist journals and presses exist that will publish feminist articles. *PMLA* publishes feminist readings of literature. It seems that the profession not only tolerates scholarship by women but encourages it. In reviewing submissions to *PMLA*, consultant readers, the Advisory Committee, and other editors do not know the author's name "until a final decision is reached." Rejecting the piece outright because the writer is a woman would be obvious bias. I don't think it happens. The readers or editors, however, may reject a piece because "the work is not appropriate to the conventions of the discipline," "the work is not methodologically sound," or the writing is "too personal," in short, because "the work is not good enough." But if Tompkins's and other feminist writers' suggestions are true, if there is no such thing as gender-neutral criterion or ideologically neutral methodology or epistemology, then both situations could be equally discriminatory—rejecting an article at first glance because the writer is female or rejecting an article because the methodology may be feminist and therefore inappropriate, although the editors may not be aware that this is the basis on which their decision is made. The latter is the Jim Crow Law—hidden, but equally oppressive. Perhaps more so, since such bias cannot be eradicated through legislation, policies, or rules.

Another way that women scholars may be discriminated against is a form of suppression in which women themselves are complicit. This is the case with Janet, of Carolyn G. Heilbrun's *Death in a Tenured Position,* who puts on academic prose in the same way that some women wear business suits. She would not want to be called "female scholar," but "scholar." This woman scholar writes academic prose very skillfully, but it is inauthentic. This woman, too, is silenced, although, ironically, her voice seems forceful and effective.

I have oversimplified the scheme of oppression laid out above for the sake of framing my discussion. The scheme ignores some crucial issues that we must also explore. For example, feminists continue to question what it means to be feminine, that is, what is the "true nature of women." And they ask, did men make conventional literary critical discourse? And third, what do we make of scholarly women who are very happy writing literary criticism in a conventional, one might say masculine, way (or, to turn it around, men who are not)? Although Jane Tompkins at the moment is not happy, she does say that there are "two voices inside," not one real voice and one inauthentic one. She says, "in reality there's no split. It's the same person who feels and who discourses about epistemology" (169). Finally, what are the implications for our profession as a whole, women and men? How we resolve the issues that I raise affects the shape of our discipline in years to come.

Feminist writers from across the disciplines suggest that the traditional conventions of our disciplinary community, with the possible exception of composition studies, may be at odds with what has been identified as a feminist value system and epistemology. I mention composition studies because, as Elizabeth Flynn suggests in "Composing As a Woman," the "emerging field of composition studies could be described as a feminization of our previous conceptions of how writers write and how writing should be taught," particularly with its emphasis on process (423). Because in this essay I focus on literary criticism rather than composition studies, I have not looked at essays about composition theory and teaching in any systematic way, although one of my examples of the adversary mode is taken from *College Composition and Communication.* While conceptions of writing and writing pedagogy might be feminist, are the essays about these subjects written using feminist forms?   *Define this*

In any event, I would not describe the conventions of mainstream literary critical writing as feminist. These conventions include the use of argument as the preferred mode for discussion, the importance of the objective and impersonal, the importance of a finished product without direct reference to the process by which it was accomplished, and the necessity of being thorough in order to establish proof and reach a definitive (read "objective") conclusion. A common denominator of each convention seems to be "to get it right," that is, establish cognitive authority. In her discussion of a feminine dialogic model of reading that may have qualities in common with a feminine model of writing, Patrocinio Schweickart writes that with the dialogic model, "the problematic is defined by the drive to connect," rather than "the drive to get it right," which is the "preoccupation of the mainstream model of reading" (54–55). Schweickart bases her model on the work of Carol Gilligan, Nancy Chodorow, and others.

Most readers are familiar with the theories of Carol Gilligan, but as a point of reference I will quote a brief passage from *In a Different Voice:*

> When one begins with the study of women and derives developmental constructs from their lives, the outline of a moral conception different from that described by Freud, Piaget, or Kohlberg begins to emerge and informs a different description of development. In this conception, the moral problem arises from conflicting responsibilities rather than from competing rights and requires for its resolution a mode of thinking that is contextual and narrative rather than formal and abstract. This conception of morality as concerned with the activity of care centers moral development around the understanding of responsibility and relationships, just as the conception of morality as fairness ties moral development to the understanding of rights and rules. (19)

To put it very simply, Gilligan, Schweickart, and others are talking about what matters to women. Gilligan means, too, what matters to women in most circumstances, not only when we are making moral decisions, but in our everyday endeavors—thinking, learning, studying, making mundane decisions like what color to paint the house or what to cook for dinner; or making more significant decisions, like whether to have this baby or not, or whether to go to this conference or not (I will miss my son's play if I go). Writing literary criticism involves such thought and decision making—thinking through ideas and making choices—and one would think that the feminine perceptual framework that Gilligan and others describe would be in operation here too. But to look at most modern literary criticism that both men and women write, one wonders if the assumption is correct. The form that literary criticism takes could not be a manifestation of that feminine perceptual framework.

This discrepancy is what Tompkins is getting at when she talks about what she should do as a critic, but what, for once in her life, she does not want to do. She has thought deeply about what matters to her at this moment, and it is something else, not an impersonal critique of Ellen's essay, and so the form of Tompkins's essay is unusual:

> But while I think Ellen is wrong in thinking that a change in episte-mology can mean a change in the kinds of things we think, I am in sympathy with the ends she has in view. This sympathy prompts me to say that my professionally correct reply is not on target. Because the target, the goal, rather, is not to be fighting over these questions, trying to beat the other person down. (What the goal is, is harder to say.) Intellectual debate if it were in the right spirit would be wonderful. But I don't know how to be in the right spirit exactly, can't make my points without sounding kind of superior and smug. Most of all, I don't know how to enter the debate without leaving everything else behind. (172–73)

The "everything" that Tompkins would need to leave behind were she to enter the debate include "the birds outside my window," the recent suicide of a dear friend and the grief that she feels, and her relationship with Ellen Messer-Davidow. Tompkins's mode of thinking, in this case as a scholar engaged in, or attempting to engage in, intellectual debate, is tenaciously "contextual and narrative rather than formal and abstract" (Gilligan 19). The suggestion is that it is difficult—I did not say impossi-ble, since so many women do it and do it very well—it is difficult for some women to engage in intellectual debate so often required in literary scholarship. The situation suggests to me a serious but imperceptible form of suppression similar to the sort of structural discrimination that femi-nist philosophers and scientists are beginning to unmask. Within our own disciplinary community, it seems to me, may exist similar implicit as-sumptions, generally unquestioned, about what is correct and what is good. Those who have power define and maintain these standards and use them to wield power, although they may not think that they are repress-ing someone or even exercising power. What they think they are doing is maintaining excellence, in a very abstract way. But in effect, these stan-dards may be used to maintain the status quo and exclude the other, that is, to undermine what Judy Lensink and others have described as femi-nine epistemic authority.

In order to see more concretely how conventional discourse might be incompatible with a so-called feminine epistemology, I would like to focus on one convention of literary criticism that seems to pervade writings in our discipline. I call it the "adversary method," a term borrowed from

Janice Moulton's discussion of the same methodology in philosophy. Using this method, the writer presents a thesis, preferably a yet unanalyzed issue or aspect of literature, and tests the thesis against the assertions of other scholars. Janice Moulton describes the adversary method in philosophy:

> [Most] important, the philosophic enterprise is seen as an impassioned debate between adversaries who try to defend their own views against counterexamples and produce counterexamples to opposing views. . . . [A] thesis which survives this method of evaluation is more likely to be correct than one that has not; and that a thesis subjected to the Adversary Method will have passed an "objective" test. (152–53)

The term "adversary" may seem quite extreme in describing a method that is used to establish the validity of a point about literature, an act usually considered a virtue. In describing quality pieces recently published in *PMLA*, the referees and editor used such words as "careful," "painstaking," "effective," "clear," "readable," "disciplined," "adroit," and, most frequently, "persuasive," all considered exemplary qualities in literary criticism. "Adversary," on the other hand, suggests rather unvirtuous qualities—combative, argumentative (the bad kind), violent, and so on. Nevertheless, it must be admitted that argument is a form of rhetoric believed to be essential for good literary criticism. But are there different kinds of argument: the bad kind, where people yell at each other and possibly hit each other, and the good kind, where people discuss in a reasoned manner and, although they might disagree, nevertheless engage in a lively debate and learn a great deal from each other? And isn't the argumentative stance in literary criticism the good kind?

What I have seen, nevertheless, is that in literary criticism there are several levels of arguments, and some of the arguments are even of the bad kind—some writers get nasty and say things that hurt other writers' feelings. I have also seen that other debates that seem innocent and in the good spirit of scholarly exchange (Is this like a "limited nuclear exchange"?) are actually not quite so innocent if one looks a bit more closely at the implications of the words that scholars use in answering their colleagues' counterarguments, as well as the general argumentative stance of the discipline as an institution. Walter Ong has suggested in *Fighting for Life* that the "agonistic edge of oratory [and by implication rhetoric] is dulled" in the present world of academe (142). But from what I have seen, it is as sharp as ever. What troubles me the most is the basic, unexamined assumption that the best way to know things about literature and to help others know things about literature is by presenting a thesis and making a case for it by answering counterarguments. Words like "careful," "painstaking," "effective," and "clear" are invariably held to be synonymous with descriptive phrases like "tightly argued" and "persuasive," the implication being that if one does not argue well or argue at all, the writing is unclear, ineffective, and unconvincing, although referees and editors, after rejecting an article, may use nicer words like "loosely constructed" or "undeveloped."

What does the adversarial method look like? To coin a phrase, every graduate student knows the adversarial method. It is the necessity of establishing credibility or cognitive authority. It is the "Critics to date have ignored _____" or the "Critical opinion about _____ differs considerably, betraying how badly _____ has been misunderstood." (Fill in the blanks with your favorite novel and theme.) In order to collect examples, I read every essay published in *PMLA* from 1975–1988 (quite a feat in itself), as well as in a scattering of other journals and literary magazines, such as *Signs, Critical Inquiry, College English,* and *The New York Review of Books.* I have focused on articles in *PMLA* because the journal purports to be the voice of our profession. The editorial policy states that the journal publishes "essays of interest to those concerned with the study of language and literature" and that the "ideal *PMLA* essay exemplifies the best of its kind, whatever the kind." All of the essays that I read, with only two exceptions, used some version of the adversarial method. As I read, I categorized what I saw to be different kinds or degrees of adversarial relationships, if one can even use those two terms together, from the very mild adversarial stance (what Sheridan Baker calls "the argumentative edge") to outright hostility. The scholar may qualify or add to what other scholars have discussed or may correct, challenge, or verbally attack another. The scholar who attacks is usually sarcastic and condescending. It may also be important to note that I use the terms "scholar" and "critic" interchangeably throughout the essay, although Gerald Graff in *Professing Literature* teaches us some important distinctions between the two. In any case, it seems that both scholars and critics use the adversary method.

Most would not question that attacks may be uncalled for, but the scholar who corrects critical misperception about a literary work, or clears up "confusion," would appear to be doing a good thing. However, it could be that the attack is a natural outcome of all the qualifications and corrections, in the same way that T.V. host Mort Downey's guests actually start punching each other because of the adversarial nature of the show to begin with. Whether the statement is seemingly innocent and appears to be useful or whether it is obviously attacking, the goals nevertheless are the same—to establish cognitive authority not only by demonstrating the value of one's own idea but also by demonstrating the weakness or error in the ideas of others. At the heart of the literary critical enterprise seems to be competition, not cooperation. In my most cynical moments I have thought of our behavior as a sort of literary Darwinism, the survival of the fittest theory or the fittest scholar.

I would like to begin with the attacks not because I think that they appear more frequently than the other types of adversarial relationships but as a frame of reference against which we can look at the other, supposedly milder, adversarial forms. I also do not intend to blame the attackers, because what takes place seems natural, almost expected, given the general adversarial tone that pervades scholarly writing. Most attacks occur in journal space set aside for exactly this sort of thing—counter-statements, pro and con, act and react. Most of the signals that we receive from our profession indicate that this is our business—to refute, repudiate, or attack.

Before I begin providing examples, I want to mention that I do not name the critics to whom I refer. It is my own attempt to avoid the adversarial method. You will note, however, that my strategy is only partly successful, because the very basis of this essay is adversarial.

In the first example of verbal fisticuffs, three critics have written a response to an essay by M concerning the difficulties of ambiguous pronoun reference, a seemingly uncontroversial topic. The three critics, S, K, and G, at first glance seem to offer relatively mild adversarial statements: "We have serious disagreements with the implication of some of these principles, M's reading and analysis of many of his examples, the lessons for writers that follow from his analysis and principles, and his final apologia."

S, K, and G are polite, but what they are saying, in short, is that they disagree with everything that M has said. He is wrong on every count. M's response is very witty and controlled:

> I would have been grateful to Professors S, K, and G for the concerted attention they have given my essay had that attention been as considered as it was close. According to their misguided argument, nearly all my views, great and small, are wrong. Although my essay must speak for itself to the unbiased reader, I will try to correct their major misunderstandings and to suggest the source of their confusion.

M's statement, highlighted here, seems harsher than it might if our eyes were to skim across it in a Letter or Comment and Response section of our favorite journal. M has used the conventional discourse that we are used to, the sorts of words that critics usually use in discussing the statements of a scholar with whom a critic disagrees, words like "misguided argument," "misunderstandings," and "confusion," words that may actually be kinder in a euphemistic sort of way than the words that the critic could have used, like "stupid," "ignorant," or "imbecile." M uses similar conventional (adversarial) discourse throughout, ending finally with the following remark: "In the light of the many inadequacies of their critique, I do not think it presumptuous of me to ask Professors S, K, and G to examine carefully (perhaps for the first time) their basic assumptions in order to see whether these need to be modified or even replaced by more valid ones." I would like to assume for a minute that words mean something and are not simply conventional rhetorical filler. What, then, has M said about S, K, and G? Their work is sloppy. They have not given M's article "close attention." They are biased. They have misunderstood M's discussion and are confused. Worse, they have willfully distorted the issues to prove their point. They have not thought carefully, that is, examined the assumptions on which their argument is based. Last, their critique is full of inadequacies. What are we to make of this response? Does M mean what he says? If he does, these are very cutting remarks. Have I lost my sense of humor? If everyone feels OK about these remarks because they are in the "good spirit of scholarly exchange," I'm with Tompkins: I don't like the spirit. Or, if after awhile critics have heard such remarks long enough that they don't take them seriously, this bothers me even more, because it seems analogous to the child who is indifferent to suffering after having watched hundreds of hours of violent TV programs. The hurt is no longer real.

The next two examples are from full-length articles about literature. The first is an article that attacks feminist readings of Shakespeare's tragedies. The second is the well known controversy over Hans Walter Gabler's *Ulysses: The Corrected Text*.

The Shakespeare article shares certain characteristics with the counterstatement that I discuss above. The critic questions how well feminists have thought through the claims that they make. The article is different from the response in that the critic takes time, in fact has more space, setting up the attack, so that the adversarial stance is very subtle. I have seen it as an attack, nevertheless, because it has those characteristics that make it an attack rather than correction or qualification: the critic not only questions the abilities of the feminist scholars (both male and female) but also questions their motives, and does so in a condescending and sarcastic manner. In fact, the entire raison d'etre of the article seems to be to attack, to discredit not only the feminist readings of the tragedies but some general tenets of feminism.

The article begins, however, in a very congenial way. In fact, it appears that it will not be an attack at all, but a synthesis of ten years of feminist criticism of Shakespeare: "In this brief period it has enlisted a number of intelligent and dedicated critics and has produced a substantial body of publications."

As I began reading, I felt some relief. I was tired of the adversarial stance. Warning bells started ringing, however, as I read the next sentence: "It seems, then, that this is an appropriate time to examine the nature of this criticism, for while some of the individual studies have been subjected to scrutiny over the years (including some searching scrutiny from the feminists themselves), there has not yet been any systematic investigation of the methodology and consequences of the enterprise itself." Here is the adversary method in a nutshell. The assumption underlying this statement, and the adversarial method in general, is that any assertion must become the subject of scrutiny. The critic, L, states a few sentences later that the purpose of his essay will be to test the feminist approach and, by implication, "similar kinds of feminist criticism in other fields." As I continued to read L's summary of the criticism to date where he generously admitted that there was "some truth" to feminists' views, I waited for the "but," which came soon after. Using sarcasm, L proceeds in the article to question the critics' assumptions, their methods, and their conclusions. We read words like "weakness," "undermined," "problems," and "illogical." Like M, L also questions the integrity of the feminist authors by suggesting that the scholars have made claims that they cannot possibly support and that to achieve their ends they have manipulated the evidence and selected only that which will support their claims: "We will not be surprised to learn, therefore, that in these studies the cause of the tragedy is located not in the particular characters but in one of those two abstractions whose opposition constitutes the theme, nor will we be surprised to learn which one always turns out to be the guilty party."

I have to ask again, as I did with M, does L mean what he says? He does seem ambivalent, as though at some level he is aware of the implications of what he is saying. I hear ambivalence or qualification in such statements as "as many of the critics acknowledge" and "they can manipulate the theme to fit the facts (again, without necessarily meaning to deceive)." L himself says that feminist critics have admitted that the assertions in their articles are "only one possible way of viewing the plays." So L believes that while feminists are using very selective evidence, they nevertheless do not intend to trick us into seeing their assertions as unqualified truth. L also does not mean it in a second way. As L talks about the "standard [strategies] of older thematists," that is, manipulation of evidence, we see that L does not see this as immoral or unethical, as "deceit." It is simply a strategy, a technique. No big deal. Everybody has done it and we all know we do it. Nothing personal. This is a crucial attitude that will help us see why women more commonly than men may feel uncomfortable with the adversary method. L's remarks indicate, not that men are mean and women are nice, but that it is very easy for him to separate the technique or the strategy from the personal, the ethical, and the moral. If what Gilligan and others say is true, then I think it is likely that women will have more trouble making this separation.

The following response to a response in a *PMLA* Forum suggests that this difficulty exists. It is important to know that the letter writer, B, is male and H is female:

> To the Editor:
> I am puzzled and distraught by H's reply to my Forum piece. Assuming that I was attacking her there personally, she proceeds by insult and innuendo to attack me. This is most unfortunate, since I had enjoyed her article and learned something from it (an impression confirmed by a subsequent rereading of it); furthermore, I believed I expressed my favorable reaction quite clearly. Perhaps H's virulence derives from a mistaken inference to the effect that I was somehow accusing her of plagiarism. I can see how such an inference is possible, and I regret it: it was certainly not intended, and I apologize for any inconvenience it may have caused her.
>
> As far as H's replies to the essence of my remarks are concerned, I wish she had included some of them in the text of her article, or in accompanying notes: they make her arguments sounder and clearer. But I do not think that a prolonged discussion of these matters would be useful.

Several things are interesting about this letter. The first is that B and H seem to be operating out of slightly different perceptual frameworks. He did not intend his remarks to be personal, but she took them as such. Such miscommunication occurs every day, and one might say that it has nothing to do with gender. But I think it's significant that it happened this way, and not the other way around. M did not take S, K, and G's comments personally. M has fashioned a couplet to make a point about the pronoun "this." The clever verse reflects his attitude: "I seek to correct my critics' faulty reasoning. / To seek this is certainly not to be the enemy of my critics." In addition, by my saying that women may have more difficulty separating the strategy from the personal, that is, abstracting or objectifying technique or strategy, it does not mean that women cannot do it. H has attacked B using the typical verbal weapons, "insult and innuendo." Nevertheless, one could also say about H that at this point, she does intend her remarks to be personal. By this time, H and B seem to be talking to each other on different emotional levels. Like H, when women attack, rhetorically speaking, they do it less dispassionately. I also think that women like H, who have learned to attack, do it at some cost to themselves.

I would now like to turn briefly to the "scandal" of Gabler's *Ulysses: The Corrected Text*. I cannot disguise the fact that I will be referring to John Kidd's critique of the new edition of *Ulysses*. Most in the profession are aware of the controversy. Kidd's article shares many of the attributes of M's and L's attacks. Professor Kidd suggests that Gabler is incompetent and careless, and he questions Gabler's motives in hastily putting together a revised text so that the Joyce estate could renew its copyright. Professor Kidd uses sarcasm masterfully by beginning with an evocative and exciting description of the rich Dublin scene and cyclist Harry Thrift "rounding the bend," a description so effective that we may come to care more for Harry Thrift than we might ever care for Hans Walter Gabler, who becomes the nondescript "anyone" of the sarcastic remark, "Did it occur to anyone to check whether Thrift was a real person before changing him to Shrift? Apparently not" (32).

For me the question of *Ulysses* has been complicated. I care about what happens to Thrift, that is, about many of the rich allusions that it seems we have lost with the revised version; but I also care about Gabler, not that I know him, but I know that as a person he must suffer from the accusation. When I first read the report on the scandal in *The New York Times*, what ran through my mind were thoughts like, Professor Gabler has worked a long time on this project. How is he reacting? What will happen to him now? Is his career destroyed? I could even see Gabler in my mind, imagined him in a suit walking down the sidewalk at his University, hair greying, mouth set and shoulders erect to hold back the turmoil in his mind. (I have no idea what Gabler looks like. We have never met.) I imagined him sitting stony-faced at dinner, his wife, or lover, or sister asking him irrelevant questions trying to get him to talk.

It is not simply a question for me of who is right and who is wrong, Professor Gabler or Professor Kidd, whose evidence is most compelling, or whose argument is most reasonable. A woman's emphasis on care "centers moral development around the understanding of responsibility and relationship, just as the conception of morality as fairness ties moral development to the understanding of rights and rules" (Gilligan 19). For me, criticism is not just a matter of following rules, that is, using conventional strategies and doing everything in the right way. I do not believe that the "problem" of Ulysses will be solved by duking it out in journal article after journal article, each claiming to have definitive evidence of the real text of Ulysses. I have also wondered why Professor Kidd did not contact Professor Gabler when he first noticed discrepancies between Gabler's revisions and the original manuscripts. I am not easily able to distance the strategies of literary criticism from the personal. I cannot objectify other writings or issues as I am working on a piece. For me, the whole endeavor is richly peopled.

In what specific ways would the epistemic framework I describe above influence the reading and writing process? Reading and writing are interactive processes that involve the whole self, so that feelings will influence thoughts. (See particularly Brand and McLeod, who discuss the role of emotion in knowing or cognition.) The simplest example is that if we are worried or distracted, or if our writing tools are unfamiliar, we will not attend very well to what we are writing or reading. Other attitudes—like anger, trust, or skepticism—will directly affect these processes in more complex ways. Trust in particular will influence cognitive processes involved in reading: a reader who distrusts a writer will be less likely to attend to details that a writer considers important, less likely to make the same distinctions between significant and insignificant details, less likely to follow a complicated train of thought to closure. An untrusting reader will, moreover, bring to individual words associations and connotations that differ markedly from those of a trusting reader.

Trust is of great importance to writers. Composition theorists and educators have documented the important role that an audience or a community of learners plays in how a writer shapes prose. Writing, like reading, is not a deterministic or behavioristic activity. A writer imagines who she is writing for and how they might respond. The motivation is intensely personal—to connect with someone else in a meaningful way. A nurturing relationship is important. Trust is important. Voicing recent views about social constructionist theories of knowledge, Daniel Calhoun writes in *The Intelligence of a People* that "intelligence is first of all a kind of social relation, not a mere trait in the observed individual" (28) and that any form of creation, "supposedly individual and private, would thrive if bound in a healthy audience relation" (31). We can assume that Calhoun is also talking about writing and reading as forms of creation (see also Bruffee and Gergen).

Calhoun and other social constructionists suggest that both women and men require healthy communities of discourse, or one might say discourse relationships. I agree. I would like to come back in a moment to the point that what in our profession may be unhealthy for women may also be unhealthy for men. Nevertheless, I do believe, especially after reading later refinements of Carol Gilligan's theories, such as Mary Field Belenky's and her colleagues' *Women's Ways of Knowing* and Jean Crimshaw's *Philosophy and Feminist Thinking,* that a lack of intellectual nurturing may be even more unhealthy for some women. The work of Belenky and her colleagues focuses on "what else women might have to say about the development of their minds on alternative routes that are sketchy or missing in [William Perry's] version [of cognitive and moral development]" (9). I will not attempt a summary of their discoveries, but I will say at least that the women, from a variety of races and classes, whom Belenky interviewed were—at each stage of moral development, particularly in their relationships to authority—in places very different from the men in Perry's study. Belenky also discovered that women and men require different sorts of educational experiences, again with respect to authority, in order to move from one developmental stage to another. For example, Belenky discovered that, in that crucial move from subjective knowledge to procedural knowledge, it was "the presence of fairly *benign* authorities" that for women was "critical to the development of the voice of reason" (90). The women's epistemological orientation throughout their development was "connected knowing" rather than "separate knowing." With connected knowing, "The focus is not on how They want you to think, as in Perry's account, but on how they (the lower case 't' symbolizing more equal status) think; and the purpose is not justification, but connection" (101). The more benign authority figures affirmed women's abilities to know, which the women more than the men of Perry's study seemed to need, and nurture the development of their own voice, their own epistemic authority, all along the road to their cognitive, emotional, and moral maturity. While a healthy community of discourse is essential for both men and women readers and writers, I do think, nevertheless, that men and women may define "healthy" differently, just as men and women may see different kinds of connecting as meaningful. I am not saying that one way of writing literary criticism is right and the other wrong. The needs and the ways are different. But as in most other arenas of life, we've got to stop assuming that one way is the best for everyone.   *yes* —

In discussing the ways of literary criticism, I have talked about only the most extreme forms of the adversarial relationship—verbal attacks, sarcasm, insults, and condescension. This does not seem quite fair and is in many ways a misrepresentation of the way that most of us write literary criticism. I do believe, however, that the adversarial method, at least less extreme forms of it, is the norm in our discipline. Sometimes the adversarial statement is very gentle and does not depend on a put-down, as is the case in the following: "A critical assessment of _____ can benefit from a focus on _____." Other statements qualify or add. Usually, however, the put-down is there, even if it is very subtle. It seems that the scholar must, at some point suggest, "I've done a better job than they have." *"locate" Having to yourself in the*

In exploring this topic, I listed the adversarial statements I found. In *larger* looking at them all in a row, out of context, I noticed a sameness to them, *conversation.* even though the articles I took them from span more than ten years. They resemble the repetitive structures of early academic oratory that Walter Ong describes. Perhaps the phrases are used as conventional rhetorical filler, like "How are you-fine and you-see you later." They may also be a sort of "presocialized discourse," an imitation of the language structures of the disciplinary community that graduate students and novice scholars pick up in the course of their training (Williams).

If, as I have suggested, many of these phrases are a sort of filler, couldn't women use them, especially the milder forms, without much trouble? Well, the answer is "yes and no." Many women actually do it and thrive on it, as I will discuss later. Some women do it and don't thrive on it. Some women won't do it. Belenky and her colleagues write,

> At times, particularly in certain academic and work situations in which adversarial interactions are common, constructivist women may feel compelled to demonstrate that they can hold their own in a battle of ideas to prove to others that they, too, have the analytical powers and hard data to justify their claims. However, they usually resent the implicit pressure in male-dominated circles to toughen up and fight to get their ideas across. (146)

Many of my feminist colleagues and I do not want to use the adversary method anymore, if we can get away with it. But this does not mean that all women or only women have trouble using it. In other words, it does not mean that it is "unnatural" for women to use the adversarial mode. Such a statement would misrepresent history in general and the histories of feminism and women's scholarship in particular, as well as the complex question of what it means to be a woman.

I would like to set aside, probably indefinitely, the question of what it is natural for women to do, that is, the question of woman's essential nature. We have debated this issue for centuries, and I won't go into various perspectives of the debate with which readers are familiar. I would recommend, however, three studies: Jane Flax's "Postmodernism and Gender Relations in Feminist Theory," Karen Offen's "Defining Feminism: A Comparative Historical Approach," and Elizabeth Spelman's *Inessential Woman: Problems of Exclusion in Feminist Thought.* Each of these feminists, and many more whom I have not mentioned, advocates what Marilyn Frye calls in her review of Spelman's book "a metaphysics and a politics of plurality" (18). In defining women and their roles, rather than making false generalizations or qualifying endlessly what we mean by woman or feminist, we must, whenever possible, locate the women we are referring to, that is, contextualize our discussions. Jean Crimshaw writes:

> But even if one is always a man or a woman, one is never *just* a man or a woman. One is young or old, sick or healthy, married or unmarried, a parent or not a parent, employed or unemployed, middle class or working class, rich or poor, black or white, and so forth. . . . Experience does not come neatly in segments, such that it is always possible to abstract what in one's experience is due to "being a woman" from that which is due to "being married," "being middle class" and so forth. (85)

It is not unnatural for women to write traditional literary criticism; however, before women adopt mainstream discourse conventions, we need to think about what we are doing and why we are doing it.

It is obvious to anyone who has researched the history of higher education, where literary critical discourse was forged, that women have played little or no role in shaping the knowledge conventions of our profession. According to Dale Spender in *The Writing or the Sex? or why you don't have to read women's writing to know it's no good,* "Literary criticism is an activity and a body of knowledge that is dominated by men; it was men who made up the rules, who constructed the theory and practice of "lit crit," who decreed what was good, bad and indifferent long before they allowed women educational and occupational rights" (24). Ellen Messer-

Davidow states that women writing conventional literary critical discourse under such circumstances are "borrowing troubles," that is, "ac-
cepting not only particular formulations, but also the particular construal
of reality, another male construction" (72). The act of writing becomes
inauthentic or alienating, as any act would be whose origins, procedures,
or goals are unexamined.

Blindly adopting critical conventions, or any methodology, is commonplace not only in literary studies but in other disciplines. Of course, there
are women who know exactly what they are doing and are comfortable. I
have no quarrel with those who knowingly adopt traditional structures,
although those are the structures I infrequently choose and infrequently
read with pleasure. What distresses me the most, however, is knowing
that there are women who know what they are doing, hate it, but are
afraid to do something different. These women fear that their degrees will
be denied, their dissertations blocked. They fear that their articles and
conference proposals will be rejected. They fear that they won't be hired,
tenured, promoted. They fear for their careers and their livelihoods. And
in listing these fears, I don't begin to touch the daily pain and frustration these women experience—the humiliation and isolation that these
women feel with each letter of rejection, the nagging self-doubt and despair when facing unsympathetic or downright hostile dissertation committees, the bewilderment, the sleepless nights, the loss of hope. But my
own hope is restored when I see feminists like Jane Tompkins continuing
to experiment, even though her most recent, unconventional work is
criticized by our colleagues, as it is by David R. Shumway in Linda
Kauffman's volume *Gender and Theory: Dialogues on Feminist Criticism.* Shumway condescendingly calls "Me and My Shadow" Tompkins's "little"
essay and implies that she has not taken her subject seriously (107–8).

But perhaps the brave experimenters will make a difference. Composition theorists are among those brave experimenters who are challenging
the knowledge conventions of our discipline. In "The Exploratory Essay:
Enfranchising the Spirit of Inquiry in College Composition," William
Zieger laments that "with overpowering frequency, college composition
classes today teach the writing of an essay which conforms to the scientific model of thesis and support" (456). He does not ask that we abandon
the argumentative essay as a way to write about literature, but that we
value other forms and other ways of knowing about literature. And in a
1988 *College English* essay, Chris Anderson wishes that scholars had greater
freedom to write in a variety of modes. He values the "essay"—belle-
tristic, personal, exploratory, distinct from the literary critical analysis—

because it is "fundamentally democratic. It enfranchises both the reader and the writer. . . . It is not exclusive. It is not secretive. . . . [It] acknowledges uncertainty and ambiguity" (303–5). Yet it is a testimony to the pervasiveness and tenaciousness of mainstream rhetorical conventions that Anderson is a little defensive and apologetic about the essay form:

> We are talking here about two very different realms, realms that both need to exist. We need more than essays to keep alive what we know about literature and the humanities. We need, for example, historical and philological scholarship, the kind of research that only the article can effectively communicate. These are privileged fraternities, rightly so, and they create valuable things for a culture. (305)

I agree with Anderson that we need more than essays and agree that other modes of literary critical writing are privileged. But I disagree that it is rightly so, and I am a little uncomfortable with his metaphor of fraternities. I would also like to note that the editors of *College English* have placed Anderson's essay in a separate (segregated?) section of its own entitled "Essay," which emphasizes that, true to Anderson's title, the essay is a second or at least a different class of things.

Both Zieger and Anderson describe what literary critical writing would look like if it were not argumentative or adversarial. There are a few other nonadversarial articles out there. I have already mentioned Tompkins's "Me and My Shadow." While Tompkins's essay is not exactly literary criticism—it is a response to another essay—it nevertheless contains characteristics of nonadversarial writing. I would also recommend a forthcoming anthology, *The Intimate Critique: Autobiographical Literary Criticism,* which two colleagues and I are editing. The essays in this anthology are personal, revelatory, nonadversarial. They are non-hierarchal and mixed-genre, often validating a variety of voices—the critic's, her students', other critics' voices. The essays sometimes incorporate poetry or journal entries. Ellen Brown's essay "Between the Medusa and the Abyss: Reading *Jane Eyre,* Reading Myself," for example, is a highly personal account that weaves together the mature voices of herself as woman and as scholar-critic, the voices of her sister, mother, grandmother, as well as Virginia Woolf, and Sandra Gilbert and Susan Gubar:

> As I think about the bee room [a junk room where bees have made their nests] from which my mother rescued *Jane Eyre* ("It was heart-breaking to clean out the room; I had to burn most of the things

myself"), I can't help but think of Bertha Mason, in a bee room of her own, madwoman in the attic at the top of the stairs. ("It was mostly a women's room," my mother writes. "Daddy had places outside to store his junk.") Bertha Mason (brain defunct), discarded, unused refuse; outgrown wife; relic of a past life; reminder of the self her husband no longer will claim. One of my students points out that Bertha only strikes out at the men who have used her: trying to burn her husband in the bed from which she has been rejected; attacking her brother, whose silent complicity in his family's deception of Rochester makes him responsible, too, for a marriage that brings the family money the color of blood. Bertha could hurt Jane but instead vents her wrath on Jane's bridal veil as if to say, Beware the wedding day. (4)

The writings in the anthology, although untraditional, are nevertheless literary criticism, another way of knowing literature.

Other writers, perhaps not so bold as to try completely new forms (Ellen Brown has asked, "Who will publish this?"), are making almost inconspicuous changes in the ways that they write literary criticism, but changes nevertheless. In the *PMLA* essays I reviewed, for example, two scholars found ways of disagreeing critically without a put-down. I don't think it was coincidence that one of these essays was a feminist reading of *The Color Purple* and *The Woman Warrior* (1988) and the other an essay on Pope's *Dunciad* (1982) in which Fredric Bogel uses the occasion to reflect on what critics do. Bogel writes in a note, "My view differs here from that of Martin Price" (854). King-Kok Cheung writes, "Hence I disagree with Stade . . ." (193). Here are two critics who have thought about how they are going to disagree and have done it, respectfully, without sarcasm or innuendo or statements suggesting "wrong-headedness," "reluctance," "confusion," or "stupidity."

What difference will it make if some of us do not use the adversarial method, or if we explore ideas without reaching any conclusions, or if we get personal in our essays about literature? I would like to think that such changes would stand knowledge on its head. The shift from "Professor A has misunderstood" to "I disagree with Professor A" involves more than just a syntactic change. It is a shift from one view of knowledge to another—from the Cartesian view that reality is fixed, that to know reality we must merely see clearly, to the social constructionist view that knowledge is created, that people and contexts shape knowledge, and that we shape it together. Such a view of knowledge allows for two *ok—yes! multiplied*

different views to be right, or partly right, or meaningful at the same time. Without the fearsome burden of exactness, we are less likely to feel compelled to beat the other down. Literary critical writing has seemed at times nothing more than competition for a limited number of resources. Competition for resources and status may actually diminish those resources and ensure lack of quality rather than survival or achievement. Again, in her article on the adversary method in philosophy, Janice Moulton shows how the method, rather than providing a definitive argument, may actually encourage illogic and distortion:

> The Adversary Method works best if the disagreements are isolated ones, about a particular claim or argument. But claims and arguments about particular things rarely exist in isolation. They are usually part of an interrelated system of ideas. . . . Moreover, when a whole system of ideas is involved, as it frequently is, a debate that ends in defeat for one argument, without changing the whole system of ideas of which that argument was a part, will only provoke stronger support for other arguments with the same conclusion, or inspire attempts to amend the argument to avoid objections. . . . Moreover, the Adversary Paradigm allows exemptions from criticism of claims in philosophy that are not well worked out, that are "programmatic." Now any thesis in philosophy worth its salt will be programmatic in that there will be implications which go beyond the thesis itself. (154–55)

I would add that any thesis in literary criticism worth its salt is also programmatic, or problematic. Literary criticism driven by the adversarial paradigm, however, necessitates treating literature as problems to be solved, and critics will frequently go to great lengths to solve them, sometimes at the expense of knowledge and understanding. We want to be right, and we don't want to be attacked. But when we are attacked, we hunker down and erect a wall in front of us. We direct all of our creative efforts toward protecting ourselves and defending our theories. It is very difficult to put our heads together under these circumstances. And our colleagues form two lines behind us, making dialogue and creative thinking even more difficult.

But is this just a rhetorical mask that we drop once we stop reading and writing? I don't think so. I see the adversary method in our pedagogy and classroom structures, in our faculty meetings, in the formats of our conferences, in informal encounters in the hall, in every corner of our public lives. The adversary method is only a symptom of a pervading ethos that stresses competition and individualistic achievement at the expense of connectedness to others.

I have mentioned how combativeness affects our work, but how does it affect us personally? In "Fighting Words," Jane Tompkins describes an all too familiar scene at a professional conference. A panelist is tearing apart a book that has recently been published: "Violence takes place in the conference rooms at scholarly meetings and in the pages of professional journals; and although it's not the same thing to savage a person's book as it is to kill them with a machine gun, I suspect that the nature of the feelings that motivate both acts is qualitatively the same" (589). I have sometimes left faculty meetings feeling bruised, and I have taken these feelings home with me. I then feel like bruising someone else. I yell at my children and snap at my husband. I am not suggesting simplistically that if we get rid of adversarial practices, everyone will live happily ever after. But larger injustices are born of the little hurts that we perpetrate each day of our lives. With Tompkins, I hope that we can "unlearn the habits of a lifetime" ("Fighting" 590).

I seem to have gone in the other direction entirely by asserting, now, that the adversary method is not just bad for women but bad for everyone. I have also taken great pains to avoid essentialism and so may have inadvertantly suggested that gender is irrelevant. In taking such a turn we are in danger of leaving women behind again. We need to keep women very firmly at the center of this issue. To put it bluntly, if it were not for women, we might not be questioning the way that we write literary criticism. If women had not been suppressed and denigrated in the particular ways that they have, and responded to their pain as they have by forming a sort of feminine subculture, we would not have new values with which to compare the conventional values of our society and our profession. Jean Baker-Miller writes in *Toward a New Psychology of Women,* "it is the woman who is motivated to make the just society come about" precisely because "[it] is she who is hurting and who deeply feels the need for change" (68). This is what Crimshaw means, I think, when she says that "women's lives often provide a space for these questions about human priorities" (196). Wherever it originates, and to a degree it doesn't matter where it comes from, the ethic of care and relationships is most commonly at the center of women's lives; it provides us with "space" to think differently, another model for doing things. Crimshaw writes:

> Despite all the dangers of being ahistorical, of overgeneralisation, and so forth, I think it is true that women commonly see "caring"

relationships for others as having a more central role in their lives than men do. There has been, as I have shown, an influential strand in feminist thinking which has stressed the frequent oppressiveness of women's "caring" role, and the need for female autonomy and independence. Against this, however, has been set a concern to criticize institutional forms, often male-dominated, that are built on an ethos of self-assertion, competitiveness and the achieving of individualistic goals. This concern has often been linked with the belief that the different concerns of women's lives, and the different psychic qualities or strengths that they possess, offer a basis for a re-evaluation of this male ethos. (178–79)

As I have suggested earlier, the relational ethic provides a critique of much more in our profession than simply the adversary method, which I have focused on here.

In the past I have avoided using the adversary method by choosing carefully the topics and audiences I would write for. In writing this paper, I have resisted the adversary method every step of the way. Sometimes I have been successful, sometimes not. I have not named some of the critics whose tactics I am uncomfortable with. In researching women's roles in our profession, my first response to Gerald Graff's *Professing Literature* was indignation. Where are the women? Was Vida Dutton Scudder the only woman worth noting in the early days of our profession? But I didn't attack. What would be gained by stressing the "scholarly omissions" and that which "seems to have been neglected in recent research"? Graff's work is invaluable. I don't think that he has intended *Professing Literature* to be the last word. (He calls it *an* institutional history, not *the* institutional history.) He has initiated a conversation that he hopes will be ongoing. An adversarial stance would draw us apart unproductively and inhumanely.

And yet, in spite of my efforts to reject the method, it's pretty clear who is wearing the white hat. As I mentioned earlier, the very basis of my essay is adversarial. All I really want is that we value other knowledge constructions, other ways of writing about literature. I didn't think I could just say that, or do that. I felt compelled to make my case: I imagined the other guys, who would oppose my suggestion or refuse to publish my writing if it were different. I felt the need to convince them of many things, particularly by showing what is wrong with the other way when I should have been just writing it. But that is easier said than done. I am not Jane Tompkins. The issue means so much to me that I will use whatever weapons (yes, weapons) I have to convince my profession that we must open up. And so, ironically, the adversary method may have been useful here, if only as a means to its own destruction. If my argument is convincing enough, later generations of writers will have more freedom to write about literature in alternative forms and to be rewarded for it: the dissertation topics supported, the articles published; the writers hired, tenured, promoted. Of course, writers have always had the freedom to write what they want. But writing that's different is usually stuck in a drawer somewhere, or it sits in a computer file, while the writer's career languishes.

The final—and for me poignant—irony will be that we will succeed, and it will have been because of the adversary method. Then I will talk about love and end with a prayer. (Love? a prayer in a journal article?) Taken from her speech at a San Francisco antinuclear rally in March 1982, the prayer is Alice Walker's response to a curse-prayer that Zora Neale Hurston discovered in 1920. My using the adversary method, and I am talking about only myself here, is reminiscent of "destroying the village to save it," like irradiating the earth to prove the dangers of nuclear weapons. Walker writes,

> Fatally irradiating ourselves may in fact be the only way to save others from what Earth has already become. And this is a consideration that I believe requires serious thought from every one of us. However, just as the sun shines on the godly and ungodly alike, so does nuclear radiation. . . . So let me tell you: I intend to protect my home. Praying—not a curse—only the hope that my courage will not fail my love. But if by some miracle, and all our struggle, the earth is spared, only justice to every living thing (and everything is alive) will save humankind. And we are not saved yet. *Only justice can stop a curse.* (265)

Ending like this, talking about nuclear weapons and the fate of the earth and such, seems inappropriately melodramatic. But for me it comes to that.

I hope I have the courage to write differently next time.

References

Anderson, Chris. "Hearsay Evidence and Second-Class Citizenship." *College English* 50 (1988): 300–308.

Anzaldua, Gloria. *Borderlands/La Frontera.* San Francisco: Spinsters/Aunt Lute, 1987.

Belenky, Mary Field, et al. *Women's Ways of Knowing: The Development of Self, Voice, and Mind.* New York: Basic Books, 1986.

Bogel, Frederic V. "Dulness Unbound: Rhetoric and Pope's *Dunciad*." *PMLA* 97 (1982): 844–55.

Brand, Alice G. "The Why of Cognition: Emotion and the Writing Process." *College Composition and Communication* 38 (1987): 436–43.

Brown, Ellen. "Between Medusa and the Abyss: Reading *Jane Eyre*, Reading Myself." Unpublished essay, 1989.

Bruffee, Kenneth A. "Social Construction, Language, and the Authority of Knowledge: A Bibliographical Essay." *College English* 48 (1986): 773–90.

Calhoun, Daniel. *The Intelligence of a People*. Princeton: Princeton UP, 1973.

Cheung, King-Kok. " 'Don't Tell': Imposed Silences in *The Color Purple* and *The Woman Warrior*." *PMLA* 103 (1988): 162–74.

Chodorow, Nancy. *The Reproduction of Mothering: Psychoanalysis and the Sociology of Gender*. Berkeley: University of California Press, 1978.

Crimshaw, Jean. *Philosophy and Feminist Thinking*. Minneapolis: University of Minnesota Press, 1986.

DuPlessis, Rachel Blau. "For the Etruscans." *New Feminist*. Ed. Showalter. 271–91.

Flax, Jane. "Postmodernism and Gender Relations in Feminist Theory." *Signs: Journal of Women in Culture and Society* 12 (1987): 621–43.

Flynn, Elizabeth A. "Composing As a Woman." *College Composition and Communication* 39 (1988): 423–35.

Freedman, Diane P. "An Alchemy of Genres: Cross-Genre Writing by American Feminist Poet-critics." Charlottesville: University Press of Virginia, 1992.

Frye, Marilyn. "Isms in Collision." *New York Times Book Review*, April 30, 1989: 18.

Gergen, Kenneth J. "The Social Constructionist Movement in Modern Psychology." *American Psychologist* 40 (1985): 266–75.

Gilligan, Carol. *In a Different Voice*. Cambridge, Mass.: Harvard University Press, 1982.

Graff, Gerald. *Professing Literature: An Institutional History*. Chicago: University of Chicago Press, 1987.

Harding, Sandra, and Merill B. Hintikka, eds. *Discovering Reality: Feminist Perspectives on Epistemology, Metaphysics, Methodology, and Philosophy of Science*. Boston: D. Reidel, 1983.

Heilbrun, Carolyn G. *Death in a Tenured Position*. New York: Dutton, 1981.

Kauffman, Linda, ed. *Gender and Theory: Dialogues on Feminist Criticism*. New York: Basil Blackwell, 1989.

Kidd, John. "The Scandal of *Ulysses*." Rev. of *Ulysses: The Corrected Text*, by Hans Walter Gabler. *New York Review of Books*, June 30, 1988: 32–39.

Lensink, Judy Nolte. "Expanding the Boundaries of Criticism: The Diary as Female Autobiography." *Women's Studies* 14 (1987): 39–53.

McAllister, Pam. *Reweaving the Web of Life: Feminism and Nonviolence*. Philadelphia: New Society Publishers, 1982.

McLeod, Susan. "Some Thoughts about Feelings: The Affective Domain and the Writing Process." *College Composition and Communication* 38 (1987): 426–35.

Messer-Davidow, Ellen. "The Philosophical Bases of Feminist Literary Criticism." *New Literary History* 19 (1987): 65–103.

Miller, Jean Baker. *Toward A New Psychology of Women*. Boston: Beacon, 1976.

Moulton, Janice. "A Paradigm of Philosophy: The Adversary Method." *Discovering Reality*. Ed. Harding and Hintikka. 149–64.

Offen, Karen. "Defining Feminism: A Comparative Historical Approach." *Signs: Journal of Women in Culture and Society* 14 (1988): 119–57.

Ong, Walter. *Fighting for Life*. Ithaca: Cornell University Press, 1981.

Schweickart, Patrocinio P. "Reading Ourselves: Toward a Feminist Theory of Reading." *Gender and Reading*. Ed. Elizabeth A. Flynn and Patrocinio Schweickart. Baltimore: Johns Hopkins University Press, 1986. 30–62.

Showalter, Elaine. "Introduction: The Feminist Critical Revolution." *New Feminist*. Ed. Showalter. 3–17.

––––––. *The New Feminist Criticism: Essays on Women, Literature, and Theory*. New York: Pantheon Books, 1985.

Spelman, Elizabeth V. *Inessential Woman: Problems of Exclusion in Feminist Thought*. Boston: Beacon, 1988.

Spender, Dale. *The Writing or the Sex*. New York: Pergamon Press, 1989.

Tompkins, Jane. "Fighting Words: Unlearning to Write the Critical Essay." *Georgia Review* 42 (1988): 585–90.

––––––. "Me and My Shadow." *New Literary History* 19 (1987): 169–78.

Walker, Alice. "Only Justice Can Stop A Curse." *Reweaving the Web*. Ed. McAllister. 262–65.

Williams, Joseph. "On Joining Communities of Discourse: Some Problems in Learning the Voice." University of Chicago Institute on Interpretive Communities and the Undergraduate Writer. Chicago, May 3, 1987.

Zeiger, William. "The Exploratory Essay: Enfranchising the Spirit of Inquiry in College Composition." *College English* 47 (1985): 454–66.

Today, when autumn colors camouflage the existence of the strip mines in the vertical West Virginia landscape of mountain and hollow, it's hard to remember actually having lived in the Mississippi Delta. What I do recall is that although the area lacks coal, it is rich in other things—soybeans, rice, and cotton—and flat as a quilt pulled tight over an old bed. From my backyard, I could see the water towers of six neighboring towns, not including the cotton boll affair in Minter City, Sunflower County.

In 1983, during the height of the job crunch in literary studies, I, a white Northern Jew—an alien by the standards of nearly everyone in Bolivar County, Mississippi—was delighted to be teaching in a tenure-line position at a small university in the state where Goodman's, Schwerner's, and Chaney's bodies had been found buried in an earthen dam near the ironically named city of Philadelphia. With the enthusiasm of a recent-vintage PH.D., I brazenly challenged my mostly white students to reconsider their understandings of Southern history and traditions, to revise their notions of what constitutes sense of place, political agenda, race, and class. I remember talking about Eudora Welty, Fannie Lou Hamer, Alice Walker. I figured, presumptuously I now see, that if no one else was doing it, then I was responsible for telling my students what I thought they should know about their past, not to mention their present.

My teaching of Alice Walker's short story "Everyday Use" and my continuing research on quilting as a metaphor in women's writing led me to ask my husband to take me to work with him, to meet a quilter he had heard about. At that time, Jack was employed in the psychiatric hospital at the Mississippi State Penitentiary, the Parchman Farm of so many blues songs. He arranged for me to meet a female inmate who had pieced a quilt for another one of the psychologists at the prison hospital.

Unlike the hospital facility, the women's unit—camp 25—had no parking area. No one from the outside was encouraged to stay. Even guards didn't want duty at 25. We stopped outside the gate, which was opened several feet to let some of the inmates out for work detail on the farm. Laughing and clowning with the guards, the blue-and-white denim-clad inmates piled into the prison bus like high school kids on a field trip. We left our keys in a wooden coffer, which was then hoisted up to the guard tower. (Many people in Mississippi leave their keys in their cars, a particularly stupid thing to do at Parchman. The administration also doesn't want to risk a visitor's dropping his or her keys inside the camp gates. Or his or her being abducted and the keys stolen, though nothing like that had ever happened.)

Inside I met the case manager, a young, neatly dressed black woman; an inmate with short cropped hair and sinewy biceps, who was wrestling with a big box, contents unknown; and finally, the quilter, Lucille Sojourner, who emerged from the Zone bathrooms, where she had been brushing her teeth and managing stray hairs into place. She wore "A" custody blues signaling her good behavior and her attending privileges. Petite, almost doll-like, the quilter wore light make-up and clean, slickly pressed prison garb. Lucille Sojourner, #46496, Unit 25, Parchman, Mississippi 38738. Immediately I thought of Sojourner Truth and recalled that etymologically the name Lucille came from the same word as *lucid* and *light,* a mythic metaphor of Truth itself, and wondered how she had come to be incarcerated. (I later learned that she had been found guilty of murder and given a life sentence.) Her name gained additional resonance when I remembered that B.B. King, the blues legend from nearby Indianola, had named his guitar Lucille.

Lucille Sojourner led me out of the Zone, a space containing both a day area and ten cubicles, each of which housed six women, and through a set of swinging doors into the cafeteria. Not realizing that we were being watched from above, I foolishly thought that we were coming and going at will, that life at Parchman was more like, say, hard-core summer camp or an Outward Bound experience without the amenity of being able to return home after the concluding celebration.

After righting two chairs set upside down upon a folding table we shook hands, and I began to tell Lucille of my growing interest in quilting. Then she began to piece together her narrative. Although her story confirmed some of what I had known about quilting as an art and a tradition, it also opened my eyes to the perspective of a black Southerner quilting behind bars.

I let Lucille Sojourner tell her story.

She had been quilting since 1980, when she was sentenced to life in prison. A quiet woman, Lucille had been approached by a white prisoner, who got her started. At that time she'd had no means of support. Soon after completing her first quilt, however, a big freeze hit northern Mississippi, and when another inmate offered to buy the cover to keep herself warm, Lucille sold it right from her bed.

Financially strapped, Lucille was emotionally depressed as well. Her family of many brothers and sisters and her own seven children did not visit her on the Farm. Her husband was in one of the men's camps. Soon she began to contract quilts with several women from Jackson, who would provide her with good material and pay her $150 a quilt. She'd recently made "an old nine-patch" for them, and those Jackson women sold it, not even a fancy patterned top, for $90. Ecstatic, she could send this money to her several sisters who were caring for her many children. At that time she was piecing for one of the counselors in the psychiatric unit a churn dash crib quilt in muted Laura Ashley tones of brick and blue. When Lucille Sojourner modestly offered "Round the World" as her favorite pattern, given the quilter's name, I was not surprised.

Parchman is a violent place. Lucille told me of one of her "friend girls" who had succumbed to gossip and gotten severely beaten. On another occasion two inmates had grabbed the freestanding quilting frame the Jackson women had bought her, destroyed it, and used the legs as clubs. As a result, she switched to a lap frame, quilting all day every day, taking time out only for trips to the bathroom. Wisely, as it turns out, she did not eat prison food: the week before I visited, seventy men in one of the camps got food poisoning, and one of them had died. Lucille told me that she got canned goods at the canteen, figuring she could survive on those and candy bars until she came up for parole. Constantly working—to make the time pass—she could piece a top in a week and quilt it in three days.

About thirty other women in the unit quilted, and Lucille spoke admiringly of a woman who worked more complicated patterns, like the lily of the valley and the double wedding ring. Yet she displayed real pride in her own skill. Some of the prison's quilters used a sewing machine to piece their tops, but she found that sometimes their seams didn't hold. Thus, she preferred, as she said, "to sew on my hands." And then she showed me her bruised fingers, swearing that they were better and had been much worse.

Why do it, I had asked. "It gives me constellation," she responded unhesitatingly, offering me an image of cosmic order.

She continued, telling of the guard who had asked her to quilt an already-pieced cover for free, since she was a convict with time on her hands. Clearly insulted by the guard's assumption that her time was of no value, Lucille noted that she was studying for her Graduation Equivalency Diploma.

This meeting with Lucille Sojourner forced me to revise my entire understanding of Alice Walker's short story, not to mention to examine my own position in the new narrative featuring the Yankee English professor's encounter with the convicted murderess. If Walker's Maggie, the stay-at-home sister of the story, was the type of meek, hard-working devoted daughter, Lucille (never mind the crime that had put her in Parchman) was the antitype, sewing for her place in the world, for her sanity. And if Dee/Wangero was the type of culturally hip daughter who desired tangible evidence of her heritage while rejecting her family, I was the antitype.

Both Dee and I had been named for family matriarchs: she had been originally named after her grandmother, and I, in the tradition of assimilated American Jews, was given a Hebrew name, Chaya—Life—after my maternal grandmother's mother. Our name changes reveal us to be cultural cross-dressers: Dee had been renamed Wangero, and I go by the English Cheryl. Lucille, too, had been renamed: #46496. Although Lucille was the only one of us to be literally incarcerated, from the perspective of Dee/Wangero's mother, Mrs. Johnson, Dee was as truly imprisoned by some institutionalized movement that had stripped her of her familial identity. And although I was privileged by education and race, I nonetheless felt a curious kinship with both Lucille/Maggie and Dee/Wangero. For in the foreign Delta culture, I felt constrained if not in many senses imprisoned as a result of my past, like Lucille; both of us, as it were, had been given "Life." But like Dee/Wangero, I was also estranged from my personal history, wanting it to confer identity, yet rejecting it at the same time. My double-bind hit home in the small synagogue in my Delta town during a Rosh Hashanah service, to which I had gone, I reasoned, to please my mother. Here the High Holy Days liturgy, sung in transliterated

Hebrew, in major modes by the members of the First Baptist Church choir, only heightened my alienation.

In Walker's story, Dee has ironically been given a sort of work-release in order to return home to appropriate the family quilts, which contain pieces of people's lives: scraps from a wedding dress and a Civil War uniform, for example. Dee/Wangero wants to hang them like museum pieces on her wall, a motive that declares with additional irony that this newly liberated dashiki-ed black woman is both a prisoner to trends in interior design and a woman bent on larceny. Seeing her reentry into the dull life of her mother and sister as a diversion from her fashionable pursuit of her black heritage, Dee/Wangero plots to take what she wants and retreat once again from her past into a world that does not validate her familial history, into a social set whose project is to write a new narrative of African-American power. Mrs. Johnson and Maggie, then, are the ones who, in Dee/Wangero's fiction, are imprisoned in their rural lives and in their "ignorance," just like the students whom I had made it my business to enlighten.

In "Everyday Use" Maggie, the plain sister, who has remained at home with Mrs. Johnson, the focus of strength in the story, is, we remember, scarred, a description that gained a metaphoric import it never had before my trip to camp 25, before my examination of Lucille Sojourner's fingers. In fact, the whole notion of "everyday use" was transformed by my own sojourn at Parchman Farm. Originally, I had understood that, like the woman to whom Lucille made her first sale, Maggie would put the quilts to everyday use—she would use them to keep her and her family warm, to preserve their bodies as well as their souls—and in that fashion perpetuate the family's heritage in a way that displaying the quilts in a museum could never accomplish. She would use them *freely*, as a woman who gains strength from the narrative of her past, which she embodies. From the quilts Maggie would derive, as Lucille would say, constellation. Most interpretations of Walker's short story follow this line of reasoning, reading Maggie as the Cinderella–good sister, and Dee/Wangero as the evil sister in the flashy clothes. But Dee/Wangero doesn't want the quilts to destroy them. True, she wants to remove them from everyday use, but her motive is, after all, preservation, of personal family history in the context of larger cultural history, and preservation, as many recent feminist readers understand, of a valid text(ile) of women's tradition.

I am similarly engaged in making my own way through both family tradition and male and female literary traditions, taking what I want: for example, the copy of *Anna Karenina* that my grandmother brought with her on the boat from her Anatevka-like village (even though I can't read a word of Russian); her volumes of the works of Sholem Aleichem (even though I can't read a word of Yiddish). Many critics have faulted Dee/Wangero for trying to "preserve" her past in the sterile, academic hanging out of the family linen as though it is the formal blazon that people like me make it out to be in our scholarship. I used to fault her, too.

But after my meeting with Lucille, who so reminds me of Maggie though her visible scars are limited to her fingertips, I feel a strong kinship with Dee/Wangero, who, had she been in my shoes, would have been called upon Passover Seder after Passover Seder to read the part of The Wicked Son, who does not believe. Like Dee/Wangero, I am trying to negotiate the old by casting my lot with the new. But whereas Walker presents no evidence that Dee/Wangero questions her own motivations, I do: call it Jewish guilt; a habit of self-reflexively examining my assumptions borne of graduate courses in literature and theory; or a rhetorical strategy to fend off an imagined reader's criticism. Why did I ask to meet Lucille Sojourner in the first place? To talk with her about quilting and do serious scholarship, or to commission a quilt for my bed? An even more fundamental question, however, is why I'm so interested in quilting. I don't quilt myself, I don't collect quilts (although I have a few), no members of my family, immediate or extended, quilt. The tradition is foreign to my family. Is it, then, that to give me some identity—cultural, professional, ultimately personal—I have wrapped myself in the critical quilt of literary theory and feminist criticism, which created the academic interest in quilting in the first place? If Lucille, Maggie, and Dee/Wangero are each imprisoned in ways both literal and metaphoric, am I a prisoner not only of literary trends but also of capitalist production and consumption, the system that, according to Michel Foucault, necessitated the existence of prisons in the first place? Admittedly, I did end up paying Lucille to make me a quilt of my own. . . .

It's been over six years since I interviewed Lucille. Although I wrote to her several times, sending her at one point a photocopy of "Everyday Use," I never heard from her. Perhaps she had been offended by my offer of the story, thinking that I was condescending to enlighten her. I hadn't thought I was, but my naive motive, thinking that it might "brighten her day," might have been condescension after all. A few years ago Parchman Farm closed camp 25 to women inmates, who were moved to Jackson, where, for what it's worth, the chief proponent of "sense of place," Eudora Welty, whose mother was a West Virginian, lives.

I wonder if Lucille was ever granted parole. I wouldn't be surprised: she was an ideal prisoner, never causing trouble, doing little other than plying her needle. In abstract terms, terms admittedly lacking any immediate meaning for a prisoner, in her quilting she established her own *parole* from the general *langue* of art and humanity. The cover she quilted for me, patched in primary colors and backed in the bright red of Isis, the goddess of creativity, is that narrative that now gives me *parole,* passing down to me, as it were, like Maggie's quilts, her stories for everyday use. Even as I write this last sentence, however, I recognize that its allusions derive from scholarship and from a culture not originally my own; that this paper, if quiltlike in its narrative, is hardly for everyday use. Rather, it is a narrative designed to be metaphorically hung, to establish an identity for myself as scholar, teacher, writer, feminist, to be used as a blazon.

Because I did not begin this essay with the requisite prefatory litany of past adventures in criticism, buying into the sort of paranoia ("If I don't cite earlier critics, my readers won't find my case credible") that the Academy seems to foster by equating scholarship and objectivity with an ability to run a CD-ROM search of the MLA Bibliography, I risk being accused of lacking professionalism and/or rigor. I'll take the risk, though, because, as Jane Tompkins writes in her wonderfully radical essay "Me and My Shadow," "This one time I've taken off the straitjacket, and it feels so good."

I take Tompkins's "feels so good" to mean "feels honest and liberating," the kind of good one feels after accomplishing a difficult, perhaps even treacherous task. Formulating the narrative of my sojourn at Parchman Farm feels so good for me because it—and its implied subtext, Alice Walker's "Everyday Use"—taught me that reading and writing and teaching with real conviction necessitate personal engagement with the text. The Parchman experience has become, conversely, my personal subtext underlying Walker's narrative, a subtext that has allowed me to reread Dee/Wangero not as some monstrous devourer of cultural treasures, but rather as a deeply conflicted young woman searching for her self in two different marginalized cultures: wanting familial memories for intellectual warmth yet able to treat them only as impersonal commodities for display. That, in turn, has given me a better sense of the teacher's responsibilities. Before visiting Parchman, meeting Lucille Sojourner, and re-envisioning "Everyday Use," I thought it my duty to teach my students about their own lives and history, about their oppression and racism. Now I see that my position was false from the outset. Like Dee/Wangero, I wanted not so much to teach as to insist on their according me, albeit tacitly, an access to their past since I couldn't cope with my own: I wanted a quilt. And since I didn't have one, I'd pay for one.

From the vantage point of a crop duster, the serpentine irrigation trenches carve the rich Delta bottomland into what resemble purposeful ancient patterns or those made by aliens—or hoaxers. I don't think this modern alien left any mark at all on the Bolivar County topography; my stay was too short. The landscape certainly left its mark on me, though. All that flatness, that horizontal experience, prepared me, in a way, for West Virginia. Living in Mississippi taught me that reading across the horizon of a text isn't enough. One must bring those vertical layers of personal texts to bear on meaning; one must not only read but also, in a sense, live a text to build to the broader view available from the mountaintops.

References

Tompkins, Jane. "Me and My Shadow." This volume.
Walker, Alice. "Everyday Use." *Norton Anthology of Literature by Women*. Ed. Sandra M. Gilbert and Susan Gubar. New York: Norton, 1985. 2366–74.

Excerpts

from Letters

to Friends

*

Susan Koppelman

January 22, 1990

Dear Sallie [Bingham]:

. . . I can't tell you how frequently I get invitations to turn one of my letters into an essay so that it can be published in one place or another. More and more I want to know why the letter form isn't sufficient? For instance, a case in point is my previous dear friend's letter, the one about Dale Spender's *The Writing or the Sex?*, a very long letter, as you may remember. Susan Davis, book review editor at *New Directions for Women* wanted to edit the letter into a "proper" book review and, with my permission, did. And she published it in that revised and more formal form. On the other hand, Janet Palmer Mullaney chose to publish the entire letter *as a letter* in the most recent double issue of *Belles Lettres*— but, since it is a *letter* and not a *review,* there is no indication in the table of contents that there is anything by me or about Dale's book in that issue. Strange.

Sallie, you ask me about my dear friends' letters and the list of people to whom they are mailed: some of the letters go out to only about ten women and others, like the last one, go out to over eighty people (including some men). It depends on many things—among others, how much money and energy I have for making and sending copies and what the letter is about. . . .

I can write more about your questions if I know that you want to use my work in letter form. I hate writing essays. I never have a clear sense of audience when I try to write that way. I know I prefer reading letters to reading essays. I like the special feeling of being addressed that letters give me—either I am being addressed, or I am eavesdropping on a personal communication. Essays are like prepackaged diet foods—no schmaltz, no seasoning, no garnish, no taste. Essays are like what I imagine sex with a sex therapist to be—no love, nothing personal, no joking asides, no memories, no plans for the future, no relationship between participants.

November 1, 1985

Dear Friends:

. . . But what about the writers who have no Great Work and a Great Many Very Good Works, all of them better than the minor works of the writer with only One Great Work. What happens to that writer? I think it is a way to describe many important women writers' oeuvres and one of the other ways that women get kept out of the canon. The problem is the Way The Selections Happen. I'm complaining about their criteria. It's like racially biased I.Q. tests. The writer, to be included in the canon, has to have had one really Great Orgasm. Having multiple regular orgasms doesn't count! IT'S BECAUSE THEY CAN'T DO IT AFTER THEY'RE NINETEEN OR SO UNLESS THEY ARE WITH A STRANGE, NEW "OFF LIMITS" WOMAN (which are the same circumstances under which sex becomes dangerous to a man who has had a heart attack. It's not dangerous with your regular partner of many years).

Looking for the One Big Orgasm is the way a lot of feminist scholars look at women writers, as they argue the case for one and then another "lost" "rediscovered" woman writer.

But the writers I love are the ones who wrote a whole lot and whose work offers one deep satisfaction after another, for years. I not only know what I like, when it comes to women's literature, I know WHY I like it. . . .

February 20, 1986

Dear Friends:

The questions on my mind tonight are these. Why do some of you write about literature in the form of essays and books instead of in the form of letters? Why do you write long essays that are speeches or position papers instead of writing letters to each other, and others, in which we discuss these issues together? Why, for instance, did Carolyn [Karcher] write her paper comparing one story by Lydia Maria Child with a story by Washington Irving (the new issue of *Legacy*)? Why, instead of writing an essay comparing the Child story and the Dall story, did I write a long letter about it, full of questions and speculations about the relationship between the two and what we might make of it and send the letter, along with copies of the stories, to Carolyn and Gary Sue [Goodman]? Why do these different things? It can't just be that you are "in" the academic world, and I am not. Or at least, that can't be the whole explanation. I think that I wouldn't do it the other way even if I was in that world. Or at least, once I had tenure somewhere, I don't think I would do it. Annette is in a good position in terms of job security and job compensation. But Annette still writes essays. And maybe if I wrote a bunch of really heavy-duty essays that got published in major juried journals, maybe despite my illness, some university would offer me an endowed professorship with just one or two classes a year of advanced graduate students and lots of money for research assistants—but even if that could be true, I don't think I could write those heavy-duty essays. I don't know how to stop and shape what is happening in my mind into one of those formal shapes that get published. I can only seem to think and talk about books when I am having conversations with friends.

Is it the patriarchy that teaches that discussion of literature has to take that kind of impersonal form, that nondialogic form, that emotional-after-the-fact form?

There are more and more women I want to bring into this correspondence, women whose work I read and think is right on, women I want to enter into dialogue with, women I know who are asking the same kinds of questions and working toward the same goals—peace and social justice, as Emily [Toth] always puts it—knowing what their achievement would require in the way of a transformation of the relation between men and women . . .

I have a suggestion. Why don't all of you who write articles and essays and books and reviews and all that stuff stop for two years. Instead, let us have an intense correspondence in which we discuss all the great issues and questions that are at the center of our radical literary political work. We could each make a commitment to participate in this correspondence and we would write to each other, responding to what we are moved to respond to in each other's letters, sending our own—having a work/talk party in which we have no formal requirements to which we have to adhere or in which we must encase our ideas.

And at the end of that period, let us publish in book form what we have done.

And then let us start a periodical or try to take over one that is already going and turn it into a correspondence journal. That's kind of what I imagined *Notes and Queries* to be before I saw it. . . .

January 6, 1988

Dear Linda [Wagner-Martin],

. . . I don't understand how or why Sylvia [Plath's] death helped other women stay alive. She makes me so damned depressed. I'm sure you have read the new *PMLA* issue with the article on V. Woolf and her manic depressiveness. What do you think of it?

I suppose there will be a rash, finally, of articles about the various sicknesses of various writers—Flannery O'Connor's lupus and her cortisone poisoning, Byron's thyroid problems, Hemingway's arterial sclerosis, Amy Lowell's thyroid problems, Joanna Russ's unilateral depressive disease, Ellen Glasgow's deafness, Alice Carey's t.b., Luther's constipation, Keats's tuberculosis, Mary Antin's bowel disease, etc. I can just see it now—an annual joint issue of *PMLA* and *JAMA*.

And there will be a general hosanna in praise of this exciting new approach to literature. The Marxists will get in on it, talking about the material base of illness in the biochemistry of the body and the feminists will get in on it by going in great gorey detail into the multitudinous examples of medical malpractice and oppression of women and the various psycho critics will get in on it by examining the language of literary art for evidence of obsession with bodily aches, pains, noises and failures. It will be wonderful and liberating; a new day will dawn in which we will finally begin to understand what literature is, and is about.

And there will be new doctoral programs developed in medical literary criticism, administered jointly by English departments and medical school specialty departments. You can get a Ph.D. with a joint major in poetry and the digestive system or psychopharmacology and the Beat Generation.

And then, ten years later, there will be a revolt of the new generation of literary critics who want to overthrow those who think of literature as something mired in shit and piss and blood and aspirin. They will alternately stage sit-ins at and invoke boycotts of joint MLA/AMA meetings, claiming that such approaches to the transcendent product of the finest ethers of the human spirit cheapen and degrade us and our understanding of the best produced by the best among us.

Their rallying cry will be something like "Hitler had piles, too," and they will kidnap the medical records of the leaders of the medical criticism movement and write scathing satires about the postnasal drip of the post-Freudian medical critics.

You asked if you could send a copy of my midnight tearstained confession of the pain of Sylvia to Annette. Of course. You can do anything you want with any letter I write you.

Social Circles:

Being a Report on

J. Hillis Miller's

Campus Visitation

*

Linda R. Robertson

The First Circle: Pear Liqueur and Pear Lacan

Though she did not really wish to go to dinner that night, she went because she was curious. The dinner was in honor of the visiting critic, J. Hillis Miller, someone who spoke the mysteries of the new postmodern, poststructuralist, deconstructionist criticism, someone who had parleyed literary criticism into a highly lucrative pursuit. Her own degree, after all, was in literature. But she had been unfortunate enough to study literature during a recession, when there were few jobs, when her first position paid $3000 per year. And she had been foolish enough to become interested in a below stairs concern in English, the teaching of writing. She was a rhetorician.

Despite her status, she remained curious about the goings-on upstairs, because lately at the conferences on writing and literature, and in the "opinion" sections of professional journals, there were the rumblings of civil war between those who professed English literature and those who professed rhetoric. She was aware that the dispute also involved the Gender Issue, because people had begun to compare the disproportionate number of male faculty members who were tenured in English and commanding rather impressive salaries with the disproportionate number of female faculty members who were teaching writing in untenured, marginalized positions.

She herself had come to this small liberal-arts college to do something unorthodox. She had started a new department detached from English, one concerned exclusively with writing. She had listened with interest at various conventions to arguments posited by chairs of English that professors such as herself ought to recognize that rhetoric was in its "adolescent" stage and ought naturally to seek its full maturity in English departments. She thought that an evening with the critic would give her a clearer insight into what that maturity might portend.

When she arrived at the provost's house, the twenty invited guests were crowded around small "television" tables in the living room, a long room overlooking the lake, its hardwood floors protected with Persian rugs, its shelves lined with old books reflecting the provost's antiquarian fervors.

After dinner, she sought the relative privacy of the sitting room for a smoke. The room was dominated by an exquisite Ferraro marble mantelpiece, carved with the modestly attired figure of Ceres dispensing Earth's Bounties (mostly grapes) in bas-relief. She was joined by a friend who taught Russian literature. From him, she discovered that she had been mistaken in assuming that J. Hillis Miller would talk after dinner, that he had already delivered his address that afternoon, when she had been sitting in a local bar, brooding over her tax bill.

They sat in Queen Anne chairs separated by an occasional table of the same period, upon which rested their cups of coffee and glasses of pear liqueur. While she smoked and he downed a bowl of ice cream and strawberries, he reviewed some highlights of J. Hillis Miller's talk on prosopopoeia (personification) in James's "Last of the Valerii." Exploring the trope of personification in the short story had seemed to her a perfectly reasonable if unsurprising approach because in it, a man falls in love with a statue.

The tale is narrated by the godfather of Martha, who loves Camillo, Count Valerio. After their marriage, they enter an idyllic life at the Count's villa in Rome. Over her husband's objections, Martha has the grounds excavated in search of ancient statues. The workmen discover first a marble hand and then a statue of Juno. Soon the Count is not acting right. He reverts to paganism, prostrating himself at night before the statue. He goes so far as to rig up an altar to it and sacrifices something—we don't know what. Martha is at first in despair: "His Juno's the reality: I'm the fiction!" she cries to her godfather. But having the pluck of an American woman, she soon orders the statue buried again on the grounds. Camillo, whose nerves by this time are shot, seems relieved when he finds the Juno is gone. At any rate, peace is restored to the couple and their villa, although the Count keeps the hand of Juno as a relic.

It was pleasant to discuss the pleasures of personification while contemplating the bountiful Ceres, but she felt obliged to mingle. She re-entered the living room and found an empty chair in a circle that had gathered around J. Hillis Miller. She joined him, two other women, and the middle-aged, ginger-haired English professor who had invited the critic to campus. The critic held the gaze of those in the circle as he explained that he would be able to visit his vacation home in Maine more often now that he was in California than he had been able to before because California had such a convenient academic calendar, and, of course, he only had to teach two graduate courses—no undergraduate—and so had plenty of time for writing. And, of course, he repeated twice, he would be able to keep the house which the University of California was building for him.

Although she was fairly accomplished at attending to the nuances of a critic's discourse, the rhetorician decided to leave the charmed circle. She moved to a small round table. Sitting at the twelve o'clock position was the associate provost, a European woman of sophisticated mind and dress. She was engaged in conversation with the provost on her right—who had before them one of his many antique volumes, a work on the early archaeological excavations of Mayan ruins. The associate provost was explaining the gist of J. Hillis Miller's talk, which the provost had not attended. She told him that the critic's point was that you couldn't really know what a text meant. The comment seemed to startle the provost. He gazed with furrowed brow at the open book which a moment before had seemed to explain a lost civilization.

Seated to the right of the rhetorician were two women, one in English and the other in French. Their attention was fixed upon a visiting literature professor from Britain. She of rhetoric overheard him say: "The masochist in a sado-masochist relationship always gazes upon the sadist, who takes his being from the gaze. So the masochist is always a repressed ecstatic, you see, and the sadist always a repressed depressive. And, of course, he is always utterly narcissistic." With this, he swept long, sensitive fingers through his long, thick, black hair, while the two women gazed at him, silently, intently.

Perhaps it was hearing the phrase "takes his being from the gaze" that made her think of Lacan's concept of the Other, of the veiled mystery, of a woman representing not simply the object of desire, but the cause of it. She had been somewhat troubled when she read Lacan by his seeming to contend that what went on between men and women ought to be a species of idolatry. But then, of course, one couldn't be sure what it was

Lacan meant. That is not to say one could ever be sure what anyone meant, but it was especially uncertain in the case of Lacan.

Averting her glance from the two women attending to their British colleague, she observed J. Hillis Miller and his small circle frozen as it were *en tableaux*. He was still talking; they were still listening. A wild-eyed thought came into the rhetorician's mind, which was evidently overcome by the pear liqueur. "Was he taking his being from their gaze?" she wondered.

Divertissement

As penance for missing the critic's address that afternoon, the rhetorician decided to attend the conversation circle, which was to gather around him at nine o'clock the following morning. It also occurred to her that as she had not heard his talk, she ought to read something he had written recently, so that she might at least contribute to the conversation.

At home in her blue velour robe, she retrieved the latest issue of the ADE (Associated Departments of English) Bulletin, which included an article by J. Hillis Miller, and a response by one D. A. Miller of Berkeley. The rhetorician settled into a leather chair, lit a cigarette, took a sip of herbal tea, shoved the cat's tail out of her face as he curled himself, purring, on her lap, and began to read J. Hillis Miller's critical commentary on Nathaniel Hawthorne's, "The Minister's Black Veil: A Parable." His article bore the telegraphic title "Theory—Example—Reading—History."

She was struck by J. Hillis Miller's claim that the story "depends on a remarkable donee or fancy": a minister who covers his face with black crepe for most of his adult life. "Why 'fancy'?" she wondered. Why would J. Hillis Miller suggest Hawthorne made the story up out of whole cloth, so to speak. She reached for the selected tales of Hawthorne, which she had placed next to her on the table and read the note he included with his story: "Another clergyman in New England, Mr. Joseph Moody, of York, Maine, who died about eighty years since, made himself remarkable by the same eccentricity that is here related of the Reverend Mr. Hooper. In this case, however, the symbol had a different import. In early life he had accidentally killed a beloved friend; and from that day till the hour of his own death, he hid his face from men." She agreed with J. Hillis Miller that this was a remarkable donee. But why had J. Hillis Miller neglected to mention that the seed for the story was an event from life? Perhaps it was an oversight. Perhaps J. Hillis Miller felt it unimportant. Or perhaps

J. Hillis Miller's criticism had led him, as it had led so many others, to remove from consideration the question of the author's intent to such a degree that the writer's role is obviated.

This last possibility troubled the rhetorician. Teachers of writing, she discovered, have to spend a good deal of time considering the writer's intent. In fact, unless the teacher of writing spends most of the time considering it, not much can happen in a writing course. Was her concern with the relation between writer and text simply a sign of the "adolescent" status of her field? On the other hand, Aristotle made rather much of the presumed ethics of the speaker, and by extension, the writer. But then, Aristotle had written when the world was yet in its adolescent stage.

She returned to her studies. She was gratified to discover that the article, like the talk she had missed, took up the problem of prosopopeia, of personification, of vesting the inanimate with human qualities. She noted that J. Hillis Miller seemed rather excited by the way he thinks or hopes the use of prosopopeia sheds light on Hawthorne's story and on reading in general:

> Have I not all along projected a human face, personality, and voice into those little black marks on the page, marks as inanimate and dead as a corpse or a stone? Just as surely as the citizens of Milford projected a face on or behind the black veil of the Reverend Mr. Hooper and assumed that the missing face was an index of a personality or a selfhood behind the veiling mask of the face itself, so have I projected faces, selves, and voices on the white pages, filigreed in black. I have thought of "Hawthorne" . . . and, most of all have thought and written of Hooper and his fellow parishioners as if they were real people, though they have no existence beyond the marks on the page. I cannot read the story without doing so, even though the point of the story is to question the activity of prosopopeia on which the functioning of the narrative depends. By the time I have, with the help of the story, come to doubt the validity of such personifying projections, it is too late to go back. I have been made the mystified victim, once more, of the piece of ideology I would "unmask." I have already committed the crime the story leads me to condemn. . . . Even the most sophisticated and theoretically aware reading of "The Minister's Black Veil," I am arguing, is no more than a permutation of this primitive and infantile fatuation. To demystify, "unmask," I must forget that I am using as the "tool" of unmasking the very thing I am unmasking, the trope of personification.

The rhetorician found herself mystified by J. Hillis Miller's use of the term prosopopeia in this passage. She could not fathom in what sense the "functioning of the narrative" in Hawthorne's tale depended upon "the activity of prosopopeia." J. Hillis Miller assumed the townspeople, in wondering about the veil, commit a figurative use of language rather than engage in reasonable curiosity. It seemed to her, that for the purposes of the story, the reader was to regard the Rev. Mr. Hooper as an animate being, not as an inanimate object, so that within the confines of the fiction itself, the townspeople wondering what the Rev. Mr. Hooper was doing with a veil over his face hardly meant they were vesting an inanimate object with human qualities.

It was devilishly hard for her to see in what sense it is true that "the citizens of Milford projected a face on or behind the black veil of the Reverend Mr. Hooper." She thought it a strange use of the word "projection" to say that folks knew he had a face but couldn't see it. Even with the mask on, they knew for certain he *had* a face. As for their projecting a face *on* the veil, well, she thought, perhaps Mr. Miller has confused this story with something he heard while viewing the Shroud of Turin.

Lighting another cigarette and stroking the cat absently, the rhetorician mused that perhaps she now understood why J. Hillis Miller had neglected to mention Hawthorne's note to the story. J. Hillis Miller wanted the story to hinge on personification, wanted to persuade his readers that the townspeople attempted to project a meaning onto the Rev. Mr. Hooper, just as J. Hillis Miller projects one onto the story. But Hawthorne himself regards the veil—both of the real Rev. Mr. Joseph Moody and the veil worn by his fictional Rev. Mr. Hooper—as a "symbol"; that is, as a device intended by the wearer to mean something to those who see him, just as Hawthorne intends his story to mean something to the reader.

She listened to the trees outside whipped by the rising wind of a storm approaching across the lake and considered the unfolding pattern in J. Hillis Miller's carpet, a criticism that went beyond ignoring the writer to suppressing the writer altogether. Although she was not particularly prescient, she foresaw the conclusion that the reader—the critic—was the real creator of Hawthorne's story. "But first, he has to murder Hawthorne," she thought.

Curious to learn how J. Hillis Miller would pull off the caper, she read again his claim that he has "projected a human face, personality, and voice into these little black marks on the page, marks as inanimate and dead as a corpse or a stone" just "as surely as the citizens of Milford projected a face on or behind the black veil." She muttered, "It is as easy to argue that the words on the page have 'projected' those human faces, personalities, and voices into your mind, J. Hillis Miller, just as they do into others, into mine, in fact. This is called reading." The cat reached out a paw and stroked her hand. As a reflex, she stroked his head, and thought of Montaigne's question about his cat—whether it was him playing with the cat when he dangled a string in front of it or the cat playing with him.

She thought it fairly obvious that J. Hillis Miller intended to administer the coup de grace to Hawthorne by means of a false analogy. But she knew, although J. Hillis Miller evidently wanted her to forget it, that words are not analogous to a corpse or a stone. Words are fit together by someone who wishes to communicate to others.

J. Hillis Miller tried another strategy. He composed a conceit which depended for its functioning upon the activity of personification, one even less likely to persuade she of the blue velour robe: "The text passively submits to whatever we say about it, but it remains silent, not saying yes or no to any speculative or theoretical formulation about its meaning. In this respect, it is like the black veil itself. . . . [T]he passivity is far from unaggressive. The patience is, in each case, an extreme violence of passive resistance. The performative efficacy of 'The Minister's Black Veil' . . . lies in this violence." Well, she thought, it is perhaps revealing that this particular man prefers an aesthetic in which he "projects" something into a written text, rather than one in which the text is understood as having been carefully prepared in the hope it will give him some enjoyment and perhaps a degree of enlightenment; prefers as well to believe that the text only seems to "passively submit" to what he has to say about it, while all the time she is really being silently and passively aggressive, so that ultimately she undoes the reader, and makes of poor him, who would use his 'tools' to unmask her, a "mystified victim," duped by an "infantile and primitive fatuation." What vixens these texts are. What do they want, anyway?

She was not surprised to find that whatever they want, J. Hillis Miller says he is required to commit a certain violence on such texts. J. Hillis Miller remarks upon his reading as "violence" because "something from the historical past is appropriated or reappropriated for my own purposes." It occurred to her, though J. Hillis Miller does not note it, that Hawthorne, too, is appropriating something from the past for his own purpose: the story of the Rev. Mr. Moody, who really did go about with a veil on his face. She wondered if, by extension, we are compelled to accept the rather odd conclusion that Hawthorne does violence to the memory of the Rev. Mr. Moody. "Interesting, isn't it," she inquired of her indifferent cat, "that J. Hillis Miller adopts the imagery of guerilla warfare, of pillage and rapine, to describe the normal, human tendency to transform experience into story?"

J. Hillis Miller had obviated Hawthorne by comparing his story to a silent, cunning tease upon which J. Hillis Miller had felt compelled to commit an act of violent appropriation. That violence, he says, engenders a birth, when that thing from the historical past (Hawthorne's story, for instance) enters "time again as a new historical act"—that is, as J. Hillis Miller's reading. J. Hillis Miller thus suggested that he as the critic serves less as a midwife than as one who gives birth, a birth resulting—confusingly—from a violent and self-serving act—a kind of rape, as he described it.

She felt suddenly tired and heavy. Contemplating his suggestion that the written words on the page—Hawthorne's words—provoke a violent act of appropriation because they are perversely silent, she thought, "I've heard this routine before." The Courtly Love tradition made of women not just the object of desire, but the cause of it, and of whatever it brought in its train. Criseyde, sitting silently and self-absorbed in a window seat or a church, is spied by Troilus and told it will be entirely her fault if he dies from desire. His violence will be caused by her, just as J. Hillis Miller's violence to the text—his projection of meaning onto it—is caused by the text's perverse silence, and just as Count Valerio is driven to killing something—a chicken perhaps—when aroused by the silent Juno. Criseyde and Juno are objectified and rendered the cause of some violence by another, which is what J. Hillis Miller seemed to think was a fitting analogue to the critical act. "But surely," she thought, "This can't be J. Hillis Miller's ethics."

Having characterized the interpretive act as a violence caused by and directed toward the veiled, silent, perverse Other, J. Hillis Miller imagined his criticism as a self-engendered act of creation. He understood his own writing as a momentous birth that will take on a life of its own, so that the effects of his words are, like our children, "unpredictable."

"Well," she thought, "which is it? Are the words on the page like the stereotypes of women—passive aggressives who deserve to be brutalized because of their provoking silence? Or the mysterious Other, who unwittingly causes the desire to know her, and who is therefore responsible for all that follows, whether she likes it or not? Or are they like children, brought forth by women with joy and pain, and released into the world, our tokens of continuity and change?" While grappling with these apparent contradictions, the rhetorician was stunned by J. Hillis Miller's claim: "The practical implications of these remarks are clear."

J. Hillis Miller called for a curriculum which would provide for "the teaching of rhetorical reading." The wind howled. The rhetorician flicked her ash. Somewhere, a goat coughed. She felt suddenly enlightened. So that is what was meant by those who said rhetoric had to "grow up" in English departments. A "matured" rhetoric would illustrate that all reading was solely a kind of personification the reader imposed upon—or projected into—the text. The desires and dreams of the writer who wrote the text would, of course, not be considered, so that properly understood, the term 'rhetoric' did not apply. J. Hillis Miller used it to mean reading as a kind of rhetorical trope—as prosopopeia—and hence as a mask for his projections of himself into a text.

"An interesting social program," she mused. She imagined teaching young men and women to suppose the closest corollary to reading was at best juvenile self-infatuation, at worst, sadism; she considered telling young writers that they do not, after all, matter at all, because they exist only to create an opportunity for someone else to "appropriate" their humanity. She read J. Hillis Miller's claim that if we would adopt this new curriculum and teach students that when they read, they are only projecting a meaning into ciphers upon a page, we would "equip citizens to resist ideological mystifications, that is, the confusion of linguistic with material reality." She turned to D. A. Miller's response and found herself agreeing with him. He confessed that J. Hillis Miller's proposed curriculum offered D. A. Miller a "prospect" which bored him either "to death or to tears." The rhetorician's cynical dismissal of J. Hillis Miller was perhaps excusable in one reading late at night, alone, in a blue velour robe, under the influence of pear liqueur.

Second Circle: The Anti-Pygmalion Effect

She arrived at the conversation circle the next morning at 9:15 to listen to the discussion of what J. Hillis Miller had said the day before about James's short story. The small group was seated in a circle around J. Hillis Miller. To his left was the ginger-haired English professor. Next to him sat a silent and wide-eyed young man, who would be introduced later as a student. There were three other males: a bearded Shakespearean specialist, a professor of religious studies, and the professor of Russian who had been her informant the night before. In addition to herself, there were two other women. One from France, a professor of Modern Languages; the other a specialist in American and Comparative Literature.

Perhaps because J. Hillis Miller had referred to it in his article, the rhetorician soon found herself thinking of speech act theory, which has, as one concern, how power or dominance is established in a group through what is said. In terms of speech acts, the conversation circle yielded predictable results. The men spoke more frequently and for longer periods than did the women. They also interrupted the women or otherwise—to use J. Hillis Miller's words—appropriated the historical moment for their own purposes. The male-initiated portions of the discussion were directed at J. Hillis Miller: a man would make an observation; J. Hillis Miller would respond.

Only the women responded to someone other than J. Hillis Miller, possibly because they mistakenly thought the group had gathered for conversation; for instance, the professor of religious studies opined that in burying the statue of Juno, Martha did not seem to be reflecting a repressive motive. He addressed this observation to J. Hillis Miller, but it was the French professor who responded levelly that Martha seemed involved in a repressive situation because she was a wealthy woman and marriageable, who is wed to a Count who had no money; her godfather regarded her as above all someone who would marry, and who ought to marry suitably. "She is like the statue," she observed, "beautiful and valuable." No one responded to her. Some time later in the discussion, however, there seemed to be a general agreement that the characters in James's story treated one another in ways analogous to statues. This confirmed another observation frequently made of discussion among men and women. A woman's remark may go unnoticed, only to be appropriated later—without acknowledging the source—by a male and then approved by the group as a whole, rather like J. Hillis Miller's notion of what a critic does to a story.

At any rate, the conversation did turn again to the matter of people in the story treating one another as statues. The rhetorician noticed, however, that this general disparagement of the ethics of the fictional characters did not prevent those present from treating each other like statues. At one point, the ginger-haired professor introduced the student as working on an honor's thesis on James which included attention to "The Last of the Valerii." The student interpreted the hand of Juno that was discovered before the statue itself as signifying the authorial hand that wrote the story and, hence, as analogous to the creative power of Juno. The professor of American and Comparative Literature was concerned about this interpretation because it seemed to make Juno the cause of the action. The student felt the statue was, indeed, the cause of what happened. The professor of American and Comparative Literature felt there was something unnerving about making an inanimate object a cause; in fact, the point of the story is that Count Valerio takes momentary leave of his senses when he vests in the statue the cause of his desires.

The rhetorician assumed J. Hillis Miller would have something to say in response. After all, her colleague's observations about misconstruing Juno as the cause of the action reflected rather clearly on the issue of personification, not only with regard to James's story, but with regard to J. Hillis Miller's own theory of reading as a violent projection of meaning caused by the text's perverse, passively aggressive silence. The rhetorician was mildly surprised when J. Hillis Miller did not respond to her colleague.

Commenting on the student's thesis, J. Hillis Miller said that while he had little to say about the hand of Juno, he did have something to say about authorial hands in another part of the book he was working on, a commentary on a short story in which the author refers to himself as the hand that is writing the words on the page. J. Hillis Miller turned this into a rather long discussion of the "ethics" of the reader.

But the rhetorician was more interested in the ethics of J. Hillis Miller. She felt that because she had not heard J. Hillis Miller's talk the previous day, she had been socially correct in letting others speak first, but that now she might ask a question or two. Still thinking of her reading the previous night, she wondered aloud whether he would say more about the hand that writes the words: "You don't seem to regard it as a synecdoche," she said, "you don't seem to take it as meaning that the hand is connected to a body, a whole person. You seem to regard it as if it is moving across the page, disembodied."

"Oh, that is how I take it."

"Well, are you comfortable with that as a way of reading, as a way of conceptualizing the writer?"

"Oh, no I think it's monstrous."

He seemed about to elaborate but the professor of Religious Studies interrupted with an observation off the subject and J. Hillis Miller gave him a lengthy reply.

Those were the only words the rhetorician spoke, although she had more she might have said. She, like the other women and the student, became as objectified as a statue, as silent as a text.

At about 10 o'clock, participants began to drift away. By 10:10 those remaining were J. Hillis Miller, the ginger-haired professor, the student, and rhetorician. The speech acts were accomplished by J. Hillis Miller and the ginger-haired professor. Henry James, who had scarcely been mentioned, must be regarded as having left the room long before.

By 10:35 the rhetorician had decided that, interesting though the participant-observation was, there was little value in confirming existing speech-act hypotheses. She commented that she had enjoyed listening but must depart. This caused no noticeable interruption in the flow of words, and but a flicker of eye movement from the two interlocutors. She slowly put on her coat and picked up her bag. She stepped directly in the line of vision of J. Hillis Miller, telling him she hoped he enjoyed the remainder of his stay. As she left, she thought she understood both the ethics and the aesthetic of J. Hillis Miller. "His Juno's the reality: I'm the fiction," she thought, confusing linguistic with material reality.

Touchstones

and Bedrocks:

Learning the Stories

We Need

*

Victoria Ekanger

I am attracted to books that encourage and teach me to listen for my own stories in the context of others' stories: touchstone tales that demonstrate the multiplicity of "*gumbo ya ya,*" which is, Luisah Teish explains, "a creole term that means 'Everybody talks at once' " (139); stories that ask me, in league with Maxine Hong Kingston's woman warrior, "to make my mind large, as the universe is large, so that there is room for paradoxes" (35); creative forms that enable, as does Ana Castillo's *The Mixquiahuala Letters,* a choice of reading sequences: for conformists, cynics, and the quixotic in turn; word uses that re-vision linguistic possibilities, as Adrienne Rich encourages, in order to "recognize how our language has trapped as well as liberated us" (35). And the writers and writings I love best tell me women's stories, which is important to me because I grew up not realizing women have very many.

Eva heard my grandfather name it indigestion. Just leave me here on the floor awhile, he said, and the pain will pass. Happens all the time, no big deal.

My Aunt Eva, his daughter, thought: maybe, unlikely, stubborn fool, can't defy him, can't cross him, and she waited, swallowing terror thick as snot. Eventually fear pushed up inside her so strong that she couldn't sit still, and she walked a small circle in her front room. She concentrated to keep her feet treading the floor, her mouth wrenched shut.

Don't scream (to herself). Don't die (to her dad).

And when she couldn't keep silence any longer, she braved his curses and called a doctor, who came to her house, because back in those days doctors still did.

It's probably not indigestion, the doctor said; he should go to the hospital.

No, Grandpa said, and his will prevailed; the doctor went on his way, only pausing to wish my aunt good luck. More time passed, and then finally, finally, the pain made Grandpa relent. All right, I guess we'll have to go get Emma (his wife, my grandmother) he said. I didn't want to worry her, but we better go get her and head over to the hospital.

This wasn't the heart attack that killed Grandpa, only the first of several. My family tells this story as a way of fondly illustrating Grandpa's character and marveling, not without some swell of awe and pride, at what a lesson in determination he was.

I am not certain what the lesson of Eva's experience is. One consequence: by breaking silence and calling the doctor, she risked her dad's wrath, which arrived very quickly. Tillie Olsen has theorized wonderfully about the role(s) of silence in the life of a creative woman, mostly about silences unnatural and oppressive, silences which are the result of, among other things: eroded confidence, leached will, bent "conviction as to the importance of what one has to say, one's right to say it" (46). Did my aunt's small breaking of silence, her public telling of my grandfather's health business, mark an increase of confidence in her right to speak up? I am not sure. I have written this version of the story to imagine something of her point of view, but circulating information about Eva is never the reason this story comes up, even when she tells it herself. My point in recalling it here, now, is neither because of Eva nor my grandfather, but because what interests me most is a detail concerning my grandmother, a piece of information I heard just one time, I think, and only by accident. The detail is this: before Grandma could accompany them to the hospital, Aunt Eva and Grandpa had to go pick her up at the fruit packing shed where she worked.

Until I heard this story I never knew Grandma worked.

Of course I knew she *worked,* but not that she worked "out," away from home, and certainly not that she worked at a fruit factory: that she was green collar, a food line worker. I think factory experience is a working-class "don't tell" story for the generation of my grandmother's children, my mom and aunts, women of determined upward mobility. Determination, one getting-to-middle-class tool, is part of my mom's heritage. The story of Grandpa denying a heart attack is about being determined, but the part about Grandma packing fruit, apparently, is not. My grandmother is bedrock to my work with literature.

You don't have anything if you don't have the stories.—Thought-Woman, the spider, a story spinner   Leslie Marmon Silko, *Ceremony*

When stories are considered—in a common sense—as efforts toward making meaning, what stories we each have constitute our grounds of being and operation; they are all those narratives which circumscribe, inform, and define our identities and choices. What I mean by this— and what Silko's Thought-Woman intends, I think, about "having" the stories—relates to knowing which ones are good for us, a determination often not simple to come by given the complexities of contemporary story circulation. (Some stories *seem* simple to denounce, yet their ubiquity resists easy analysis: the story TV tells, for instance, about Sugar Chomps being an important part of a balanced breakfast or the one Shakespeare tells about taming a wife.) It is knotty business to assign value to stories we hear and see and read, and perhaps harder yet to evaluate the wisdom of teaching, telling, or writing into circulation any particular story. Yet we all have profound responsibility for the stories we circulate—from the jokes we repeat to the stories we assign students if we are teachers to the texts we invent if we are writers.

Too often ways of knowing and kinds of knowing get plotted as hierarchies in traditional U.S. education, so that we consider ourselves uncultured (which really means differently cultured) when we don't have knowledge of certain stories. (Plato's one about the cave, for example, or Melville's one about the whale.) Both are wonderful stories, I think, but not necessary ones, and the difference is significant.

When belief in a category (or canon) of *necessary* stories is promoted, values and visions about story possibilities are fettered. Such belief de-ludes us into calling whole our partial pictures of creatively imagined human experience and results in mistaking stories that rend us culturally for stories that hold us together. It seduces us into finding universals before we've experienced *enough* stories for this to be likely.

The nurse held a small bottle containing a premeasured dose of antibiotic in one hand, and with her other hand she worked to fit it to the IV tube. The bottle slipped, and in attempting to recover it she knocked over the water that sat on the bedstand next to my mom's hospital bed. She wiped up the water and examined the antibiotic bottle, then successfully attached it.

"Did any of it spill?" I asked, noticing that the bottle was only about three-quarters full.

"Not a significant amount," she smiled.

I wanted to ask, "Was it full to begin with? Isn't a quarter of the total amount significant? Are you sure you know what you are doing?" But I didn't say anything, instead telling myself not to insult her, not to be inappropriately argumentative. After she left, I regretted not asking, and I worried that my challenge to the nurse was all that stood between my mother and postsurgical infection. I was there, after all, to be assertive on her behalf. I decided I must track down this nurse and grill her about the derelict decision to use the partial bottle of antibiotic solution.

But almost immediately my mom's surgeon came in. "I'm concerned," I began, "that my mom might not be getting the full dose of antibiotic intended. Some of the solution was spilled when the bottle was installed." Then, stepping aside from the IV stand—with dramatic flair, I thought—I said in an incriminatingly low tone, "This is all the solution the bottle contained when it was connected."

"Yes, that looks about right," the doctor responded with a marked lack of concern, an attitude not nearly satisfactory to me. Was I going to have to interrogate him too? This man was a top-rated neurosurgeon at the city's premier hospital, and he was someone my mom had a pressing need to think of as godlike. He had recently completed hours of surgery on her lower back, her second back surgery, and all my wishes would also have him be a god who might really effect a lumbar fix this time. I too wanted his responses, even when casual, to be supernaturally informed.

But this doctor looked mortal to me, and I had grave doubts. I said evenly: "I know the antibiotic is being administered as insurance, but if it turns out she's actually fighting an infection, I worry about whether the blood level of medication will have been adequate the required length of time."

I observed three things in fast sequence. One: My mom's doctor examined the bottle very closely, as if seriously considering my words for the first time. Two: I heard him say "Yes, three-quarters is the full mark for this solution. Are you in medicine, then?" Three: My mother, watching this verbal interchange, beamed.

I tend to imagine that my mother thinks *I'm* a little godlike. Not perfect, but optimally effective and oldest-child capable, no matter what I set my mind to. I wish. At any rate, talking to doctors is not something at which she ever expects to be expert, so for major concerns she delegates this responsibility to me. She wants me there, to be the person in command of language, the formulator of just the right questions. My mother knows I can't protect her from what being in a hospital might mean, but she has a certain faith that—by sheer force of *articulate* will—I might potentially re-story a threatening outcome. I am the family delegate to hospitals, the language wielder.

I felt like apologizing to the nurse for thinking her inept. And I was irritated by the doctor's assumption that there was anything necessarily "medical" (as opposed to merely informed) about what I asked. I curtly responded: "No, I'm not in medicine. I'm in English." Let him figure how to make conversation of that, I thought.

Was I surprised.

"My wife is in English too," he said. "She's doing graduate work at the university here."

Well, knock me over with a tongue depressor. It's a small world and so forth, I said. It turned out I knew who she was.

My mom told me later she thought my use of the term "blood level" sounded most medical. How did I know to say that? she wondered. I wasn't sure, but guessed it was from watching TV.

My mother is bedrock to my work with literature. Because of my mom I never underestimate the power of language nor of my formal education to word use. I am the first person in my family to attend college, and her expectations were vital to this. Like Alice Walker's mom did for her, my mother "handed down respect for the possibilities—and the will to grasp them" ("In Search of Our Mothers' Gardens" 242). She identifies in me a relationship to words that makes almost anything possible. What she sometimes means is a literacy she feels closed out of.

We know different things, I tell her. (She reads a lot too.)

I don't understand *A Room of One's Own,* she says. Touchstone for me, I think this book has been an albatross around her reading time since I gave it to her years ago.

So don't bother with it, I say; it doesn't matter.

But *you* love it, she points out. She wants to know books I read. I want to share them. More often than not it doesn't work out. She doesn't need me to give her books. I suspect she thinks I need to give them, and perhaps this is true.

Here, I love this book too, I say, giving her *With Wings.* Its stories are by and about women with disabilities (I don't add: like you). The characters in Mary Wilkins Freeman's "A Mistaken Charity" will remind you of Grandma and her sisters, and Alice Walker writes wonderfully about her loss of sight in one eye, and, Mom, I think I know you even better when I read "Affliction" by Muriel Minard:

> Affliction
> Is ice
> On a summer pond.
> And the pond
> Not dead,

> But subtly robbed
> Of pondness.

I notice that *With Wings* is often in my mom's hands the day I give it to her. I also notice, whenever she puts it down, that she isn't getting further than the first pages. How can being public about disability be a literary project? Why would women with disabilities be public about them at all? Don't tell. Don't tell these private things. I am afraid this is what she thinks, although perhaps she is saving the book to be alone with. Next time we visit I'll ask, and I'll listen very hard. I am a storyteller, and I'm selfishly desperate to understand her "don't tell."

The guinea should be earmarked "Rags. Petrol. Matches. Take this guinea and with it burn the college to the ground." And let the daughters dance round the flames. —Virginia Woolf, *Three Guineas*

I have daughters, and they too are bedrock to my work with literature. If I don't endorse torching schools in the stories I pass on to them, they nevertheless know and ask that the stories schools tell them be accountable to their lives, and not the other way around. They think about which stories are good for them and about the ones that are their right to have available. I think about all the stories I want them to have, and I realize there is not enough time for me to get to all those before they leave home. And besides, just as I come to what I think is a most crucial story, their thoughts will sometimes be on phoning a friend or dishing up ice cream. So: time is short, inevitably they will spend part of it on ice cream, and I am convinced there is no one very most important set of stories for them to have anyway. My goal is to provide a selection and a direction: a range of stories to encourage them beyond being knowers of narrow selves. Like me, my daughters are happily engaged in a lifelong process of learning which stories are needed. They know far more stories of women than I knew at their ages, and I take great pleasure in recognizing they are wise to the stories about Sugar Chomps and Shakespeare's shrew as well.

References

Castillo, Ana. *The Mixquiahuala Letters*. Binghamton, New York: Bilingual Press, 1986.

Freeman, Mary Wilkins. "A Mistaken Charity." *With Wings*. Eds. Saxton and Howe. 143–51.

Kingston, Maxine Hong. *The Woman Warrior*. 1975. New York: Vintage-Random, 1977.

Minard, Muriel. "Affliction." *With Wings*. Eds. Saxton and Howe. 10.

Olsen, Tillie. *Silences*. New York: Laurel, 1965.

Rich, Adrienne. "When We Dead Awaken: Writing as Re-Vision." *On Lies, Secrets, and Silence*. New York: W.W. Norton and Company, 1979. 33–50.

Saxton, Marsha, and Florence Howe, eds. *With Wings: An Anthology of Literature By and About Women with Disabilities*. New York: Feminist Press, 1987.

Silko, Leslie Marmon. *Ceremony*. 1977. New York: Penguin, 1986.

Teisch, Luisah. *Jambalaya: The Natural Woman's Book of Personal Charms and Practical Rituals*. San Francisco: Harper & Row, 1985.

Walker, Alice. "Beauty: When the Other Dancer is the Self." *With Wings*. Eds. Saxton and Howe. 152–58.

Walker, Alice. "In Search of Our Mother's Gardens." *In Search of Our Mother's Gardens*. San Diego: Harcourt Brace Jovanovich, 1983. 231–43.

Woolf, Virginia. *A Room of One's Own*. San Diego: Harcourt Brace Jovanovich, 1929.

Woolf, Virginia. *Three Guineas*. San Diego: Harcourt Brace Jovanovich, 1938.

PART II

Critical

Confessions

*

We need to support each other

in rejecting the limitations of

a tradition—a manner of

reading, of speaking, of

writing, or criticizing—which

was never really designed to

include us all.

—Adrienne Rich, "Toward a

More Feminist Criticism"

Creative Voices:

Women Reading and

Women's Writing

*

Frances Murphy
Zauhar

I read with avidity a variety of books, previously to my mind's being sufficiently matured, and strengthened to make a proper selection. I was passionately fond of novels; and, as I lived in a state of seclusion, I acquired false ideas of life. The Ideal world which my imagination formed was very different from the real. My passions were naturally strong, and this kind of reading heightened my sensitivity, by calling it forth to realize scenes of imaginary distress. . . . As I always read with great rapidity, perhaps few of my sex have perused more books at the age of twenty than I had. Yet my reading was very desultory, and novels engaged too much of my attention. . . . Reading much religious controversy must be extremely trying to a female whose mind, instead of being strengthened by those studies which exercise the judgment, and give stability to the character, is debilitated by reading romances and novels, which are addressed to the fancy and imagination, and are calculated to heighten the feelings.—Hannah Adams, *A Memoir*

Hannah Adams, an eighteenth-century American historian, thus defines the legacy of her early reading of literature. The novels to which she was directed as a young girl as the only appropriate genre for feminine reading created in her a habit of mind which made her later religious, philosophical, and historical reading confusing and distressing to her; they required that she "unmake" the world of her earlier reading in order to pursue the "serious" reading and writing that she would make her career and life's work. I focus on Adams as I begin my essay on women editors, women's reading, and women's writing, because she so candidly articulates the attitude widely held about the fate of women who "read too much." Adams views herself as a "ruined reader," a woman who has suffered considerably because the only reading matter permitted to her as a young girl did not prepare her for the "adult" (i.e., "male") world of history, science, and ideas. She believed that the early reading which she had absorbed as exemplary did not prepare her to approach the language of academic research and that reading scholarly material required her to undergo an agony of relearning unlike that of any male reader of academic texts. She believed, she *knew,* that she should have had access to the process of learning available to boys and young men in order to prepare herself to read and learn as they did. While most readers would agree that she did indeed learn "how to read," Adams was never sure of her accomplishments, perhaps because she believed that what came for her with such effort was second nature to the men around her, who had been taught to read rigorously from childhood.

I cherish Hannah Adams's work, and I read her *Memoir* quite regularly; I teach it every semester in my Survey of American Literature to 1860, paying particular attention to the analysis of her "ruination." Part of why I read her again and again is because her description of herself corresponds so closely with the sense I have had of how I have become a reader/writer of and about literature. I have shared her impression that the boys and men around me have not had the same experience with reading that I and many of the women I know have had. I could and can easily remember the times in high school, in college, in graduate school, and even at work, when I have felt that there was something I hadn't been told that my male classmates knew, that I had to find out if I wanted to continue with the work I had chosen, and that what I *had* learned was somehow inappropriate to the task at hand. Looking at Adams's life, and looking at my own, I have come to think that, while I may or may not have had anything withheld from me deliberately, I and many other women have been taught that the heightened sensitivity, the heightened feeling, the sense of relationship that we often developed through our girlhood reading have no place in our professional lives. I recognize one significant difference between Hannah Adams and myself: I no longer consider myself a "ruined" reader. And I consider myself to have been "redeemed" primarily by the writing of other women who, like Hannah Adams and myself, seem for a time to have considered themselves also to be women who "read too much." I have been heartened to find such inspiration, not only in the work of widely recognized, relatively secure, or influential writers, but also in writing by women who, like myself, are still tentatively practicing, trying to find our most expressive voice.

Hannah Adams is not the only writer to observe her early reading and what it did to her. George Eliot remarks about her early reading: "I shall carry to my grave the mental diseases with which [novels] have contaminated me" (Eliot 22). And Catharine Sedgwick often expressed her regret that she had not been allowed the academic education regularly afforded to men. These early writers develop the convention that what girls read ruins them for what they will read as women; the convention has lived and prospered until very recently.

Many of us—when we decided to leave the world of the leisurely reader to become English majors and then English professors—learned that the way we responded to literature as professionals ought to be authoritative, objective, and engaging, but that we should not focus on ourselves as readers or on the way that a particular book may have affected us personally. The language of enthusiasm, of heightened sensitivity, had no place in our professional writing and was not involved in an articulate, perceptive analysis of/response to literature. We might write in strong words about our subject, we might even be enchanting in the arguments we make, but if we are personal, intimate, if we try to create for our readers, or between our readers and ourselves, the affiliation we feel with the texts most important to us—we will be emoting, we will not be working, we will not be writing criticism.

However, what our reading, early and subsequent, has taught many of us is that this is simply not the case. Our reading and a variety of other experiences in our lives do connect to make us very capable, dynamic respondents to the worlds around us and within us—and effective, learned readers of the texts we study. *definitely — the relationship btw writer ⇄ text ⇄ reader*

Like most women who become English teachers and scholars, I read a lot as a girl and loved it. My mother and my grandmother could always find me curled up in "the circle," the left corner of our parlor sofa, proverbially, with my nose in a book. If I was in the middle of reading something, they would have to make me go outside to play. If I had finished something, they would have to make me wait to start another book. In spite of their concern for my social life, both women were always eager to drive me to the public library, where we would all exchange armsful of already-read books for books-to-be-read-this-week; both Mom and Nana contributed to my "ruination" by their own example. It was a wonderful experience to share.

I found other pernicious examples of excessive female reading at school; my Catholic grade school and, later, my high school, were staffed by nuns. The sisters from both schools lived at the same convent, and so my high school teachers had it on sound information that I was someone who read almost anything put into my hands; they shared their own favorite novels with me. Most girls got punished for talking during class; I got put on detention once for reading *Emma* during a Biology lecture, but the sister in charge of detention that day let me leave when I told her why I was there, because *Emma* was her favorite novel.

I continued to find models for my reading when I got to college—a Catholic women's college, again taught mostly by nuns. My teachers shared books with me and my friends both in the classroom and outside—not just the traditional canon of English and American novels, or the most recent "serious," contemporary literature, but lots of other books, as well—detective fiction, science fiction, romantic fiction—you name it, someone was in a reading group reading it or passing it around. It really wasn't until I got to graduate school that I felt that the ways I approached my work reading and my play reading were somehow different from the ways that my (mostly male) professors did. It was here that I "discovered" that I had some catching up to do.

"Catching up" mostly involved developing an authoritative tone rather than a personal one in the essays I wrote about literature. I looked back recently at papers I wrote while I was in graduate school, and I was struck with how my writing changed. I still consider some of those changes to be good ones, for they involved my awakening to the importance of writing for an audience that might possess a different perspective from yours. What saddened me a bit is the gradual diminution of what I can only call "enthusiasm" for the literature I took as my subject. I became a strong writer—focused, organized, direct, a creator of active, readable prose—but I also became formal, distant. I find it interesting that I occasionally recovered an "engaging" voice in papers I wrote for two courses taught by women: one on English Romantic novelists and another on Elizabethan tragedy. I think that most of what I wrote was informed, not only in idea but also, and more significantly, in tone, by secondary material, the literary criticism with which I also dealt.

Mainstream literary criticism has, until very recently, reinforced the convention that the "good" reader remains detached from the reading, unaffected in a moral or developmental sense; and only under those conditions is he (or sometimes she) able to make a responsible assessment of the text at hand. Such a model assumes that the writer, on some significant level, intended that the reader remain uninvolved with the work. On the contrary, most literature was meant to be read by a totally engaged, emotionally involved reader.

I would probably never have written very much beyond my dissertation if I had not started reading feminist literary criticism, for it was not until I did so that I rediscovered a voice that helped me think about what I valued in the texts I read. A significant number of feminist scholars who deal primarily with the work of women writers have relinquished the model of the detached analytical reader and begun to create a model of the reader engaged in and even transformed by the literature she reads. This reader creates good readings in the academic sense of that term by working from the understanding that what the writer wrote mattered to that writer, who intended it to matter to the reader, as well. Such a reader examines the text in relation to the experiences of her own life and thought, to discover, among other things, what in the text might matter to her. Much feminist scholarship focuses on those texts that enable the reader to articulate her understanding of the intricacies of her life and its relationship to the experience of others. Many contemporary critics present themselves as co-readers, providing a different model for the practice of reading, for they share with their readers the experience of enjoying and being engaged with the text as an appropriate and learned response.

In the eyes of these recent critics, a good reading requires that the reader allow herself to be informed or, as George Eliot described it, "contaminated," by the writer's values and concerns. These readers, unlike Eliot, do not consider the values or habits of mind developed by the literature to be diseases or deviations; rather, they can and do view these tendencies as deliberately created differences from the ideals of male-centered fictions, and as they reread them and recover them for their own use, they actively model (without prescribing) a way of reading this material for others. In contrast to prevailing theories of reading, feminist critics tend to see the relationship between the reader and the text as collaborative rather than submissive, demonstrating that the reader's choice to listen to the speaker in the text is not a matter of subordination but of cooperation, because she finds her own voice enabled rather than silenced by the influences of the text.

Three well-known scholars, Rachel Brownstein, Blanche Gelfant, and Judith Fetterley, provide particularly helpful models for this practice of interactive criticism in the reader-writer relationship; they have engaged me in my reading and in my own writing in important ways. Although only Fetterley's writing editorially prefaces an actual anthology of literature by other writers, the process in the works of Brownstein and Gelfant also presents groups of works by various authors to their readers and seeks to engage those readers by presenting a reading of the presenter, as well as of the text. One can discover a significantly incremental relationship among their work that parallels the growing importance of the reader's response in feminist criticism; each more recent work demonstrates a fuller figuring forth of the importance of affiliation between reader and writer through the text.

Rachel M. Brownstein's book, *Becoming a Heroine: Reading about Women in Novels,* was first published in 1982, although portions of the book, including her autobiographical first chapter, "My Life in Fiction," appeared somewhat earlier. While Brownstein says that she "make(s) no attempt to articulate a theory or to follow a particular method of feminist criticism" (Brownstein xx), the shadows of a theory and the germs of a method are nevertheless present. In her introduction, Brownstein several times praises the autobiographical impulse of some women critics in distinctly positive terms, as when she points out that "in the past twenty years, women have written a great deal about women as women. Feminists, like many others in our time, have been keenly conscious of what it means to write and to be written; they have been *generously frank* about their relationships with their own and other people's pens" (Brownstein xvi, emphasis mine). Brownstein speculates about the significance of the fact that "the popular rebel heroines of Erica Jong and Marilyn French, closer to home, are women who studied English Literature in graduate school, who were marked for life, *as I was*, by having been English majors" (Brownstein xvii, emphasis mine). Brownstein's references to herself never distract her readers from a serious consideration of the texts she presents; rather, they always bring readers back to considering, first, the text, and second, a reader's response to it: initially, readers consider Brownstein's response, but they are invited, eventually and inevitably, also to consider their own. Thus, in her own writing, she recreates a heroine who holds herself before the reader as a mirror in which the reader may see herself, much like the mirror/heroine that Brownstein found in the fiction about which she now writes. Brownstein openly declares her interest in the effect of her own reading, and her method of weaving autobiographical responses to her reading into the text of her book, which also records what she reads, seems designed to evoke in most readers their own memories of the reading of these same books. She also wants to suggest to her readers that the nature of their responses to these works has some significance, which they can discern if they examine it. It is only after the readers' memories of reading are evoked that Brownstein suggests the significance of what she herself has read and invites her readers to do the same. The result of her text is not an open-ended "appreciation" of the novels she reads, but a closely detailed anatomy of the aspirations and limitations worked on many readers through the heroine(s) of the nineteenth-century English novel.

Brownstein takes for granted that girls and young women who read novels about young women care about these characters and allow their fictional stories to matter in their own lives. As an English major-turned-professor, she can articulate the significances of meaning derived from this care and its effect on her life even while she distinguishes it from the effect of the detached critical method she has learned as a professional. And she questions the propriety of excluding this type of reading from professional use. In ways parallel to those in which nineteenth-century women writers hesitated to call their fictions "literature," Rachel Brownstein hesitates to call her process a "method," but she does imply, if not in so many explicit directions then at least in presenting her text to other readers, that allowing a text to matter and considering what matter it makes in one's life affords a reader a legitimate and good reading of a text.

My own first experience with Rachel Brownstein's work came in the summer after I started teaching full time. I was taking a break from preparing my American survey to read some criticism, and her book was on the top of my pile. It took me several days to read because I could not believe at first that I was learning so much about literature while I was learning about her. As I considered how much I had discovered, I went back to reading eighteenth- and nineteenth-century literature and found myself making new connections between writers. I saw then what I had not seen before largely because finally I was thinking, as Brownstein's work suggested, of how the writer's intentions and her activities paralleled my own.

Like Brownstein, Blanche Gelfant also demonstrates the importance of the reader's response to what she reads in *Women Writing in America,* first published in book form in 1984. Like Brownstein's work, some of Gelfant's essays appeared earlier in other forms. She has gathered essays—"disparate pieces," she calls them—into a single volume which she describes as a "collage." Gelfant does this, she says, "to suggest a preference for criticism that is open-ended, capable of surprise, and subversive of traditional standards and forms. In these respects, it seems to me congenial of a feminist inquiry. For the analogy valorizes a continuously open canon, since collage is an open form" (Gelfant 7). She admits that enabling the individual's creation of her own "canon" is more important to her than reiterating the praise of already famous texts; her attitude on this issue differs somewhat from Rachel Brownstein's. Brownstein deliberately chooses well-known works by (mostly) canonical authors, although she emphasizes that her list might "compose a sort of personal version of The Great Tradition," which "only in the fullest, most ambiguous sense of that word" does she mean to "propose as [a] model" (Brownstein xx). Blanche Gelfant shares Brownstein's assumption that the reader's "personal involvement" with the text is central, even when, as she says, she cannot pinpoint its exact nature. Also, like Brownstein, Gelfant takes the model for her life and work from her reading. In her first chapter, which she calls "*An* Introduction" (the indefinite article reminds readers that what she says will not be definitive but simply alternative to more traditional ways of approaching these and other works), she recognizes that she has "enjoyed listening to highly distinctive voices and hearing them sound, singly and contrapuntally, certain themes common to American writers, and particularly, to women. Seeing these essays grouped together, I realize that I too pursue certain themes. . . . I saw how pervasively I deal, as a critic, with . . . events that usually shape women's lives" (Gelfant 1). Gelfant thus recognizes her interest in a particular kind of story, as well as its effect on her own work:

> Only as I was completing a description of the city's "hungry" heroines did I realize how urgently I was pursuing images of survival, how much I wished to find in American writers and their characters salient examples of women who were not mad, suicidal, starving, raging, or sinking into inanition. Like the heroines I was delineating, I wanted to hear the sound of voices strong enough to have shattered women's well-known "silence." Perhaps that desire has motivated all these pieces, for as a critic I seem to have been gathering assurances of the strength of American women writers (Gelfant 3).

In the autobiographical notes she writes to introduce each of the essays, Blanche Gelfant reiterates the personal importance of each writer to her and the empowering effect which that personal sense has on her reading. Rather than clouding her perspective or dimming her vision, the sense of the personal sharpens her perceptions of what each writer attempts. She thus sees evoking relationship rather than maintaining detachment as an alternative and positive way of reading well. She also sees these personal connections as the foundation for a literary tradition, as she reveals in an anecdote about herself, Tillie Olsen, and their shared legacy from Willa Cather:

"evoking relationship" vs. "maintaining detachment"

I date an important insight back to Olsen's [campus] visit of 1973, a significant year to me, since it was Willa Cather's centennial. The occasion was marked on my campus by a display of photographs from a new book that traced Cather's life pictorially. Tillie Olsen was deeply moved to see in the photographs of Nebraska the landscape of her own childhood. I began to sense then, dimly perhaps, what has now become clear: that women writers have common roots, not necessarily geographic, as in this instance; that they inspire and give strength to each other; that when one finds or recovers her voice, she enables many others to speak (Gelfant 60).

This insight and others like it underscore the commitment with which Gelfant praises the common ground, the relationship between writer and reader. More specifically than Rachel Brownstein, Gelfant demonstrates the enabling potential of one woman's voice for another's, and the significance for one reader of perceiving the relationship between another reader and herself when they have shared the same text, as she and Tillie Olsen share Willa Cather's work.

Gelfant most deliberately takes a place with these evocative writers as an evocative writer herself, when, in the preface to her essay on "The City's 'Hungry' Heroine," she remarks, "I liked these characters and was to discover that others liked them too. When in various lectures I described the hungry heroine, women in the audience reacted personally, said they were hearing the story of their own lives. They were academic women, professors and students, and yet in images of hard-working, idealistic, and often lonely characters—many of them poor immigrants in the city—they saw admirable reflections of themselves (Gelfant 204–5). By recognizing her role in creating certain evocations from her listeners, Blanche Gelfant recognizes more explicitly than Rachel Brownstein not only the importance of creating affiliational responses between the reader and the writer but also the necessity of recognizing the responses that arise from readers as a result of her work.

I first read Gelfant's book in the same summer as I read Rachel Brownstein's, and her work likewise helped me clarify my thinking about the women's literature I had been reading. As I tried to identify books I would use in my survey course, as well as books I could use in a course focused on women writers, I felt overwhelmed by the quantity of material available. I worried about how I would do justice to the variety of styles and voices and how I could be sure I would choose texts that would "represent" the material "accurately." Blanche Gelfant's work reminded me that the idea of "coverage" offered by the "canon" can be a vast trap. Her metaphor of the collage enabled me to put my choices into perspective, recognizing that they are not the last word on the subject—nor should they be. Gelfant's practice in *Women Writing in America* also reinforced the importance of personal involvement in reading. I have learned to refuse to be the sole chooser of assignments in my classes: my students share in choosing the readings and the subjects for discussion. The resulting conversation, lively and often intense, creates the sense of empowerment and understanding that Gelfant describes in her book. It likewise creates a community of readers, rather than a hierarchy of teachers and students.

The most deliberate and explicit of the three critics I am presently considering, Judith Fetterley, like Rachel Brownstein and Blanche Gelfant, takes the affective model of the fiction she reads as an appropriate paradigm for the criticism she writes. In the Introduction to her anthology, *Provisions: A Reader from Nineteenth-Century American Women,* published in 1985, she writes, "If I was struck by the degree of self-consciousness and self-confidence that many mid-nineteenth-century American women writers exhibited in their writing, I was equally struck by the apparent ease with which they chose to write about women and their lives—or, in other words, with which they chose to write about themselves" (Fetterley 7). Like the two contemporary writers who slightly precede her, Judith Fetterley values the impulse to autobiography in the writers whose work she reads, and like them, she recognizes the sense of pleasure a reader derives from reading a text as an appropriate critical response. Also like Brownstein and Gelfant, she openly invites her readers to form their own vision of "the literary tradition"—as she herself has done—by examining the short stories of other women who wrote in the nineteenth century, by considering whether or not her own comments on the short stories are equally applicable to the novels of this period, and, most significantly, by reading works not anthologized but listed in Fetterley's "Alternate Table of Contents," or by looking for lost writers and works themselves.

Much more deliberately than either Brownstein or Gelfant, Fetterley fosters an affiliation among herself, other readers, and writers by offering an anthology of other works with her own history of reading appended to it. In doing this, she prepares her readers to practice a method of reading similar to but not necessarily identical to her own. In addition, almost as an index to the process of reading her readers may discover, she presents the difficult and often painful experience of trying to present these texts to a community as a counterpoint to the pleasurable experience of the texts themselves.

In her title and in her essay, Fetterley constantly reminds her readers that her anthology is *a* reader, not *the* reader of writing by women; it is not exhaustive, nor is it meant to be. Like Blanche Gelfant, she is aware of her role as an evocative writer, one who can give voice not only to her own words, but to the words of other writers and readers, as well:

> My decision was also inspired by the desire to break the silence surrounding these writers. I wished to contradict the prevailing assumption that their voices were not heard because their texts have nothing to say and thus nothing can be said about them. I wished instead to demonstrate the counter position, that these texts are capable of sustaining significant critical inquiry and discourse. And in so doing, I sought to begin the process of developing that discourse and the concomitant community of readers so central to the work of recovering and reviewing the literature of nineteenth-century American women (Fetterley 32).

Fetterley admits that her desire is eventually to be able to read these works in the same context with which she has read the works of the literary canon: a context filled with readers who share a knowledge of the same texts and who come to those texts aware that others have read them and have written about them. As she proceeds in the task of composing that context, however, she discovers that the methods of reading and analyzing that have developed and been given to her through the canonical tradition can only disable her reading of these noncanonical texts and that the task of providing them with the matrix she desires will be far more difficult than she initially believed.

Judith Fetterley develops her autobiography of reading into an actual theory of reading in her discussion of the process by which she came to create the matrix for the stories collected in the anthology. She comments that her struggle as editor came not from the texts but from their existing context—the absence of information and literary history about this material. Like many women before her, Fetterley realizes that the tradition has not prepared her to read nontraditional material, and so she begins her search for a way of reading otherwise.

Deliberately foregoing the agony of reading authorized by Harold Bloom and other traditional critics, Fetterley suggests that "when one works with the prose literature of nineteenth-century American women writers, there is no 'anxiety of influence': there is rather the 'anxiety of absence.'" Indeed, she goes on to say, "there were many times during my work on this project when I would have given a great deal for a little

So much of Summary / Fetterley I where's I going with this?

'influence'" (Fetterley 35). Fetterley's wish for a relationship with other readers mirrors the impulse of the fiction about which she tries to write: both seek to create meaning and relationship, especially in the simplicity of the daily life of a woman.

While Fetterley admits that the silence of the critics temporarily silenced her, she recognizes that first the fiction and then the responses of other readers with whom she shared it created the context that enabled her to engage her own writing with this work again. When she began to see the reading of these texts as related to her self and the evocation of self that enabled her to begin writing again, her "self-concept as a critic," Fetterley recognized a new way of looking at the texts, at their relationship to other readers, and her relationship to other reading. She says: "I wanted my words to serve as a medium and instrument, not interference and armament. . . . I was no longer an antagonist, I was a lover" (Fetterley 36–37). For Judith Fetterley, the appropriate practice of criticism became transformed from agony to joy, from competition to affiliation, from warfare to lovemaking.

Even as she embraces her newfound affiliation to her primary texts, Judith Fetterley recognizes the most radical implications of her choice to revise the canon and read anew: she may find that her own voice will be silenced within the critical tradition. Nevertheless, by recognizing the risk she takes, she is able to view it as not so hazardous a prospect. She recalls that "The final factor that traumatized my first few months of writing was my recognition of what would constitute success. If I did what I set out to do right, my work would rapidly become obsolete, overwritten by the dialogue they had started" (Fetterley 37). Fetterley declares that the feminist critic, in evoking the voice of the writers she reads, gains her own voice. By speaking with them, she does not silence them, but allows others to hear them as well, and thus evokes still other voices who speak to and about what they have read. By doing this, she risks her own obsolescence, but she advocates this loss of immortality by authority. In taking this instrumentalist posture, as she calls it, Fetterley privileges the coequal importance of other voices with her own.

Fetterley may take some comfort in the figure of the "hungry" heroine as described by Blanche Gelfant. These heroines read to quench their hunger as Fetterley read to feed her sense of the writer's absence—first of the writer's texts and then of her own. So other readers may read her work; in evoking first her voice and then their own, they will continue the network of care which bespeaks their common ground and understanding. This sustaining web of understanding, of which Judith Fetterley is clearly a part, is figured in the image she invokes in the final paragraph of her introduction: "The literature of nineteenth-century American women speaks to the contemporary reader. In my various experiences of sharing it with others, I have found this to be so. It nourishes and feeds. In the spirit of feeding, I offer it to you" (Fetterley 38). Fetterley recognizes the potential for communion, for community, that the mutual reading and speaking of these texts creates.

The work of Rachel Brownstein, Blanche Gelfant, and Judith Fetterley inspire and permit a variety of activities that I now pursue as a teacher and writer. They particularly encourage me to discover a voice of my own and to look for places to speak my own voice in everyday life (i.e., at work and at play). They have also taught me how to listen for and enable the voices of others whenever I can. This work is perhaps most often done in the classroom, but I think that the classroom metaphor can become pernicious when we forget that we are not always teachers of students; often, we are also and more appropriately colleagues and, sometimes, still protégés ourselves. The three women I have focused on stand in the midst of a larger community of readers who, as Elaine Showalter suggests, have turned their consideration from the images of women in fiction to the life and mind of the one who reads. Significantly, each of these women celebrates her relationship to this larger community, and each clearly articulates her reading while evoking the voice of the writer she reads and the voices of other readers as well.

Many feminist critics thus have extended their reading to consider "unread" works from literary history, works that have lain unread for so long that they appear before us almost as new texts. I have found these critics the most helpful in teaching me to think and speak about women writers, some of whom I have read since childhood, but many more of whom I never encountered, not even in the classroom. I felt their work said something important to me. I felt the connection their work created between myself and other readers. I felt these works worthy of serious consideration, even though my academic training prepared me to see them otherwise. And I have responded to their work and the work of other feminist scholars who have helped me to value the way I learned to read.

It is important to realize the power of such reweavings of criticism and autobiography. Since I became interested in looking at how women readers connect themselves to the work they read, I have found many works of literary criticism that incorporate readings of the literary text with articulations of the reader's self. By any definition, these readings are "good," "close," "strong" *because* they are coupled inextricably with the reader's personal response. The criticism implicit and explicit in these works is complex and rich, achievable primarily, if not only, through their ability to relate the real and personal to the literary experience. It is important to acknowledge that the personal functions in the work of all of these writers is *to create criticism*. These essays demonstrate that reading the self through the text, reading the text through the self, is significant. Such reading and writing enrich the reader, her reading, and the others who read her work. As Judith Fetterley figures this relationship, in the spirit of feeding, each writer offers and shares her feast of words.

Something that I didn't accomplish.

References

Abel, Elizabeth, ed. *Writing and Sexual Difference*. Chicago: University of Chicago Press, 1982.

Adams, Hannah. *A Memoir of Miss Hannah Adams; with Further Continuances by a Friend*. Boston: Gray and Bowen, 1832.

Belenkey, Mary Field, Blythe McVicker Clinchy, Nancy Rule Goldberger, and Jill Mattuck Tarule. *Women's Ways of Knowing: The Development of Self, Voice, and Mind*. New York: Basic Books, 1986.

Brownstein, Rachel. *Becoming a Heroine: Reading about Women in Novels*. New York: Viking, 1982.

Fetterley, Judith. *Provisions: A Reader from Nineteenth-Century American Women*. Bloomington: Indiana University Press, 1985.

Flynn, Elizabeth A., and Patrocino P. Schweickart. *Gender and Reading: Essays on Readers, Texts, and Contexts*. Baltimore: Johns Hopkins University Press, 1986.

Gelfant, Blanche. *Women Writing in America: Voices in Collage*. Hanover, N.H.: Dartmouth College and the University Press of New England, 1984.

Hoffman, Lenore, and Margo Culley, eds. *Women's Personal Narratives: Essays in Criticism and Pedagogy*. New York: Modern Language Association, 1985.

Breaking Silence:

THE WOMAN

WARRIOR

*

Shirley Nelson
Garner

I have filled my office door with quotations. Those on the right are mainly sexist; those on the left, feminist—interspersed here and there with the wisdom and humor of my two children. As I began to think about writing this article and about "breaking silence" as part of a feminist tradition— for some feminists even a rite of passage—I remembered one of the quotations on the right side (that is, the wrong side) of my door. It is from a sixteenth-century collection of proverbs, advertised as containing "new additions" from the Dutch scholar and theologian Erasmus, renowned in his time and still as a Humanist. The proverb, "Mulierem ornat silentium," is translated by Richard Taverner, "Silence garnisheth a woman," and elaborated: "Assuredly there is no tire [attire], no apparel that better becometh a Woman than silence. Which thing also the Apostle Paul requireth, while he forbiddeth Women in the Church or congregation to speak, but willeth them to ask their husbands at home, if they be in doubt of anything." When I read the quotation on separate occasions to two women colleagues, who are specialists in Renaissance literature (as I am), they both immediately remembered King Lear's lament over his dead Cordelia: "Her voice was ever soft, / Gentle and low, an excellent thing in woman" (*Lear* 5.3.274–75).[1]

I have long known that our cultural heritage defined chastity as the essential virtue for women, just as it made bravery essential for men. It now occurs to me that silence or quietness has been just as unquestioned a virtue for women as chastity. Isn't the shrew always garrulous? I recall that Hamlet, at a moment when he has the greatest contempt for himself, mourns that he "must, like a whore, unpack . . . [his] heart with words / And fall a-cursing like a very drab" (*Ham.* 2.2.592–93).

For women born into such a cultural tradition, speaking itself becomes an act of assertion. Speaking in public becomes a radical act—a movement away from woman's role, a vast impropriety. To speak with anger relegates one to the realm of whores, witches, and madwomen. It is no wonder, then, that feminist artists and writers talk about "breaking silence" as a crucial experience. For Adrienne Rich, Audre Lorde, and Tillie Olsen, it becomes a central theme.

Maxine Hong Kingston's breaking of silence is at the center of *The Woman Warrior.* It means becoming an adult woman as well as a writer; it is a rite of passage, the emergence of a new self. Her breaking of silence makes her a woman warrior. To be a woman warrior one must fight the reticence inside the self as well as the oppression outside. Her particular mode of warfare is her writing; her mother's was becoming a doctor and practicing medicine. Significantly, both know how to "talk-story," the mother teaching her daughter that art through example. In the simplest sense, her mother gave Kingston the means to become a woman warrior by teaching her the song of Fa Mu Lan, a "girl who took her father's place in battle." [2]

I am interested in Kingston's association of silence with punishment and madness and her need to break her silence as a moral act as well as a necessity for the preservation of her sanity. These associations have personal resonance for me, and I am engaged with them also because they represent the particular configuration for Kingston of a common and powerful feminist experience.

Her book begins as an antithesis to a story. Instead of "Once upon a time," we hear, "You must not tell anyone . . . what I am about to tell you," the warning of Kingston's mother as she tells her story of "No-Name Woman," Kingston's paternal aunt. *The Woman Warrior* begins, then, with both the breaking of silence and the telling of a secret. The central fact of the secret, bluntly told, is that Kingston's aunt committed suicide: " 'In China your father had a sister who killed herself. She jumped into the family well' " (3). But the essential fear—what is unspeakable—is not of suicide, but of women's sexuality. Both the occasion for Brave Orchid's revealing No-Name Woman's history and the circumstances surrounding her suicide reveal this deeper fear.

After No-Name Woman had been married only a few days, her husband left China for America. Years later, she became pregnant, and on the eve of her child's birth, her neighbors and friends (including perhaps the father of her child) raided her family's house. Wearing white masks, their hair hung over their faces or made to stand on end, they slaughtered animals and threw and smeared blood over the house, broke up its furniture, spilled its comestibles, and reduced her aunt's personal effects to shards and scraps and pieces. The aunt gave birth later that night alone in a pigsty. In the morning, she drowned herself and her baby in the water well. " 'Don't tell anyone you had an aunt,' " Brave Orchid warns. " 'Your father does not want to hear her name: She has never been born' " (18).

The story of No-Name Woman is the sort that Kingston recognizes as one of her mother's stories "to grow up on." Brave Orchid tells her the story as a warning when she reaches puberty: " 'Don't let your father know that I told you. He denies her. Now that you have started to menstruate, what happened to her could happen to you. Don't humiliate us. You wouldn't like to be forgotten as if you had never been born. The villagers are watchful' " (5).

Kingston comes to see that her family's silence about her aunt, and her own silence, is in fact their continued punishment of the aunt:

> I have believed that sex was unspeakable and words so strong and fathers so frail that "aunt" would do my father mysterious harm. I have thought that my family, having settled among immigrants who had also been their neighbors in the ancestral land, needed to clean their name, and a wrong word would incite the kinspeople even here. But there is more to this silence: they want me to participate in her punishment. And I have.)
>
> In the twenty years since I heard this story I have not asked for details nor said my aunt's name; I do not know it. People who can comfort the dead can also chase after them to hurt them further—a reverse ancestor worship. The real punishment was not the raid swiftly inflicted by the villagers, but the family's deliberately forgetting her. (18)

For Kingston, then, telling No-Name Woman's story is a moral act, a way to stop participating in the punishment. But even though her breaking of silence is freeing, it is also fraught with anxiety:

> My aunt haunts me—her ghost drawn to me because now, after fifty years of neglect, I alone devote pages of paper to her, though not origamied into houses and clothes. I do not think she always

means me well. I am telling on her, and she was a spite suicide, drowning herself in the drinking water. The Chinese are always very frightened of the drowned one, whose weeping ghost, wet hair hanging and skin bloated, waiting silently by the water to pull down a substitute. (19)

The punishment implicit in the silence is not merely directed against the aunt, but against women's sexuality and hence against Kingston herself. That it is so directed is made clear through the various constructions Kingston imagines of her aunt's life. So frightened is Kingston's father and his family of disgrace that they cannot take into account the aunt's needs or rights as a woman and a human being, nor can they understand, much less appreciate or sympathize with, her position as a woman in her society. Kingston's constructions are an attempt to see No-Name Woman as real and to make it impossible to judge her as her family does: merely as a woman who disgraced them through her sexuality—either because she had ordinary sexual desires or was pressed, through rape or seduction, into a forbidden sexual relationship.

The personal resonance that this story has for me is that it recalls my mother's telling me a family secret, shortly after I was divorced in my late twenties. She told me that my maternal great-great-grandmother Gilles had two illegitimate children before she married, one of whom was my great-grandmother Hankins. I did not think of this story as a warning. I thought merely that my mother had decided that since I was now sexually experienced and divorced, I was fallen enough to know this darkest of family secrets. Far from feeling any shame in my ancestry, however, I found it, for the first time, interesting.

Now that I think about it, I imagine my mother, like Brave Orchid, meant her story as a warning: Your great-great-grandmother got pregnant out of wedlock; you might too. Even though you're a divorcee (and she would have thought of me with that word and the pity and scandal it evokes), don't sleep around. That was probably the message, which I didn't get—so great was my fascination with my mother's story. The secret in my family history undoubtedly explains why my illegitimate great-grandmother Hankins (though her family were "big Baptists," as my mother describes them) was sent to a Catholic convent at eleven, to be brought home only shortly before she was married at a very young age; and why my own grandmother Pope was married at fifteen, not to be given any time for illegitimate children.

The fact that Brave Orchid tells No-Name Woman's story to Kingston when she reaches puberty further affirms that the fear it expresses is that of women's sexuality. Kingston is asked to experience her aunt's fate vicariously, and she is reminded that to menstruate, to become an adult woman, is to come newly into danger and guilt. When I taught *The Woman Warrior* in "Women's Autobiography," the four autobiographers we read who described the beginnings of their menstruation—Emma Goldman, Mary McCarthy, Lillian Hellman, and Maxine Hong Kingston—associate it with embarrassment, pain, and punishment. Emma Goldman, for example, remembers that her mother struck her hard across the face and explained, "This is necessary for a girl . . . when she becomes a woman, as a protection against disgrace."[3] There is no moment of celebration or ritual, as there is in Faulkner's *Go Down, Moses* when Ike McCaslin reaches puberty and participates in the ritual hunt described in "The Bear." Instead, at the moment when we might begin to experience pleasure in our creative powers, many of us—most of us—are made to feel guilty and afraid.

Kingston's telling her aunt's story—as well as the story of her mother's telling her the story—breaks the circle of shame. The guilt and fear that the story awakens is not that she is likely to share No-Name Woman's history, but that she has the mere *potential* for sharing it. Not being ashamed to tell the story means not being ashamed of the woman and of the self.

The fear of unwanted and disgraceful pregnancies hovered over the women in my family. They were haunted by the notion of social stigma common to their time and place as well as the burden of their family's past, located in what they knew of my great-great grandmother's "indiscretions." When I was nine or ten, my mother and father, who had been divorced by the time I was four, flirted with an unpromising and unrealistic hope of reconciliation. I remember my grandmother crying, hugging me tightly and rocking me in her arms, and warning me, "Your mother could get pregnant again."

Though we rarely spoke of it to each other, girls in my generation were terrified of becoming pregnant before we married. As teenagers, we felt curiosity, desire, loneliness—all the things that might draw us into sexual experience. Terror alone kept us chaste. The few boys who understood our fears and to some extent shared them reined in their surging hormonal passions when they threatened to conquer. But others pressed to satisfy their desires, depending upon the girls to stop them, prevent them from "going all the way." On the other side of giving in, girls risked, at the least, acquiring a bad reputation; at worst, of becoming pregnant "out of wedlock," as it was termed. Boys had the leisure of forgetting the possible consequences of fulfilling their desires. Many did not forget, but rather calculated shrewdly that if satisfying themselves culminated in a pregnancy, the girls alone would suffer. It was easy enough for boys to escape the entanglement of a messy aftermath. So they pleaded in tones no less urgent or determined than those of a courtly lover that your reluctance would send them to prostitutes or tried to goad you into compliance by threatening that they would respect but not love you unless you gave in to them.

Unlike No-Name Woman, pregnant girls that I knew did not suffer punishment or death. But pregnancy meant disgrace and the end of possibilities. I remember meeting a girl from out of town who had become pregnant in high school. Her family had sent her to a home for unwed mothers to bear her child and give it up for adoption. My friends and I knew her history—and I assume she knew that we knew—but we did not speak of it to her, and she didn't allude to it. Though beautiful, wealthy, and intelligent, she had an aura of sadness and detachment. She had grown up before her time, and the marks of it showed in her face and in her dimmed enthusiasm. I remember noticing in my junior year that the skirts of one of the most popular girls in my high school were beginning to pull at the waist and then feeling sick when I heard that she and her boyfriend would marry. I thought of it as the end of everything for her.

When I first read the story of No-Name Woman, it chilled me to the core. I recalled that after I was divorced, sometime before the saving decision of Roe vs. Wade, I measured my security by my ability to afford an abortion. Even as a graduate teaching assistant, I kept enough money in my savings account to allow me to travel outside the United States should I need one. From the time I was a young girl, I was wary of my blossoming sexuality. Instead of bringing me joy, puberty put me in peril, brought me fear of disgrace, taught me to keep guard.

Before Kingston can tell the story of No-Name Woman, breaking the silence of her writing voice, she must break other silences of her speaking voice. I do not mean to imply that she would have made a neat separation between her writing and speaking voice. Since she continually describes her art as "talking-story," she clearly would not have. But the last section of The Woman Warrior, entitled "A Song for a Barbarian Reed Pipe," recounts her personal struggle as a child literally to speak and later to speak for and to defend herself. After winning that struggle, she can see herself as the poetess Ts'ai Yen, whose voice is "so high and clear, it matched the flutes" (243). Combining one of her mother's tales and her own, Kingston concludes the book with the story of Ts'ai Yen, with whom she clearly identifies herself.

As a child, Kingston was obsessed with the notion that her mother had cut the frenum of her tongue when she was an infant, and she evidently still feels that she has an ugly voice: "A dumbness—a shame—still cracks my voice in two, even when I want to say 'hello' casually, or ask an easy question in front of the check-out counter, or ask directions of a bus driver. . . . A telephone call makes my throat bleed and takes up that day's courage. It spoils my day with self-disgust when I hear my broken voice come skittering out into the open. It makes people wince to hear it" (191). When she went to kindergarten and had to speak English, she became silent. She describes herself as silent for her first three years of school, during which time, she "covered . . . [her] school paintings with black paint" (192). As she observed that other Chinese girls had trouble talking in school, she decided that "the silence had to do with being a Chinese girl" (193). Only when she went to Chinese school did she begin to be able to speak.

She associates her silence with masochism and insanity. Her vivid account of two incidents relates her attempts to resist oppression and to retain her sanity. The first was her persecution of the younger sister of a Chinese classmate because she never talks. "She would whisper-read but not talk. Her whisper was as soft as if she had no muscles. She seemed to be breathing from a distance. I heard no anger or tension" (201). One day after school, when Kingston found herself alone with the girl in the lavatory, she threatened her, " 'You're going to talk . . . I am going to make you talk, you sissy-girl' " (204), and taunted her, pinched her cheeks, and pulled her hair until she cried. But no matter how Kingston tormented the child, she would not speak, and the episode defeated Kingston: "I was getting dizzy from the air I was gulping. Her sobs and my sobs were bouncing wildly off the tile, sometimes together, sometimes alternating. 'I don't understand why you won't say just one word,' I cried, clenching my teeth. My knees were shaking, and I hung on to her hair to stand up." (210–11). After this moment, on the eve of her entrance into junior high school, Kingston became ill with a "mysterious illness" and spent the next eighteen months sick in bed.

The child, who is unnamed and possibly associated with No-Name Woman, clearly represents Kingston's alter ego. Her hatred of the girl is her hatred of the unassertive self. What is so terrifying about the moment is that the girl cannot or will not defend herself in the most minimal way.

Kingston's inability to make her talk—or even scream—can only be a negative victory for the child, won as it is through her own pain and humiliation. What brings on the mysterious illness is Kingston's fear that as she was not able to get the child to talk, so she will not be able to rescue her own reticent self, that she is doomed to be a victim.

This episode with the silent Chinese girl prepares for Kingston's linkage of silence and madness. It parallels the scene in which Brave Orchid drags her sister, Moon Orchid, to see the husband who has deserted her, the event at the center of the book's preceding section, "At the Western Palace." Leaving her in China, Moon Orchid's husband came to America and took a second wife. After years of planning, Brave Orchid brought Moon Orchid to America to reclaim her husband, who had become a successful doctor. In the terrible and darkly humorous scene in which they confront the wayward husband, Brave Orchid cannot get Moon Orchid to speak. Even though Brave Orchid pinches her cheek and slaps the insides of her arms, she cannot give her energy to say a word. When she sees her husband, "All she did was open and shut her mouth without any words coming out" (176). Ultimately Moon Orchid must be placed in a mental institution, where she dies.

Kingston watches the woman next door have a mental breakdown and be taken to Napa or Agnew, California's state mental institutions. Observing another neighborhood girl, Crazy Mary, she concludes: "I thought talking and not talking made the difference between sanity and insanity. Insane people were the ones who couldn't explain themselves. There were many crazy girls and women" (216).

To save herself, Kingston begins daily to confess to her mother the two hundred and seven items of shame she has toted up. She observes that her mother acts as if she has not heard. As she speaks to her mother, she hears her "duck voice," which she does not use with her family; and finally, her mother reprimands her: " 'I can't stand this whispering. . . . Senseless gabbings every night.' " But then one night when the whole family is seated around the dinner table, Kingston stands up, addresses her mother and father, claims her self, and makes demands.

The pressure that creates this moment is the fantasy or the actuality that her family wishes her to marry a mentally retarded, unattractive man, who is supposedly rich and who follows her everywhere, carrying around with him cartons "stuffed with pornography—naked magazines, nudie postcards and photographs" (229). After he has hung around for days, she tells us, her throat begins to "hurt constantly, vocal cords taut to snapping" (233).

She begins without uncertainty: " 'I want you to tell that hulk, that gorilla-ape, to go away and never bother us again.' " She insists that if he follows her once more, she will leave. She asserts determinedly, " 'I am not going to be a slave or a wife' " (234)—defined early in the book as the opposites of the woman warrior.

The breaking of silence is saving:

> The very next day after I talked out the retarded man, the huncher, he disappeared. I never saw him again or heard what became of him. Perhaps I made him up, and what I once had was not Chinese-sight at all but child-sight that would have disappeared eventually without such struggle. The throat pain always returns, though, unless I tell what I really think, whether or not I lose my job, or spit out gaucheries all over a party. (239)

Though speaking frees her, she knows that a person can't do it once and for all, but must do it over and over. She also knows that whatever the cost of breaking silence, the cost of keeping it is greater.

Notes

1. William Shakespeare, *The Complete Signet Classic Shakespeare,* ed. Sylvan Barnet (New York: Harcourt, 1972). Subsequent quotations from Shakespeare are from this edition.
2. *The Woman Warrior: Memoirs of a Girlhood Among Ghosts* (New York: Random House, 1977). All quotations from *The Woman Warrior* are from this edition.
3. *Living My Life,* 2 vols. (London: Dover, 1970) 1: 21.

Different

Silences

*

Traise Yamamoto

habit
+ protection
caught btw
speaking and
not-speaking
— is writing a
way to break
this binary?
I wonder.

Last night, dinner with friends. At some point, we decide to go for a walk because it is a beautiful evening, and because the rhythms of walking bring out the rhythms of talk; speech syncopated between steps. There are four of us. We are all dressed in the easy sloppiness of the middle class. There is a baby strapped to the stomach of one of the two men.

We walk through a neighborhood where poverty is nonexistent, then through one where Hondas and fancy import cars, flower gardens and freshly painted house-fronts give way to older American cars, low-maintenance shrubs, shabby window casings, and faded brown front doors.

Paired off and talking movies, the four of us move slowly down the street. As we approach a yard in which three young boys are playing, I hear, "Look!" (the long drawn out "oooo" of childish fascination), "A Chinese Lady!" The boy who has spoken, the youngest of the three, is about nine. And he is African American. The other two stare dutifully; they are also African American.

To speak or not to speak? How many times have similar things been said within my hearing, shortly followed by the yo-yo-ed vowels parodying "Oriental" speech? How many times has the next question been, "When did you get off the boat?" To be silent is to give in, to not-face and so to lose face; to be silent is what is expected of "a Chinese lady." But to speak is to risk intensified "chink talk." To speak is to risk losing my temper and having to see the satisfied grins, the mean pleasure of having gotten a reaction. It hardly matters that I am almost twenty years older than the boy who has spoken. The space into which I have suddenly been flung—keenly conscious that I am not simply one of four friends, but one Asian American with three white friends—is nontemporal: it could be a scene from anywhere between the time I was five to now. The neighborhood resembles the one I grew up in, though the low income of the residents is less evident; the boys are the boys that were inevitably part of every school year, the boys that have become the men fascinated by the erotic exotic.

We are not yet past the house. To speak or not to speak? The boy is young. Is it simply a statement that he has noticed my difference? Just one of those things kids bravely call out from the safety of their own front yard, an honest inquiry? Is there an Asian kid at school whom he picks on, whom he is identifying with me? "Not Chinese," I say, "Japanese. I am Japanese American."

I have to say it twice because he asks again; this is a new angle on the universe. "I am Japanese American." Then: "What are you?" "Oh," he answers, surprised, "I'm Black." I say, "Yes. You are not Chinese either, I take it." "Oh no," he giggles. Suddenly, he is just a child again. "Not me," he says as we—finally—pass by. My friends, silent this whole time, wait the space of a two-beat pause. Then, movie-talk.

You ask me to speak. You tell me at parties how lucky I am to be Japanese (always forgetting "American"), how you wish you could be Japanese so you too could "be so graceful," or so you could have straight black hair, or because you always *have* liked kimonos. You tell me in classes that you are glad I talk because when I do, you learn something, learn something about yourself. You tell me in clothes stores that I should get the red blouse because "Orientals look so nice in red," that I should get the A-line dress because it makes me look "so doll-like." You suggest that housecleaning is a good way to make extra summer money, then say I'm a snob when I tell you that my grandmothers did not clean other women's toilets, other women's children, other women's dirtiness so that I could grow up and do the same thing. You ask me to speak. Sometimes, I do. And sometimes when I do, you say, "You're so unlike most Japanese women. You are very articulate (funny, loud, strident, etc.)." And if I speak in anger, you are surprised, call me bitter, tell me I'm lucky I'm not Black, Chicana, Native American; or, worse, you apologize for all whites of all time, want me to "forgive" and "absolve" for all Asians of all time. Or you tell me you feel you can talk to me because I am not threatening ("as . . . as" implicitly bookending "threatening").

"I am weary of starting from scratch each time I speak or write, as if there were no history behind us, of hearing that among the women of color, Asian women are the least political, or the least oppressed, or the most polite" (Yamada 71).

But there are other things besides frustration and fear that keep me silent, that keep me stuck between speaking and not speaking. If you grow up Japanese American, you grow up with the intense insider/outsider mentality that the Isseis brought from a country where therapy is still not widely practiced or participated in. The boundaries begin with oneself, then the family ("This is family business," my Nisei mother would say, "and you are not to go blabbing it around to the outside"), then ring gradually outward: must stay within the Japanese American community, the Asian American community. What belongs within must stay within: don't lose face, don't spill your guts, don't wear your heart on your sleeve. Fifty years after the war, most of those interned in the "relocation camps" will not speak of it. Boundaries. Self-containment: don't bother other people. *Shikata ga nai.* It can't be helped. There is nothing to be done. Its goodness lies in a certain acceptance, a giving of oneself to the world as it is. But it can modulate into resignation, passivity. So one doesn't speak because there is no use in it, *shikata ga nai*, no use to calling so much attention to oneself, to one's family; no use to shame others, both inside and outside.

"You who understand the dehumanization of forced removal-relocation-reeducation-redefinition, the humiliation of having to falsify your own reality, your voice—you know. And often cannot say it. You try and keep on trying to unsay it, for if you don't they will not fail to fill in the blanks on your behalf, and you will be <u>*said" (Trinh 80)*</u>.

Between the impulse to speak and the impulse to not speak is the desire to not be said, the desire to not speak others—which means speaking to them so that they can speak for themselves, so they can speak themselves—the desire to work through what is most fraught in myself and in my relations with others. But between silence and speech the skeins, the angles tangle and blur.

Some of those skeins and angles involve the attempt to speak over differences that work like the floating *X*. Between Isseis and Niseis and Sanseis there are differences of culture, of history; generational blips difficult to speak over. Between Japanese Americans and Chinese Americans. Established Asians and newly arrived Asians. There are Asians I speak to who do not understand why I am interested in the liberal arts; liberal arts folk who ignore or overemphasize "the Japanese stuff" in my poetry, in me. Feminists who don't understand that silence is not always a bad thing, that it doesn't always signify passivity. Asian men who feel rejected because I live with a white man. Lesbians who tell me that my life with another woman is "canceled out" because I now live with a man. Women who say my writing is not feminist enough; Asian writers who say my poetry is too white. Nonwriters who tell me what I write is impenetrable; one, who told me it was "inscrutable."

And there is that in me that silences others. There are angles in me that turn others away, gaps in my understanding. Within myself there is a voice that turns another into the Other, a voice that shouts over the painful particulars of other people's lives. A voice with whom I make a deal: I'll let you rage inwardly if you will not speak through my mouth, which I will keep closed, in which I will keep you closed. And the dishonesty of that act becomes inseparable from the fear that if I speak, I will meet that voice in someone else.

In my life now, the boundaries are still there, though I am trying to push them outward. I speak with other women of color about what it is like to grow up, to live as a woman of color in a racist and sexist society; of the problematics of (white women's) feminism and its assumption that gender is extractable from and to be privileged over race, ethnicity, and class. I speak to Coleen about the distances between Japanese Americans, about the silences or tension-relieving jokes that often make dialogue between Japanese American women impossible. I speak to Eileen about the similarities and differences between African Americans and Asian Americans, about the often fraught relations between African American and Asian American women. I speak knowing that each step from silence is a risk, and that I must understand it as a good one, not as one that betrays the principles I grew up with, that betrays myself.

I speak, knowing that to speak is to begin trust. But to speak at all, there must already be trust, or a reason to believe trust will be possible. You ask me to speak: I am telling you what keeps me from speaking. I am telling you that, for me, silence is part of speaking; silence is also habit, protection. I am telling you that your desire for me to speak, to tell you where I am, is synonymous with asking me to take a risk that I have taken too many times before, with asking me to repeat and repeat and repeat myself without getting anywhere. Endless repetition is not simply to say, and then to say again. It is language circling round its own opacity. To say and not be heard, to say and have to say again is to be silenced, to be spoken, to be made invisible in a skein of language not one's own. Who has access to the what and wherefores of articulation also has the power to separate, make distinctions, make selves and others. And with the power to name and shape speech comes the power to name and shape silence. My desire to speak, that I will speak, means that I am taking that risk for myself, for the sake of those connections I sometimes feel are impossible, for the sake of the possibilities I feel exist.

"The strongest prisons are built / with walls of silence," writes poet Janet Mirikitani. In the writings of Asian Americans, especially Asian American women, silence is something to be broken, shattered, shredded; it is something solid through which one must pass in order to join one's voice to the voices on the other side. It sits stone-heavy in the body, or is a stifling enclosure within which the body suffocates. The act of writing itself becomes the broadest stroke toward speech. But sometimes that stroke is too difficult against the current of self-doubt, the belief that what one has to say isn't important or "universal" enough.

It took me years to discover that there was such a thing as a Japanese American writer. I had begun to believe what I had been told for so many years: Asian Americans are nonverbal, unimaginative, and, above all, too quiet to be writers and poets. "Of course there aren't any," a white friend informed me, "they're all engineers or social workers." I had begun to believe that we had nothing to say and no way of saying it. But when I finally began to find and read the writing of Japanese Americans, I myself became one of the silencers. It wasn't good enough or complex enough; it wasn't metaphysical, lyrical, memorable enough. That there was none of Eliot's extinction of personality seemed proof positive that this writing was of a lesser order. After all, how could a literature be great that was so imbued with the temporal, historical, experiential, and personal? If good, was it as good as Shakespeare, Donne, Auden, Stevens? In short, did the work of Asian Americans meet up to the literary standards of academia and *The Norton Anthology*?

Inevitably, the answer was no. What I saw when I read the work of Asian Americans was myself. My experience was suddenly reflected back to me; I saw rooms in which I could see myself walking, heard conversations in whose accents and timbres I could hear my family's voices. Instead of Virginia Woolf's *Boeuf en Daube* and Proust's *madeleine*, there were *tofu* and *takuan*, *sashimi* and *sake*. But this couldn't be the stuff of literature: it was too like myself. In devaluing the worth of my own experience, I dismissed Asian American literature, assuming it to be a simple rendering without the subtlety of art.

Even now, it is difficult for me to silence the one-eyed critic I hear in my head: not good enough no one will be interested not universal dull minor literature self-indulgent simplistic not really art hack writing no good only about yourself.

"If you sing too often of woe, yours or your sisters', you may be charged with being 'too personal,' 'too autobiographical'. . . . You believe, almost too simply, that you are establishing your own traditions, becoming your own role model. . . . And you are angered by the arrogance of some articles that would tell you that Virginia Woolf is your spiritual mother, your possible role model, for the work you have to do: to write" (Wong 178).

Mine is not the individual talent Eliot had in mind when he spoke of its relation to literary tradition, and I sometimes wonder whether Whitman addresses me when he calls out to the poets of the future to look for him under their boot-soles (my sense is that he does address me—but it's the fact of wondering about it at all that I call attention to here). I do know that when I tell people I write poetry, they often go on to tell me how much they like haiku, as if it were inconceivable that I might write in Homeric dactyls or Dantean *terza rima*. I know that I don't like it when a poem or manuscript is rejected with what is thought to be a helpful bit of advice: write poems on the "Asian American experience." I think of Paul Laurence Dunbar: when he was invited to read his poetry, the audience wanted to hear only his dialect poems—poems of the "Negro experience" in "Negro tones"—and drowned him out when he attempted to read his nondialect poetry. It's not that I don't write about and out of my experience as a third generation Japanese American, but that I don't feel compelled to trot out the particulars of "Asian stuff" on demand and for display.

And yet, those particulars are what I respond to when I read Asian American writers. When I read the section in Maxine Hong Kingston's *Woman Warrior* where she tries to bully a silent classmate into speech, I know what it is like to be both the silent girl and the girl frustrated by the stereotype of the quiet Chinese female. When I come across the Japanese words in David Mura's or Garrett Hongo's poems, there is always for me a pleasant thrum of recognition; I feel a sense of a shared past, that we share the language of our grandparents. Every internment camp poem speaks my parents' and grandparents' past, speaks their silence. Every short story, novel, memoir guides me and tells me what I knew but could not know enough: we have something to say and we have ways to say it.

Every poem I write silences those who assume my aptitude in nonverbal fields (I first came to understand the use of the collective "you" when math teacher after puzzled math teacher would say, "But you're usually so good at this kind of thing") or my limited abilities in what must surely be my second language ("Where did you learn to speak English so well?").

But every poem I write also testifies to what has increasingly become the uneasy relationship between the desire to speak the invisible mysteries that move my inner life and the desire to speak what Blake called "the minute particulars" of which my daily life is comprised. I suppose it is much the same for every writer, the struggle to balance the timeless and the temporal. But for me, whose experience of daily life is inseparable from my identity as an Asian American woman, there is always the question of whether gender and ethnicity will become the filtering lenses through which my work will be judged, by which my work will be obscured. Yet, to write out of some "universal" mode in an attempt to avoid those lenses would be to erase myself with each stroke of the pen. "She who 'happens to be,'" writes Trinh Minh-ha, "a (nonwhite) Third World member, a woman, and a writer is bound to go through the ordeal of exposing her work to the abuse of praises and criticisms that either ignore, dispense with, or overemphasize her racial and sexual attributes" (6).

For me, none of this can dampen the pleasure of articulation, the sensual satisfaction of words on the page, and, most of all, the sense that to speak is necessary—because the alternative is the silence that comes from without, the silence that cannot speak through fear, frustration, doubt, and the words of the other. But I must also remember that speech for the sake of speech only works to keep me tied to those who would assume my silence. It means forgetting, too, that mine is a heritage that knows the beauty of silence, the many ways in which it articulates what speech cannot. There is a silence that comes from within, what the famous Zen koan calls the soundless sound of one hand clapping. There are silences of difference, different silences.

References

Trinh, Minh-ha. *Woman, Native, Other: Writing Postcoloniality and Feminism.* Bloomington: Indiana University Press, 1989.

Mirikitani, Janice. *Shedding Silence.* Berkeley: Celestial Arts, 1987.

Wong, Nellie. "In Search of the Self as Hero: Confetti of Voices on New Year's Night." *This Bridge Called My Back: Writings By Radical Women of Color.* Eds. Cherrie Moraga and Gloria Anzaldua. Watertown: Persephone Press, 1981. 177–181.

Yamada, Mitsuye. "Asian Pacific American Women and Feminism." *This Bridge Called My Back: Writings By Radical Women of Color.* Eds. Cherrie Moraga and Gloria Anzaldua. Watertown: Persephone Press, 1981. 71–75.

The question of color takes up much space in these pages, but the question of color, especially in this country, operates to hide the graver questions of the self.—James Baldwin, 1961

. . . blood, darky, Tar Baby, Kaffir, shine . . . moor, blackamoor, Jim Crow, spook . . . quadroon, meriney, red bone, high yellow . . . Mammy, porch monkey, home, homeboy, George . . . spearchucker, schwarze, Leroy, Smokey . . . mouli, buck, Ethiopian, brother, sistah. . . .—Trey Ellis, 1989

I had forgotten the incident completely, until I read Trey Ellis's essay, "Remember My Name," in a recent issue of the *Village Voice* (June 13, 1989). But there, in the middle of an extended italicized list of the by-names of "the race" ("the race" or "our people" being the terms my parents used in polite or reverential discourse, "jigaboo" or "nigger" more commonly used in anger, jest, or pure disgust) it was: "George." Now the events of that very brief exchange return to mind so vividly that I wonder why I had forgotten it.

My father and I were walking home at dusk from his second job. He "moonlighted" as a janitor in the evenings for the telephone company. Every day but Saturday, he would come home at 3:30 from his regular job at the paper mill, wash up, eat supper, then at 4:30 head downtown to his second job. He used to make jokes frequently about a union official who moonlighted. I never got the joke, but he and his friends thought it was hilarious. All I knew was that my family always ate well, that my brother and I had new clothes to wear, and that all of the white people in Piedmont, West Virginia, treated my parents with an odd mixture of resentment and respect that even we understood at the time had something directly to do with a small but certain measure of financial security.

He had left a little early that evening because I was with him and I had to be in bed early. I could not have been more than five or six, and we had stopped off at the Cut-Rate Drug Store (where no black person in town but my father could sit down to eat, and eat off real plates with real silverware) so that I could buy some caramel ice cream, two scoops in a wafer cone, please, which I was busy licking when Mr. Wilson walked by.

Mr. Wilson was a very quiet white man, whose stony, brooding, silent manner seemed designed to scare off any overtures of friendship, even from white people. He was Irish, as was one-third of our village (another third being Italian), the more affluent among whom sent their children to "Catholic School" across the bridge in Maryland. He had white straight hair, like my Uncle Joe, whom he uncannily resembled, and he carried a black worn metal lunch pail, the kind that Riley carried on the television show. My father always spoke to him, and for reasons that we never did understand, he always spoke to my father.

"Hello, Mr. Wilson," I heard my father say.

"Hello, George."

I stopped licking my ice cream cone, and asked my Dad in a loud voice why Mr. Wilson had called him "George."

"Doesn't he know your name, Daddy? Why don't you tell him your name? Your name isn't George."

For a moment I tried to think of who Mr. Wilson was mixing Pop up with. But we didn't have any Georges among the colored people in Piedmont; nor were there colored Georges living in the neighboring towns and working at the mill.

"Tell him your name, Daddy."

"He knows my name, boy," my father said after a long pause. "He calls all colored people George."

A long silence ensued. It was "one of those things," as my Mom would put it. Even then, that early, I knew when I was in the presence of "one of those things," one of those things that provided a glimpse, through a rent curtain, at another world that we could not affect but that affected us. There would be a painful moment of silence, and you would wait for it to give way to a discussion of a black superstar such as Sugar Ray or Jackie Robinson.

"Nobody hits better in a clutch than Jackie Robinson."

"That's right. Nobody."
I never again looked Mr. Wilson in the eye.

But I loved the names that we gave ourselves when no white people were around. And I have to confess that I have never really cared too much about what we called ourselves publicly, except when my generation was fighting the elders for the legitimacy of the word "black" as our common, public name. "I'd rather they called me 'nigger,' " my Uncle Raymond would say again and again. "I can't *stand* the way they say the word *black.* And, by the way," he would conclude, his dark brown eyes flashing as he looked with utter disgust at my tentative Afro, "when are you going to get that nappy shit *cut?*"

There was enough in our public name to make a whole generation of Negroes rail against our efforts to legitimize, to naturalize, the word "black." Once we were black, I thought, we would be free, inside at least, and maybe from inside we would project a freedom outside of ourselves. "Free your mind," the slogan went, "and your behind will follow." Still, I value those all too rare, precious moments when someone "slips," in the warmth and comfort of intimacy, and says the dreaded words: "Was he colored?"

I knew that there was power in our name, enough power that the prospect frightened my maternal uncles. To open the "Personal Statement" for my Yale admission application in 1968, I had settled upon the following: "My grandfather was colored, my father is Negro, and I am black." (If that doesn't grab them, I thought, then nothing will.) I wonder if my daughters, nine years hence, will adapt the line, identifying themselves as "I am an African American." Perhaps they'll be Africans by then, or even feisty rapper-dappers. Perhaps, by that time, the most radical act of naming will be a return to "colored."

I began to learn about the meanings of blackness—or at least how to give voice to what I had experienced—when I went off to Yale. The class of 1973 was the first at Yale to include a "large" contingent of Afro-Americans, the name we quickly and comfortably seized upon at New Haven. Like many of us in those years, I gravitated to courses in Afro-American studies, at least one per semester, despite the fact that I was premed, like almost all the other black kids at Yale—that is, until the ranks were devastated by organic chemistry. (The law was the most common substitute.) The college campus, then, was a refuge from explicit racism, freeing us to read and write about our "racial" selves, to organize for recruitment of minority students and faculty, and to demand the constitutional rights of the Black Panther party for self-defense—an action that led, at New Haven at least, to a full-fledged strike in April of 1970, two weeks before Nixon and Kissinger invaded Cambodia. The campus was our sanctuary, where we could be as black as the ace of spades and nobody seemed to mind.

Today the white college campus is a rather different place. Black studies, where it has survived—and it has survived only at those campuses where *someone* believed enough in its academic integrity to insist upon a sound academic foundation—is entering its third decade. More black faculty members are tenured than ever before, despite the fact that only eight hundred or so black students took the doctorate in 1986, and fully half of these were in education. Yet for all the gains that have been made, racial tensions on college campuses appear to be on the rise, with a monitoring group finding incidents reported at over one hundred and seventy-five colleges since the 1986–87 academic year (and this is just counting the ones that made the papers). The dream of the university as a haven of racial equity, as an ultimate realm beyond the veil, has not been realized. Racism on our college campuses has become a palpable, ugly thing.

Even I—despite a highly visible presence as a faculty member at Cornell—have found it necessary to cross the street, hum a tune, or smile, when confronting a lone white woman in a campus building or on the Commons late at night. (Once a white coed even felt it necessary to spring from an elevator that I was about to enter, in the very building where my department was housed.) Nor can I help but feel some humiliation as I try to put a white person at ease in a dark place on campus at night, coming from nowhere, confronting that certain look of panic in their eyes, trying to think grand thoughts like Du Bois but—for the life of me—looking to them like Wille Horton. Grinning, singing, scratching my head, I have felt like Steppin Fetchit with a Ph.D. So much for Yale; so much for Cambridge.

The meanings of blackness are vastly more complex, I suspect, than they ever have been before in our American past. But how to explain? I have often imagined encountering the ghost of the great Du Bois, riding on the shoulders of the Spirit of Blackness.

"Young man," he'd say, "what has happened in my absence? Have things changed?"

"Well, sir," I'd respond, "your alma mater, Fair Harvard, has a black studies department, a Du Bois Research Center, and even a Du Bois

Professor of History. Your old friend, Thurgood Marshall, sits like a minotaur as an associate justice on the Supreme Court. Martin Luther King's birthday is a *federal* holiday, and a black man you did not know won several Democratic presidential primaries last year. Black women novelists adorn the *New York Times* Best Seller lists, and the number one television show in the country is a situation comedy concerning the lives and times of a refined Afro-American obstetrician and his lovely wife, who is a senior partner in a Wall Street law firm. Sammy Davis, Jr.'s second autobiography has been widely—"

"Young man, I have come a long way. Do not trifle with the Weary Traveler."

"I would not think of it, sir. I revere you, sir, why, I even—"

"How many of them had to die? How many of our own? Did Nkrumah and Azikwe send troops? Did a nuclear holocaust bring them to their senses? When Shirley Graham and I set sail for Ghana, I pronounced all hope for our patient people doomed."

"Nor sir," I would respond. "The gates of segregation fell rather quickly after 1965. A new middle class defined itself, a talented tenth, the cultured few, who, somehow, slipped through the cracks."

"Then the preservation of the material base proved to be more important than the primal xenophobia that we had posited?"

"That's about it, Doctor. But regular Negroes still catch hell. In fact, the ranks of the black underclass have never been larger."

I imagine the great man would heave a sigh, as the Spirit of Blackness galloped away.

From 1831, if not before, to 1965, an ideology of desegregation, of "civil rights," prevailed among our thinkers. Abolitionists, Reconstructors, neoabolitionists, all shared one common belief: that if we could only use the legislature and the judiciary to create and interpret the laws of desegregation and access, all else would follow. As it turns out, it was vastly easier to dismantle the petty forms of apartheid in this country (housing, marriage, hotels, and restaurants) than anyone could have possibly believed it would be, *without* affecting the larger patterns of inequality. In fact, the economic structure has not changed one jot, in any fundamental sense, except that black adult and teenage unemployment is much higher now than it has been in my lifetime. Considering the out-of-wedlock birthrate, the high school dropout rate, and the unemployment figures, the "two nations" predicted by the Kerner Commission in 1968 may be upon us. And the conscious manipulation of our public image, by writers, filmmakers, and artists, which many of us *still* seem to think will bring freedom, has had very little impact in palliating our structural social problems. What's the most popular television program in South Africa? The "Cosby Show." Why not?

Ideology, paradoxically, was impoverished when we needed it most, during the civil rights movement of the early 1960s. Unable to theorize what Cornel West calls "the racial problematic," unwilling (with very few exceptions) to theorize class, and scarcely able even to contemplate the theorizing of the curious compound effect of class-cum-race, we have—since the day after the signing of the Civil Rights Act of 1965—utterly lacked any instrumentality of ideological analysis, beyond the attempts of the Black Power and Black Aesthetic movements, to *invert* the significa-tion of "blackness" itself. Recognizing that what had passed for "the human," or "the universal," was in fact white essentialism, we substi-tuted one sort of essentialism (that of "blackness") for another. That, we learned quickly enough, was just not enough. But it led the way to a gestural politics captivated by fetishes and feel-bad rhetoric. The ultimate sign of our sheer powerlessness is all of the attention that we have given, in the past few months, to declaring the birth of the African American and pronouncing the Black Self dead. Don't we have anything better to do?

Now, I myself happen to like African American, especially because I am, as a scholar, an Africanist as well as an African Americanist. Certainly the cultural continuities among African, Caribbean, and Black American cultures cannot be denied. (The irony is that we often thought of our-selves as "African" until late into the nineteenth century. The death of the African was declared by the Park school of sociology in the first quarter of this century, which thought that the hyphenated ethnicity of the Negro American would prove to be ultimately liberating.) But so tame and unthreatening is a politics centered on onomastics that even the *New York Times,* in a major editorial, declared its support of this movement.

> If Mr. Jackson is right and blacks now prefer to be called African-Americans, it is a sign not just of their maturity but of the nation's success. . . . Blacks may now feel comfortable enough in their standing as citizens to adopt the family surname: American. And their first name, African, conveys a pride in cultural heritage that all Americans cherish. The late James Baldwin once lamented, "No-body knows my name." Now everyone does (December 22, 1988).

To which one young black writer, Trey Ellis, responded recently: "When somebody tries to tell me what to call myself in all uses just because they come to some decision at a cocktail party to which I wasn't even invited, my mama raised me to tell them to kiss my black ass" (*Village Voice,* June 13, 1989, p. 38). As he says, sometimes African American just won't do.

Ellis's amused rejoinder speaks of a very different set of concerns and made me think of James Baldwin's prediction of the coming of a new generation that would give voice to blackness:

> While the tale of how we suffer, and how we are delighted, and how we may triumph is never new, it always must be heard. There isn't any other to tell, it's the only light we've got in all this darkness. . . . And this tale, according to that face, that body, those strong hands on those strings, has another aspect in every country, and a new depth in every generation (*The Price of the Ticket*).

In this spirit, Ellis has declared the birth of a "New Black Aesthetic" movement, comprising artists and writers who are middle-class, self-confident, and secure with black culture, and not looking over their shoulders at white people, wondering whether or not the Mr. Wilsons of their world will call them George. Ellis sees creative artists such as Spike Lee, Wynton Marsalis, Anthony Davis, August Wilson, Warrington Hudlin, Joan Armatrading, and Lisa and Kelly Jones as representatives of a new generation who, commencing with the publication in 1978 of Toni Morrison's *Song of Solomon* (for Ellis a founding gesture) "no longer need to deny or suppress any part of our complicated and sometimes contradictory cultural baggage to please either white people or black. The culturally mulatto *Cosby* girls are equally as black as a black teenage welfare mother" ("The New Black Aesthetic," *Before Columbus Review,* May 14, 1989). And Ellis is right: something quite new is afoot in African-American letters.

In a recent *New York Times Book Review* of Maxine Hong Kingston's new novel, Le Anne Schreiber remarks: "Wittman Ah Singh can't be Chinese even if he wants to be. . . . He is American, as American as Jack Kerouac or James Baldwin or Allen Ginsberg." I remember a time, not so very long ago, when almost no one would have thought of James Baldwin as typifying the "American." I think that even James Baldwin would have been surprised. Certainly since 1950 the meanings of blackness, as manifested in the literary tradition, have come full circle.

Consider the holy male trinity of the black tradition: Wright, Ellison, and Baldwin. For Richard Wright, "the color curtain"—as he titled a book on the Bandung Conference in 1955 when "the Third World" was born— was something to be rent asunder by something he vaguely called the

"Enlightenment." (It never occurred to Wright, apparently, that the sublime gains in intellection in the Enlightenment took place simultaneously with the slave trade in African human beings, which generated an unprecedented degree of wealth and an unprecedentedly large leisure and intellectual class.) Wright was hardly sentimental about Black Africa and the Third World—he actually told the first Conference of Negro-African Writers and Artists in Paris in 1956 that colonialism had been "liberating, since it smashed old traditions and destroyed old gods, freeing Africans from the 'rot' of their past," their "irrational past" (James Baldwin, *Nobody Knows My Name*). Despite the audacity of this claim, however, Wright saw himself as chosen "in some way to inject into the American consciousness" a cognizance of "other people's mores or national habits" ("I Choose Exile," unpublished essay). Wright claimed that he was "split": "I'm black. I'm a man of the West. . . . I see and understand the non- or anti-Western point of view." But, Wright confesses, "when I look out upon the vast stretches of this earth inhabited by brown, black and yellow men . . . my reactions and attitudes are those of the West" (*White Man, Listen!*). Wright never had clearer insight into himself, although his unrelentingly critical view of Third World cultures will certainly not make him required reading among those of us bent upon decentering the canon.

James Baldwin, who parodied Wright's 1956 speech in *Nobody Knows My Name,* concluded that "this was, perhaps, a tactless way of phrasing a debatable idea." Blackness, for Baldwin, was a sign, a sign that signified through the salvation of the "gospel impulse," as Craig Werner characterizes it, seen in his refusal "to create demons, to simplify the other in a way that would inevitably force him to simplify himself. . . . The gospel impulse—its refusal to accept oppositional thought; its complex sense of presence; its belief in salvation—sounds in Baldwin's voice no matter what his particular vocabulary at a particular moment." (Craig Werner, "James Baldwin: Politics and the Gospel Impulse," *New Politics* [Winter 1989].) Blackness, if it would be anything, stood as the saving grace of both white *and* black America.

Ralph Ellison, ever the trickster, felt it incumbent upon him to show that blackness was a metaphor of the human condition and yet to do so through a faithful adherence to its particularity. Nowhere is this idea rendered more brilliantly than in his sermon "The Blackness of Blackness," the tradition's classic critique of blackness as an essence:

"Brothers and sisters, my text this morning is the 'Blackness of Blackness.'"

And a congregation of voices answered: "That blackness is most black, brother, most black . . ."

"In the beginning . . ."

"At the very start," they cried.

". . . there was blackness . . ."

"Preach it . . ."

". . . and the sun . . ."

"The sun, Lawd . . ."

". . . was bloody red . . ."

"Red . . ."

"Now black is . . ." the preacher shouted.

"Bloody . . ."

"I said black is . . ."

"Preach it, brother . . ."

". . . an' black ain't . . ."

"Red, Lawd, red: He said it's red!"

"Amen, brother . . ."

"Black will git you . . ."

"Yes, it will . . ."

". . . an' black won't . . ."

"Naw, it won't!"

"It do . . ."

"It do, Lawd . . ."

". . . an' it don't."

"Hallelujah . . ."

"It'll put you, glory, glory, Oh my Lawd, in the WHALE'S BELLY."

"Preach it, dear brother . . ."

". . . an' make you tempt . . ."

"Good God a-mighty!"

"Old aunt Nelly!"

"Black will make you . . ."

"Black . . ."

". . . or black will un-make you."

"Ain't it the truth, Lawd?"

(Ellison, *Invisible Man*)

Ellison parodies the idea that blackness can underwrite a metaphysics or even a negative theology; that it can exist outside and independent of its representation.

And it is out of this discursive melee that so much contemporary African-American literature has developed.

The range of representations of the meanings of blackness among the post-*Song of Solomon* (1978) era of black writing can be characterized—for the sake of convenience—by the works of C. Eric Lincoln (*The Avenue, Clayton City*), Trey Ellis's manifesto, "The New Black Aesthetic," and Toni Morrison's *Beloved,* in many ways the ur-text of the African-American experience.

Each of these writers epitomizes the points of a post-Black Aesthetic triangle, made up of the realistic representation of black vernacular culture: the attempt to preserve it for a younger generation (Lincoln), the critique through parody of the essentialism of the Black Aesthetic (Ellis), and the transcendence of the ultimate horror of the black past—slavery—through myth and the supernatural (Morrison).

The first chapter of Eric Lincoln's first novel, *The Avenue, Clayton City* (1988), contains an extended recreation of the African-American ritual of signifying, which is also known as "talking that talk," "the dozens," "nasty talk," and so on. To render the dozens in such wonderful detail, of course, is a crucial manner of preserving it in the written cultural memory of African Americans. This important impulse to preserve (by recording) the vernacular links Lincoln's work directly to that of Zora Neale Hurston. Following the depiction of the ritual exchange, the narrator of the novel analyzes its import in the following way:

> But it was playing the dozens that perplexed and worried Dr. Tait the most of all when he first tuned in on what went on under the streetlight. Surely it required the grossest level of depravity to indulge in such willful vulgarity. He had thought at first that Guts Gallimore's appraisal of talking that talk as "nasty" was too generous to be useful. . . . But the truth of the matter was that in spite of his disgust, the twin insights of agony and intellection had eventually paid off, for suddenly not only the language but the logic of the whole streetlight ritual finally became clear to him. What he was observing from the safety and the anonymity of his cloistered front porch was nothing less than a teenage rite of passage. A very critical *black* rite of passage! How could he not have recognized it for so long? The public deprecation of black men and women was, of course, taken for granted in Clayton City, and everywhere else within the experience of the Flame Gang. But when those black

men and women were one's fathers, mothers, and sisters, how could one approaching manhood accept that deprecation and live with it? To be a *man* implied responsibilities no colored man in Clayton City could meet, so the best way to deal with the contradiction was to deny it. Talkin' that talk—that is, disparaging one's loved ones within the in-group—was an obvious expression of self-hatred, but it also undercut the white man's style of black denigration by presupposing it, and to some degree narcotizing the black boys who were on the way to manhood from the pain of their impotence. After all, *they had said it first!* Playing the dozens, Tait reasoned, was an effort to prepare one to be able to "take it." Anyone who refused to play the dozens was unrealistic, for the dozens were a fact of life for every black man. They were implicit in the very structure of black-white relations, and if one didn't "play," he could "pat his foot" while the play went on, over and around him. No one could exempt himself from the cultural vulgarity of black debasement, no matter how offensive it might be.

Trey Ellis, whose first novel, *Platitudes,* is a satire on contemporary black cultural politics, is an heir of Ishmael Reed, the tradition's great satirist. Ellis describes the relation of what he calls "The New Black Aesthetic" (NBA) to the black nationalism of the sixties, engaged as it is in the necessary task of critique and revision:

> Yet ironically, a telltale sign of the work of the NBA is our parodying of the black nationalist movement: Eddie Murphy, 26, and his old *Saturday Night Live* character, prison poet Tyrone Green, with his hilariously awful angry black poem, "Cill [sic] My Landlord," ("See his dog Do he bite?"); fellow Black Packer Keenan Wayans' upcoming blaxploitation parody *I'ma Get You Sucka!*; playwright George Wolfe, and his parodies of both "A Raisin in the Sun" and "For Colored Girls . . ." in his hit play "The Colored Museum" ("Enter Walter-Lee-Beau-Willie-Jones. . . . His brow is heavy from 300 years of oppression"); filmmaker Reginald Hudlin, 25, and his sacrilegious *Reggie's World of Soul* with its fake commercial for a back scratcher, spatula and toilet bowl brush all with black clenched fists for their handle ends; and Lisa Jones' character Clean Mama King who is available for both sit-ins and film walk-ons. There is now such a strong and vast body of great black work that the corny or mediocre doesn't need to be coddled. NBA artists aren't afraid to publicly flout the official, positivist black party line.

This generation, Ellis continues, cares less about what white people think than any other in the history of Africans in this country. "The New Black Aesthetic says you just have to *be* natural, you don't necessarily have to *wear* one."

Ellis dates the beginning of this cultural movement with the publication of *Song of Solomon* in 1978. Morrison's blend of magical realism and African-American mythology proved compelling. This brilliantly rendered book was an overnight bestseller. Her greatest artistic achievement, · however, and most controversial, is her most recent novel, *Beloved,* which won the 1988 Pulitzer Prize for Fiction.

In *Beloved,* Morrison has found a language that gives voice to the unspeakable horror and terror of the black past, our enslavement in the New World. Indeed, the novel is an allegorical representation of this very unspeakability. It is one of the few treatments of slavery that escapes the pitfalls of *kitsch.* Toni Morrison's genius is that she has found a language by which to thematize this very unspeakability of slavery.

> Everybody knew what she was called, but nobody knew her name. Disremembered and unaccounted for, she cannot be lost because no one is looking for her, and even if they were, how can they call her if they don't know her name? Although she has claim, she is not claimed. In the place where long grass opens, the girl who waited to be loved and cry shame erupts into her separate parts, to make it easy for the chewing laughter to swallow her all away.
>
> It was not a story to pass on.
>
> They forgot her like a bad dream. After they made up their tales, shaped and decorated them, those that saw her that day on the porch quickly and deliberately forgot her. It took longer for those who had spoken to her, lived with her, fallen in love with her, to forget, until they realized they couldn't remember or repeat a single thing she said, and began to believe that, other than what they themselves were thinking, she hadn't said anything at all. So, in the end, they forgot her too. Remembering seemed unwise. They never knew where or why she crouched, or whose was the underwater face she needed like that. Where the memory of the smile under her chin might have been and was not, a latch latched and lichen attached its apple-green bloom to the metal. What made her think her fingernails could open locks the rain rained on?
>
> It was not a story to pass on.

Only by stepping outside of the limitations of realism and entering a realm of myth could Morrison, a century after its abolition, give a voice to the silence of enslavement.

For these writers, in their various ways, the challenge of the black creative intelligence is no longer to *posit* blackness, as it was in the Black Arts movement of the sixties, but to render it. Their goal seems to be to create a fiction *beyond* the colorline, one that takes the blackness of the culture for granted, as a springboard to write about those human emotions that we share with everyone else, and that we have always shared with each other, when no white people are around. They seem intent, paradoxically, in escaping the very banality of blackness that we encountered in so much Black Arts poetry, by *assuming* it as a legitimate grounds for the creation of art.

To declare that race is a trope, however, is not to deny its palpable force in the life of every African American who tries to function every day in a still very racist America. In the face of Anthony Appiah's and my own critique of what we might think of "black essentialism," Houston Baker demands that we remember what we might characterize as the "taxi fallacy."

Houston, Anthony, and I emerge from the splendid isolation of the Schomburg Library and stand together on the corner of 135th Street and Malcolm X Boulevard attempting to hail a taxi to return to the Yale Club. With the taxis shooting by us as if we did not exist, Anthony and I cry out in perplexity, "But sir, it's only a trope."

If only that's *all* it was.

My father, who recently enjoyed his seventy-sixth birthday, and I attended a basketball game at Duke this past winter. It wasn't just any game; it was "the" game with North Carolina, the ultimate rivalry in American basketball competition. At a crucial juncture of the game, one of the overly avid Duke fans bellowing in our section of the auditorium called J. R. Reid, the Carolina center, "rubber lips."

"Did you hear what he said?" I asked my father, who wears *two* hearing aids.

"I heard it. Ignore it, boy."

"I can't, Pop," I replied. Then, loud-talking all the way, I informed the crowd, while ostensibly talking only to my father, that we'd come too far to put up with shit like this, that Martin Luther King didn't die in vain, and we won't tolerate this kind of racism again, etc., etc., etc. Then I stood up and told the guy not to say those words ever again.

You could have cut the silence in our section of that auditorium with a knife. After a long silence, my Dad leaned over and whispered to me, "Nigger, is you *crazy*? We am in de Souf." We both burst into laughter.

Even in the South, though, the intrusion of race into our lives usually takes more benign forms. One day my wife and father came to lunch at the National Humanities Center in Research Triangle Park, North Carolina, where I'm currently a fellow. The following day, the only black member of the staff cornered me and said that the kitchen staff had a bet and that I was the only person who could resolve it. Shoot, I said. "Okay," he said. "The bet is that your Daddy is Mediterranean—Greek or Eye-talian, and your wife is High Yellow." "No," I said, "it's the other way around; my Dad is black; my wife is white."

"Oh, yeah," he said, after a long pause, looking at me through the eyes of the race when one of us is being "sadiddy," or telling some kind of racial lie. "You, know, *brother,*" he said to me in a low but pointed whisper, "we black people got ways to *tell* these things, you know." Then he looked at me to see if I was ready to confess the truth. Indeterminacy had come home to greet me.

What, finally, is the meaning of blackness for my generation of African-American scholars? I think that many of us are trying to work, rather self-consciously, within the tradition. It has taken white administrators far too long to realize that the recruitment of black faculty members is vastly easier at those institutions with the strongest black studies departments, or at least with the strongest representation of other black faculty. Why? I think the reason for this is that many of us wish to be a part of a community, of something "larger" than ourselves, escaping the splendid isolation of our studies. What can be lonelier than research, except perhaps the terror of the blank page (or computer screen)? Few of us— and I mean *very* few—wish to be the "only one" in town. I want my own children to grow up in the home of intellectuals, but with black middle-class values as common to them as the air they breathe. This I cannot achieve alone. I seek out, eagerly, the company of other African-American academics who have paid their dues, who understand the costs, and the pleasures, of achievement, who care about "the race," and who are determined to leave a legacy of self-defense against racism in all of its pernicious forms.

Part of this effort to achieve a sense of community is understanding that our generation of scholars is just an extension of other generations, of "many thousands gone." We are no smarter than they; we are just a bit more fortunate, in some ways, the accident of birth enabling us to teach at "white" research institutions, when two generations before we would have been teaching at black schools, overworked and underfunded. Most of us define ourselves as extensions of the tradition of scholarship and academic excellence epitomized by figures such as J. Saunders Redding, John Hope Franklin, and St. Clair Drake, merely to list a few names. But how are we *different* from them?

A few months ago I heard Cornel West deliver a memorial lecture in honor of James Snead, a brilliant literary critic who died of cancer this past spring at the age of thirty-five. Snead graduated valedictorian of his class at Exeter, then summa cum laude at Yale. Fluent in German, he wrote his Scholar of the House "essay" on the uses of repetition in Thomas Mann and William Faulkner. (Actually, this "essay" amounted to some six hundred pages, and the appendices were written in German.) He was also a jazz pianist and composer and worked as an investment banker in West Germany, after he took the Ph.D. in English Literature at the University of Cambridge. Snead was a remarkable man.

West, near the end of his memorial lecture, told his audience that he had been discussing Snead's life and times with St. Clair Drake, as Drake lay in bed in a hospital recovering from a mild stroke that he had experienced on a flight from San Francisco to Princeton where Drake was to lecture. When West met the plane at the airport, he rushed Drake to the hospital and sat with him through much of the weekend.

West told Drake how Snead was, yes, a solid race man, how he loved the tradition, and wrote about it, but that his real goal was to redefine *American studies* from the vantage point of African-American concepts and principles. For Snead, taking the black mountaintop was not enough; he wanted the entire mountain range. "There is much about Dr. Snead that I can understand," Drake told West. "But then again," he concluded, "there is something about his enterprise that is quite unlike ours." Our next move within the academy, our next gesture, is to redefine the whole, simultaneously institutionalizing African-American studies. The idea that African-American culture was exclusively a thing apart, separate from the whole, having no influence on the shape and shaping of American culture, is a racialist fiction. There can be no doubt that the successful attempts to "decenter" the canon stem in part from the impact that black studies programs have had upon traditional notions of the "teachable," upon what, properly, constitutes the universe of knowledge that the well-educated should know. For us, and for the students that we train, the complex meaning of blackness is a vision of America, a refracted image in the American looking glass.

Snead's project, and Ellis's—the project of a new generation of writers and scholars—is about transcending the I-got-mine parochialism of a desperate era. It looks beyond that overworked masterplot of victims and victimizers so carefully scripted in the cultural dominant, beyond the paranoid dream of cultural autarky, and beyond the seductive ensolacements of nationalism. Their story—and it is a new story—is about elective affinities, unburdened by an ideology of descent; it speaks of blackness without blood. And this *is* a story to pass on.

Poetry and

the Age:

"A Girl

in a Library" to

Randall Jarrell

*

Sandra M. Brown

I don't read poetry. At least that's what I've always said. I've never said I didn't like it, only that I don't read it. I have said that poetry is too often obscure and I'm too busy to take time to unscramble somebody's puzzle. At the very moment I see a poem, I feel a moment's guilty hesitation, and then I say, sometime later I'll read this, when I have more time to think, when I am more prepared for intensity. In the meantime I will read everything else in the magazine I am reading, fiction or nonfiction. That may well take me a very long time and may even make me think, but I will never get back to the one little poem.

Obviously then, I do not see myself as qualified to talk about poetry and its importance. However, in September of this year I had to think about poetry whether I wanted to or not, because I was assigned to teach a class called "Introduction to Creative Writing," a course that is half fiction-writing and half poetry-writing. I wasn't worried about the fiction. I've written stories long enough and been in enough writing workshops to think that writing and teaching fiction is something I do.

Though I claim to know *no* poetry and to have *no* interest in it, last summer, as I prepared for teaching my course, I was haunted by one line of poetry. (So I can't legitimately say that I know *no* poetry. It actually is a fabrication how little I've been exposed to poetry, but I've never before had to think out why I've insisted on it.) The line that haunted me and which by late August had me in a pitch of high anxiety about who was I to think I could teach poetry was this one from "A Girl in a Library" by Randall Jarrell:

> (Tanya, they won't even *scan*)

I feared my students faced the double scandal of having a poetry teacher who didn't read poetry and knew nothing (and cared less) about meter. I was reminded of a recurring nightmare I had as a child in which I was required to perform at a piano recital without knowing a note of music.

I went to undergraduate school in another era, an era of right readings and absolute professorial authority. Their authority mirrored the culture. I can personally key into the time and place with the single word "scan." In that word "scan" and the emphasis placed on it (I can actually hear Jarrell's voice), I find almost the whole of the poem. On the single syllable scan rests class conflict and intellectual collision between educated professors and the mass that comes into a university to learn something. In those days learning something pretty much meant that we the mass needed to be made human by mainline infusions of the intellectual legacy of the past.

Jarrell said that "A Girl in a Library" is about the New World and the Old. (He was most likely explaining things to students like this imaginary girl who asked him obvious questions, such as, if you have something you want to say, why don't you just say it in dog and cat English?)

The poem doesn't read as an overt cultural collision, because we read it from only one point of view—the poet's. The girl is asleep. But this is a poem about cultural collision: the collision between High Culture represented by the past (on the shelves of the library) and by the inheritor of that past, the poet persona (who in real life was a poet, teacher, and critic) and Low Culture, as represented by the student, a somewhat stereotyped Southern girl.

But to get back to the word *scan*. The stanza it's in begins like this:

> Poor senseless Life:
> When, in the last light sleep of dawn, the messenger
> Comes with his message, you will not awake.
> He'll give his feathery whistle, shake you hard,
> You'll look with wide eyes at the dewy yard
> And dream, with calm slow factuality:
> "Today's Commencement. My bachelor's degree
> In Home Ec., my doctorate of philosophy

In Phys. Ed.
> (Tanya, they won't even *scan*)
> Are waiting for me. . . ."

I chose this poem because I have long been intrigued by it. In fact I've never understood it all, but it has so far remained in my life because it has things in it that are and have been meaningful to me and a few that I am interested in knowing more about. This is the approach to reading I suggested to my class for any writer. I chose the poem for other reasons also, none of which I was aware of until I needed to write this particular essay.

Jarrell composed the poem roughly at the time when I was a student at the college at which he spent most of his teaching career, the Woman's College of the University of North Carolina. Once he represented High Culture and I, the Low. Now a generation later, I am a graduate teaching assistant, and compared to my students—who have grown up on TV and videos and Heavy Metal—I, to my surprise, represent both High Culture and the institution in which I once "did time" for four years.

And so I took copies of "A Girl in a Library" to my class and eagerly awaited the response. One of the things I wanted to know was if they identified with being peasants the way I once did, aided by the general atmosphere of impregnable authority and a few cranky teachers who tried to impress upon me how high a place in life a Ph.D. put a person in. (One professor was so successful that I am continually taken aback that that is what I now do—teach in a college.)

I say I had read the poem often but this time, it had been ten years since I had read it. I say I've liked this poem. I suppose I like it most because a writer where I had lived wrote about someone sort of like me—on the surface "the girl" is a fairly typical Woman's College student of the fifties and early sixties, the bane of the existence of the teaching faculty, because they had the career misfortune of landing jobs in an all female institution and she was their only raw material, the only legatee in sight for receiving "the best that has been thought and said" in Western Civilization, and all this girl cared about was Friday coming and finding a ride from Greensboro to Chapel Hill, where Life was.

But there are other poems of Jarrell's that I read fifteen years ago which then and now feel more important to me. I discovered them in 1976 when my children were out of diapers and the dust had cleared and I understood that a revolution in expectations was taking place, and though I was on the wrong side of the first revolution I was caught in the middle of, I was quite certain that I didn't want to make the same mistake twice.

Anyway, in 1976 I found some of Jarrell's "woman" poems. They were given to me by a poet in a community poetry class that I wandered into to think about my life. It is interesting to me now that the first chance I got to look for Life, I went to a poetry class. I wonder why I didn't take up hot air ballooning. It's something I've always wanted to do.

When I say Jarrell's "woman" poems, I mean "The Face," "Seele im Raum," "Next Day," "The Lost Children," and "The Woman at the Washington Zoo." There are some others too, but these are the most important to me, and I wish someone would put all of them in a volume by themselves, because I know only a very few writers of the twentieth century who have written so well about women, and without obvious misogyny, who have identified so completely, who have thought us important enough to write about. Jarrell, a poet and a critic recognized in his time, and knowing himself to be one of society's appointed knowers, recognized in women particular kinds of knowing. He was known early as a born genius, and his mentor was John Crowe Ransome, a central figure in establishing criticism in the university as an academic discipline. So everyone knew that Randall Jarrell knew a lot. But I never knew it until 1976 when I read his woman poems. The one I liked best was "The Face":

> *Die alte Frau, die alte Marschcallin!*
>
> Not good any more, not beautiful,
> Not even young.
> This isn't mine.
> Where is the old one, the old ones?
> Those were mine.
>
> It's so: I have pictures,
> Not such old ones; people behaved
> Differently then . . . When they meet me they say:
> You haven't changed.
> I want to say: You haven't looked.
>
> This is what happens to everyone.
> At first you get bigger, you know more,
> Then something goes wrong.
> You are, and you say: I am—
> And you were . . . I've been too long.
>
> I know, there's no saying no,
> But just the same you say it. No.

I'll point to myself and say: I'm not like this.
I'm the same as always inside.
—And even that's not so.

I thought: If nothing happens . . .
And nothing happened.
Here I am.
                But it's not right.
If just living can do this,
Living is more dangerous than anything:

It is terrible to be alive.

I read that, and I figured I knew a poem when I saw one. Last year in General Writing, I twice taught an essay by the critic Stanley Fish called "How to Recognize a Poem When You See One." Basically, Fish claimed that you know what a poem is because someone has told you what one is, has taught you to see with poetry-seeing eyes. Fish, in his own way, makes a certain cold-hearted sense. People spent a lot of years talking to me about what poetry was and why it was important. But to me, personally, I never *knew* what a poem was until I read "The Face."

So as far as I'm concerned, Jarrell was a first class knower. However, he wasn't a perfect one. Men can be sympathetic toward women (and in the history of literature, we've had precious little sympathy), but men can't *be* women. That became evident to me when my class and I read "A Girl in a Library" together.

I had told them that this was a poem about a student who didn't like poetry. I thought they might identify with her. And then we talked about point of view, persona, and voice, which we had been talking about since we started the fiction half of the course. We talked about who was seeing whom, what the situation was. What did the man think of the girl? How did he see her? And what did Tatyana Larina think? (Of course, I had to explain who Tatyana Larina was, but that is part of Jarrell's point—she is a woman in a little-read poem-novel, *Eugene Onegin* by Alexander Pushkin. She is also a little-appreciated literary heroine whom Jarrell considered a rich and exemplary woman and a knower of important things, many of which she learned in her ex-lover's library.) And then I asked, when we were almost done, and what about the girl? What do you suppose she thought?

And that's when I got mad, partly at the poem, partly at myself. Why had it never occurred to me to ask what the girl might be thinking, even though the poet says she doesn't think?

I know as well as anyone else who ever graduated from the Woman's College what this girl thought and/or why she refused to think. Most any Southern woman knows why she refused to think, if she thinks about it long enough. And it's not because the girl couldn't think, or didn't want to think, it's that she had already thought so much that she knew serious thinking for a girl in the days of racial segregation and sexual polarization caused a person to have to live in basic contradiction in the schizophrenic society in which she had grown up. Thinking was so confusing and/or downright dangerous that she had decided at least to act as if it *looked* like she wasn't thinking, or sometime before eighteen, she just blotted out large sections of "knowing" altogether.

I sat at my desk in the circle I sit in with my students, restless with anger that I thought it a little late and useless to have. I tried to explain. I felt like a traitor doing this to Jarrell's poem, Jarrell having been so important to me—one of the few poets I've cared about, and an exceedingly fine teacher. But I kept going anyway, even though as a new teacher, I try to refrain from telling stories (which I really love to do) mainly because when I do it, their eyes glaze over.

I happen to know for dead certain that that girl did think, even though the poem says she didn't. She sat in classes and wondered why anybody ever thought Milton was important. She didn't think he was important. She felt a little guilty to defy authority that way. One's elders knew best. She'd always said "Yes, m'am," and "No, sir." Everyone said Milton was important. The past was important. Books were important. She knew books were important, because she had already read books. But she had no books and no guide for what was happening outside the very library window she spent hours staring through.

The girl, after sleeping for decades in the library window, woke up one day and saw four colored boys walk by. They were from A & T College, the Negro college down the street. The boys were dressed up respectable in coats and ties, their Sunday best. She'd seen one of them on her long bus rides home to the other side of the state, though she would have ridden in the front of the bus, and he would have ridden in the back.

Later she found out where the four boys were going. They were going down to Woolworth's 5 and 10. They went to Woolworth's, and all four sat down at the lunch counter where no Negroes had ever been allowed to sit, even though Negroes were welcome to spend money in the store. Negroes were not allowed to sit any place in the South that was implicitly understood to be for "whites only." The four boys ordered coffee, and they were asked to leave. They didn't. They sat there for six months, until the people of Greensboro said they would be allowed to get their coffee.

And when the girl went back to her dorm, she would listen to a girl from New Jersey with hair clear down to her waist play her guitar and sing about free love. The girl thought she would fry in hell if she was not a virgin when she got married. And the only reason her parents had sent her to the Woman's College (no freshman females could then be admitted to the University at Chapel Hill, then called the intellectual center of the South) was so that she could be qualified to be a teacher (of children), so that when she got married (that was supposed to be the week she graduated, or she would be branded an Old Maid), she would have something to fall back on. Teaching was something you learned to do "in case"—in case your husband died or for some reason failed to support you and, god forbid, you had to go to work. But actually she started losing interest in school the day she saw the boy from her town walk by in his suit and tie. She thought he must know something worth knowing. And she had some things she knew too.

One of the things she knew was that by the time she was eighteen, she had read a lot of books, most of which she had enjoyed. But for the time being, she thought she had read enough books. She thought her "soul had no assignments," a line she was later to learn from a local poet. Another one of the things she knew was that everything as she knew it was about to change. A whole society was on the edge of upheaval. The border line dividing white people from black people was three centuries old. Personally she didn't think Milton nor Plato was a great help to her in what she saw happening. Being a student just didn't seem important when so much was going on *outside* the library. But instead of finding the language she needed to say that to somebody, she just always said (after she graduated and taught phys. ed. or home ec. or English), "I don't read poetry."

Now one woman who was once in a library, a genuine representative of Low Culture, tried to use this poem to teach writing and somehow bring together her past and her students' future. Her Low Culture view of writing led her to statements like this: you are the writer. You are in charge of your art and responsible for its power.

Her High Culture training (osmosis) led her to point out that stereotypes were undesirable, even when used by Randall Jarrell. A few wanted to know what was wrong with stereotypes.

Low Culture Woman heard a voice in her head and said something like this: as a writer—and you are writers—ultimately you will be known

(known in the sense that I know "The Face") by the quality of your sympathy. When you write you have power, whether you admit it or not. And my position is that you must be responsible with your power, that no matter who you are when you write, what goes on the page has a life of its own. You have to think for the future. You have to think of what you'll give to others and how you might be a shaper of the future. You need (in fact the state of the world requires of you) a vision of reconciliation wider and more generous than that of most of your predecessors, a vision big enough to allow a bridging of all borders of race, gender, and religion and national origin.

No one liked what I had to say. They knew a preacher when they heard one. What I called sympathy, they called censorship. One young man said, I have to be responsible in every thing I do. Why can't I do what I want to do here? Low Culture Woman replied that he could indeed do what he wanted to do, be as irresponsible as he wanted to be, but did he want to add to any person's suffering with his angry demarcation of "fucking faggots"? Did he know what he was doing? He didn't.

When the first poems came in, it turned out all the poetry anxiety was mine. My class liked poetry, and they weren't intimidated by the Poetry of the Past. They had never known anyone who scanned. Most of them were the first of their families to go to college, but they didn't consider their inability to scan a sign of their social or intellectual inferiority, as once I did. I asked them to write poems, and they did. Two early responses follow. I rejoiced. I still can't scan, but I do read a lot of poetry now, and these look like poems to me:

> Guardian Dear
> What with
>> The shine from the votives before me—
>> The flickering rows in wine-red glass cups
>> Sending up waves, not of smoke, but of heat;
>> An underwater shimmer—and the scent all around
>> (A sleepy church-smell, of warm wax and spice;
>> Incense, like decay-covered cinnamon),
>> And the marble beneath me, so hard as to make
>> My knees seem soft in comparison,
>> Like the rippled air;
>>> What with
>> All that, it was not so strange to think I heard
>> A sharp crack above me (and a bit to my right)

And to imagine I'd see, if I'd just turn my head,
The window
—You know the one; Jacob's ladder, it shows—
With a clear patch of sky at the second rung
(Like the hole in the dough when the cookie-cutter's been
And gone).
And to see the angel in translucent glory,
The one who, with a sly smile, had always kept
Half-turned to me, not toward yawning Jacob;
I say, to see the angel, wrenched free, hover
And shake the shards from his back in a sparkling rain.
    And what with
The wind so sudden on the back of my neck,
I was sure I'd soon hear in descent
The brittle snap of wings long held from flight
And feel a cold glass hand on my shoulder.
—(Stacy Hoffman, 20)

(Unsure of a Title)

Upon the sidewalk my barefeet burned
to the roar of a revving engine my eyes turned
and there was the car my brother's friend owned
with its shabby, vinyl top, and its color two toned.
It rolled toward my house; I knew it would stop,
but I walked on, finishing a grape soda-pop.
Step after step avoiding each crack
my mother didn't need a broken back.
Distant horns filled the air; across the street a baby
    cried.
My house was getting closer with every stride.
Pausing outside this house, callow where I stood
staring at the once white picket fence and all its broken
    wood.
Through the jungled yard I walked, coming to the door
the screen that kept the bugs out was crinkled on the
    floor.
I traveled through the hallway knowing where mother would be
sitting there, chain smoking, mesmerized by the TV.
The smell of stale tobacco smoke lingered in the air
empty, green wine bottles scattered everywhere.

my oldest brother was killed in the Vietnam war,
and cancer killed my daddy when I was only four.
    On the mantle their dusty pictures lay
    their noble faces stare as if to say,
    "we are sorry for leaving you this way."
And upstairs, my other brother with the help of his friend
sits in that room and tries to pretend
that he can beat reality. And he can,
he has been smoking that stuff since death began.
I walked through the loud music out in front of his door
and smelled the sweet smoke like so many times before.
I went into my room and laid back on my bed
and suddenly I realized, my whole family is dead.
—Dennis Hasch, 19

My class didn't identify with Randall Jarrell, or rather they didn't see that they did. But look at these two poets. They are doing what poets have always done best and with the same passion and power and grace. They address the central issue of being human—are you alive or dead? Are you present or not? Awake or asleep? "Poor senseless Life, When, in the last light sleep of dawn, the messenger / Comes with his message, you will not awake. . . ."

For this class ('90) their issues on coming of age are less dramatically defined than Life was for Randall Jarrell or for me—the Depression and the Second World War for Jarrell, the Civil Rights Movement and the Viet Nam War for me—but their issues are none the less pressing (the pollution of the planet), and coming of age has the same urgency it has ever had.

In conference, one young man said, "My adviser wants to talk to me about my courses. I want someone to talk to me about my life."

I believe in change. So I told him that. I have been present for and lived through two social revolutions. Once I was a girl in a library when four men of the lowest class in my culture, Negro students at A&T College in Greensboro, N.C., sat down at Woolworth's lunch counter on February 1, 1960, and they didn't get up until they got their coffee. I thought they couldn't win. I was wrong.

The first revolution precipitated the second. In 1976, I found myself in a man's poems. I thought about them while I pushed my child's stroller. I thought about the woman sitting in the Washington Zoo and the leopard crawling inside her and I heard her cry, "Change me, change me."

I answered this student with the best I learned from the four years I spent window-gazing and squirrel-watching in Greensboro. I told him that time is on his side and that his soul has no assignments.

October, 1988

References

Jarrell, Randall, *Complete Poems.* New York: Farrar, Straus & Giroux, 1968.

Lowell, Robert, Peter Taylor, and Robert Penn Warren, eds. *Randall Jarrell 1914–1965.* New York: Farrar, Strauss & Giroux, 1967.

Students' poems printed by permission of Stacy Hoffman and Dennis Hasch.

Joseph McNeil, of Wilmington, N.C., was one of the four young men from A&T College who began the Greensboro sit-in on February 1, 1960. Reported by the *Wilmington Journal.*

My Friend,

Joyce Carol

Oates

*

Brenda Daly

Perhaps I should correct my title—which, after all, I borrowed from Elaine Showalter—and instead use the title, "By Reading Joyce Carol Oates I have Learned to Be My Own Best Friend." For, unlike Elaine Showalter who works with Joyce Carol Oates at Princeton, I am an older, academic woman constantly on the verge of unemployment. Ironically, it is my love for Oates's fiction—and my commitment to writing a book about her development as a writer—that helps to keep me in this precarious state. Nevertheless, Joyce Carol Oates is my friend: by speaking *for* me (when my own voice was not yet strong), her fiction has taught me to speak for myself; by courageously developing and changing (through the past twenty-five years), her fiction has taught me to insist on growth and change; and by continuing to insist on the value of a woman's perspective—despite often hostile criticism—her fiction has also taught me to persist, despite the sometimes harsh attacks on my own work.

Recently, for example, I was introduced to an English class as "the woman who would talk about Oatmeal Mush," the male instructor's derogatory name for Joyce Carol Oates. This introduction was rather a surprise to me, but perhaps it should not have been. It took place on February 9, 1987, at a private liberal arts college in Georgia where, in the English department, all the women had M.A.s (and taught composition only) and the men had Ph.D.s. Clearly, the men liked it that way. I was there for a job interview, invited at the insistence of a newly hired woman dean who had met me at MLA. It became rapidly apparent that I had been invited to the campus so that the department could *appear* to support the new dean. What would she have done, I wonder, had she heard a young man in the department introduce me to his students as "the woman who would talk about Oatmeal Mush?" Rather than answer him, rather than defend Oates or myself, I turned to the students and said: "Oates writes so much, but not so much mush. Let's talk about this story." We then began an animated discussion of Oates's well known, frequently anthologized short story, "Where are you going, where have you been?"

I shall return to this violent story, in which a rape-murder is anticipated after the story's ambiguous conclusion, but first I would like to place it within the context of Oates's development as a writer, because the power of Oates's "daughters" has grown from the 1960s to the present. This growth in power occurs on a number of levels: (1) her women characters survive violent assaults; (2) they survive economically; (3) they compete in the professions, yet they recognize the dangers of becoming exclusively male-identified, and (4) they gradually develop a feminist consciousness in the 1970s and 1980s. Oates's more articulate women, after a period of trying to think of themselves as "ungendered," recognize their mothers in/as themselves.

Although the details of Oates's life are not strictly parallel to those of any of her heroines, the trajectory I will outline has autobiographical implications which, I believe, are helpful in understanding the development of Oates's feminist consciousness. "All art," Oates has said, "is autobiographical," if not in particular details, then in the kinds of problems articulated—and sometimes "solved"—in a given work. I will focus in this essay upon an act of violence that Oates reworks obsessively in her fiction (both in novels and short stories). Specifically, for Oates, this violence is rape, and for me, rape *within* the family: incest. In an autobiographical essay in 1982 called, "Stories That Define Me," Oates has stated that she was the victim of "not quite clinical molestation." I will illustrate how this "playground" violence enters Oates's fiction, in novels published in 1966 and 1986, but first I would like to give my own autobiographical response to "Stories That Define Me." In this essay Oates describes how she became a writer—a process that each time yields a different (revised) Joyce Carol Oates—out of a desire, not simply to escape a world of violence, but to transform it. "I write," she says, "with the enormous hope of altering the world—and why write without that hope?" Now this is a bald, powerful statement, nothing timid about it, and it empowers me.

What does not empower readers like me—a reader who has witnessed her father's sexual abuse of a sister who slept in the same bed, abuse that continued for many years—are writings like Jane Gallop's "The Father's Seduction," in which Gallop cites Luce Irigaray in order to critique Freud and, finally, to defend psychoanalysis. Gallop writes, "The recent emphasis on real incest threatens to deny important psychoanalytic insights in the same gesture that it perhaps correctly accuses Freud of a blind spot." Gallop goes on with her defense of psychoanalysis, arguing, "Irigaray's more complex accusations—'not simply true . . . nor completely false'—about father Freud's defensiveness are finally more useful to a feminist understanding of the binds of the father-daughter relationship." How has Gallop determined that Irigaray's "more complex accusations" are "more useful" to feminists than are accusations by victims of actual incest? Certainly accusations of both actual and psychological rape are equally complex! Finally, Gallop insists that mental seduction is more damaging than actual rape: "Briefly, the veiled seduction, the rule of patriarchal law over the daughter, denying her worth and trapping her in an insatiable desire to please the father, is finally more powerfully and broadly damaging than actualized seduction" (*Daughters and Fathers,* 107).

Why the necessity to put into competition psychological and actual forms of paternal rape? (I wish, Jane, you could have observed my mother, a victim of that more "veiled" seduction, a woman so trapped in her "insatiable desire to please the father" and the father-husband, that she did nothing to rescue my sister from abuse, and, in fact, denied the abuse until all three of my sisters became victims.) Finally, I do not think it surprising, as Gallop apparently does, that paternal rape (by fathers, or uncles, or older cousins) is so widespread. In this culture, men readily assume that, because they "own" women and children, they have the right to use them as they see fit. Slave owners made this same argument. How useful, I wonder, is psychoanalysis to slaves?

Not until my father's funeral in 1976, when I wrote, "I am my father's daughter" in the funeral register, could I begin to write. And not until this moment have I written so openly about my origins in shame, in family shame. Even now I feel that my testimony on this topic will be discredited, that it will "taint" my authority (which must remain lofty and theoretical to be "important"). I also wonder: will my story merely arouse male readers (assuming men will read such writing as this)? As Christina Froula says in *Daughters and Fathers,* Judith Herman "notes that incest victims frequently report that men find their histories arousing, as though they too envy the place of bad father" (135). Will a story that I write to liberate myself become the stimulus for a man's pornographic fantasies? Another (childhood) fear ignited by this writing: will I be rejected, will I be abandoned? (Victims of incest often remain silent for this very reason, and certainly they/we have been abandoned.) Victims also fear that they may destroy their families: I have certainly said nothing for years because of this fear; nevertheless, my family of origin has been destroyed because of this violence. Victims also learn to protect their fathers, whom they recognize as financially more powerful and emotionally more independent than mothers. While my father still lived, I could not speak openly. Now, however, I gain courage because of publications like *Daughters and Fathers,* and I continue writing.

Few such feminist publications were available when I first began to read Joyce Carol Oates in 1972. At that time, her fiction helped me to feel that, one day, I too might speak out against violence and injustice. It certainly helped me to complete my master's degree and then to insist upon my right to graduate school in 1978. By 1983, as I wrote my dissertation, I kept dumping this explosive autobiographical material into a fifth chapter, a chapter that I never wrote. It was my strategy for delaying a writer's block until a time when I could better afford it. Sure enough, my fear emerged again in the summer of 1988, as I wrote an essay on teenage runaways—many of them victims of sexual abuse. With perfectionism bordering on self-censorship—which Madelon Sprengnether describes as symptomatic of abuse victims—I wrote and rewrote my essay until my body was so contorted by pain that I required physical therapy. As I stood to read my essay at a conference the next fall, I nearly fainted. At the end of the session, I was able to continue, but not in my own voice: I read a poem by Joyce Carol Oates. Her voice saved me, once again.

Even Oates's title, "Stories That Define Me," liberates me, for it insists that one life may consist, not of a single story—the story perhaps of childhood victimization—but rather of "stories," and not stories imposed by others, by those who assume language belongs to them, but *stories* created by me, in the company of other women. How splendid to read Oates in the company of other women (past and present) who imagine new worlds into existence. And in "Stories That Define Me," Oates reminds us that our reading, not only our actual lived experience, shapes our writing, or sometimes (mis)shapes a woman's writings. Oates writes:

> Hadn't I absorbed the unmistakable drift of certain prejudices, certain metaphysical/anatomical polarities? Even the otherwise egali-

tarian Thoreau, whose *Walden,* I read at the age of 15 or 16 and have prized forever, even Thoreau, who understood that slavery is obscene because all men are equal, tells us matter-of-factly in "Reading" that there is a "memorable interval" between spoken and written languages. The first is transitory, a dialect merely, almost brutish, "and we learn it unconsciously, like the brutes, of our mothers." The second is the mature language, the written language—"our father tongue, a reserved expression."

Oates continues, "one wonders if brutes achieve a written language, are they no longer brutes? Or is their writing merely defined (by others) as brutish?" A blank space follows and, in the next paragraph Oates shares the fact of her being molested repeatedly and, later in her life, repeatedly attacked for writing that is violent. "Why is your writing so violent?" "Why is your writing so brutish?" So frequently has Oates been attacked, under the guise of this "innocent" question, that she finally replied, in a *New York Times Book Review* essay appropriately called, "Why Is Your Writing So Violent" (1981). The question, Oates rightly states, is always "ignorant," always "sexist." The violence in her fiction does not come from her fantasies, it is obviously everywhere, and women are its frequent victims. Is there a connection between such acts and Thoreau's widely shared (unconscious) view that the language belonging to men is civilized whereas the "mother tongue" remains brutish?

Yes. I believe so. The "father tongue" which Oates constantly challenges and revises seems to me an elaborate (mythical) denial system, an "official" language that allows men to define women, not as rightful users of language, but as outside it, as "brutes" or "sleeping beauties." From the beginning of her writing career, as, for example, in *A Garden of Earthly Delights* (1966), Oates has challenged such stereotypes. Her heroine in *A Garden,* for example, is at once brutish—that is, uneducated and illiterate, born into a family of migrant workers—and angelic, a beautiful golden-haired child, a favorite of her father's because she embodies his dying soul. Oates grew up not far removed, historically or geographically, from poverty (six miles south of Lockport, New York, in Niagara County), and her depiction of migrant workers contains certain fictionalized autobiographical elements. The most important, for my purposes, are her depictions of Clara's mother—(whose outlines remain blurry)—and her depictions of sexual abuse. In *Marya, A Life* (1986), written twenty years later, Oates returns to these images, but with significant differences: Marya's mother, unlike Clara's, comes into clear focus at the end of the novel, and Marya, unlike Clara, not only survives, she prevails: she becomes, in fact, an academic and a writer.

On a structural level, as well, the differences in the two novels are significant. In *Marya,* the first five chapters center upon Marya's encounters with different men—her father's corpse, her cousin, her eighth grade teacher, Schwilk, Father Shearing, Emmet Schroeder—but this "personal" novel shifts focus. In chapter six, Marya's friendships with women, with Imogene Skillman in particular, become central. What Marya discovers is that competition sometimes destroys friendship or love. Marya also discovers that, like many a heroine of romance, she has been seeking her mother in men, such as Maxmillian Fein, her father-professor-lover. In the final chapter, Marya searches directly for her lost mother. By contrast, in *A Garden of Earthly Delights,* Clara never recognizes her need for a mother; she defines herself solely in terms of her relationships to men. Oates divides the novel into three parts, each bearing the name of a significant man in Clara's life: Carleton, her father (Part I), Lowry, the lover who abandons her (Part II), and Swan, the son who nearly kills her (Part III). Swan finally shoots his surrogate-father, Clara's husband, aptly named "Revere," and then turns the gun on himself.

Clara survives the slaughter, but only physically. In her midforties she enters a nursing home where, sustained by Revere's money, she watches television, endlessly. Oates writes, "She seemed to like best programs that showed men fighting, swinging from ropes, shooting guns, and driving fast cars, killing the enemy again and again until the dying gasps of evil men were only a certain familiar rhythm away from the opening blasts of the commercials, which changed only gradually over the years" (384). Clara, then, never escapes the world of violence; it has penetrated her imagination, victimizing her. Furthermore, her author, Joyce Carol Oates, has not yet discovered structures that will enable her to transform a heroine defined exclusively by her relationships to men: to father, lover, and son. As in the novels of George Eliot, Oates's earlier heroines did not become her equals. The problem is that in order to claim language, Oates, like Eliot, had to first imagine herself as male or, at best, genderless. As Oates has explained, she recognized very early that it was better to be Lewis Carroll, the writer, than to be Alice, his character. It is better to be a writer than to be written, better to be an author than to be authored.

Some critics, such as Myra Jehlen in "Archimedes and the Paradox of Feminist Criticism," have suggested that the novel imposes restraints that force a woman to write as a man. I would agree that, during the 1960s when Oates was learning the craft—that is, before she had begun to

revise the novel's conventions—this gender issue caused her difficulty. In
A Garden, for example, despite Clara's centrality in the novel, Oates keeps
her heroine at a "safe" distance. What I mean is that Clara's experiences,
her poverty and sexual vulnerability, parallel Oates's own experience so
closely that she can not yet bring her past (or Clara's) into closer focus. In
A Garden, although Oates protests against the view of "a fall" into sexuality, she splits the act of rape—incestuous rape—into the experience of
two characters, Clara and Rosalie, one a survivor, the other a victim. Clara
escapes her father's incestuous fantasies, though her father seeks her
everywhere before his death as if Clara might redeem him; Clara's friend
Rosalie does not escape incestuous rape. The two little girls had played
together in an abandoned car lot, a setting that recurs in *Marya,* but only
Clara has the power—the seductive appearance, intelligence, and good
fortune—to escape poverty by charming a man who is "fatherly" toward
her and who marries her. Rosalie, however, bears her *biological* father's
child. When the people in a nearby town find out, they beat to death
Rosalie's father, Bert, a migrant worker.

The scene is violent and, to me, terrifying. It is a scene that many a
victim of incest imagines might happen if she tells. She pictures the
townspeople who

> were dragging Bert out of his shanty. One man jumped down,
> another was behind Bert, and with a shove they got him out. He lost
> his balance and fell in the mud. Then some of the men in the town
> rushed over and began kicking him. Clara saw a spurt of red. She
> saw his face lifted by someone's boot, his head snapped back, and
> then he was lost in a rush of legs. The only shouting came from that
> group. Everyone else waited. People around Clara were inching
> back. "You let him alone, I'll kill you!" Clara screamed. . . . Then she
> saw Rosalie's mother in the doorway. She was screaming at the men
> who were beating her husband. . . . Clara could not make out any-
> thing except two words—"His property, his property." (79)

Rosalie's mother, like the mother of many victims of family sexual abuse,
believes in father-right, in father-law. Before this law women, children,
and the poor of all races are helpless "property." Patriarchal law itself
engenders violence and chaos, as this mob scene suggests.

In this scene, I believe, Oates also depicts the chaos of her own
emotions: her anger and pity, her grief and perhaps shame. As people
around Clara "inch away"—as victims of incest expect others to inch
away—Clara pleads for the life of the father, the sexual abuser, and in this

moment the author's self-division seems evident to me: if she takes on the power of the father (his law, his language) will she become a destroyer? If she rejects this power, will she perish? In this novel Oates does not resolve the dilemma; the problem remains like a frozen memory, left behind in the abandoned car lot. The two girls in *A Garden of Earthly Delights,* separated forever by Rosalie's fate (her victimization by her father), never return to their childhood playground, a vacant lot where "junked auto-mobiles all around them looked as if they had crawled . . . and died." As they played in abandoned cars, they had smiled, these two girls, not knowing why, and Clara had seen "windows everywhere . . . cracked as if jerking back from something in astonishment; the cracks were like spider webs, like frozen ripples in water" (65). Sexual abuse destroys their friendship.

Moving forward twenty years, from 1966 to 1986, Oates creates another abandoned car lot, another "playground," this time in *Marya, A Life.* This time Oates brings the scene of sexual abuse into closer focus. Rather than "jerking back from something in astonishment," an astonishment that freezes memory and creative movement, Oates now identifies that vague "something": the repeated scenes of molestation by a cousin. Marya, who later becomes an academic and a writer, has been abandoned by both parents, left in the care of an aunt and uncle, when the sexual abuse occurs. Chapter Two of the novel opens, without introduction, with these words:

> He instructed her to hold still. Not to move. *Not* to move. And not to look at him either. Or say a word.
>
> Marya froze at once. "Went into stone," as she called it. And stared at the grimy partly broken windshield of the old car. And said nothing.
>
> It was only Lee, her cousin Lee, who liked her. Who liked her most of the time. Who meant her no harm. . . .
>
> He was 12 years old, Marya was eight. He didn't mean to hurt her and he never *really* hurt her unless by accident. . . .
>
> In the smelly old Buick at the back of the lot, Marya knew how to go into stone; how to shut her mind off, to see nothing without closing her eyes. She was afraid only that her neck might snap: she knew how chickens' necks were rung, how a garter snake might be whipped against the side of a barn and its secret bones broken. Lee

was strong—it was a joke around the house how strong he was. [Here the scene shifts but Oates courageously returns to a fictionalized version of a painful memory.]

"Be quiet," Lee would say, grunting. "Or I'll wring your skinny little neck."

She never closed her eyes because—how did she know this?—the gesture might anger him, might make him rough.

She stared at, must have memorized, the windshield of the old wreck. It was cracked in cobweb-like patterns that overlapped with one another, doubly, trebly, dense and intricate and fascinating as a puzzle in a picture book. A maze; such things were called, a labyrinth. *"Can you get to the center without raising your pencil point and without crossing any line?"*

[Marya tries, as my sisters have told me they had tried, to lose their pain by intense concentration, as if leaving their bodies behind.]

Sometimes Marya could do it at the first try, sometimes she couldn't. If she got angry, she cheated: but then getting to the center didn't count.

[Marya wonders how many people have died in these cars. She sees bloodstains. She waits for Lee to finish, as my sisters must have waited.] When it was over Lee wouldn't wait to catch his breath but drew back from her at once, flush-faced, panting, his wet lips slack. He never looked at her—they never looked at each other at such times. He rarely spoke except to mutter, "Don't you tell anybody, you."

Hold still. Don't move. Don't tell. (15–18)

These are familiar injunctions, *"Don't move. Don't tell."* Victims of incest, and other categories of rape, are either killed or cautioned against speaking out. And society often conspires with the abuser, shaming the victim, forcing her to bear the responsibility for the rapist's violence. To give a recent example of blaming the victim: a number of students in my freshman English class at St. Olaf College, on reading Oates's story "Where are you going, where have you been?" blamed the victim of rape. She should have obeyed her mother, wrote the students, she should have stayed home like her "good" sister June. When I returned these papers, for revision, I showed them photographs of three young women—ages thirteen, fifteen, and seventeen—all of them victims of rape and murder, all of them pictured in a (1966) *Life* magazine article called, "The Pied Piper of Tucson." These, I said, these are photographs of rape victims, the "raw material" of Oates's story. Do they deserve violent deaths for disobeying their parents? (I ask this question with open anger.)

"What do you mean," I asked Joyce Carol Oates in an interview in 1973, "What did you mean when you wrote in *The Edge of Impossibility* that 'violence is always an affirmation' "? In her reply she used the rapist as an example. "The rapist," she insisted, "seeks to unite himself with something beyond himself, but his desire for this union has been twisted." Perverted. Love twisted into violence, into a wish to obliterate the other, to swallow up the other's threatening identity. Clara, staring into the violence of a television program, gets lost, but Marya, Marya is found. After she receives a letter and a photograph from her mother Vera Murchison, Marya stares into the blurry photograph, "waiting for the face to shift into perfect focus" (310). Although the picture is still slightly blurred, Marya sees more clearly (and looks more closely) than did Clara, who saw only a series of "formless" women with "formless" bodies who took her biological mother's place. It is knowledge—that we are "of woman born"—everywhere violently repressed. What Oates affirms in *Marya,* and in many other novels, is the possibility of dreaming into existence a culture which doesn't require us to define ourselves at the expense of an other, a culture which allows each of us a center, a voice, a face, a story.

As I complete this essay in the winter of 1989, I am a tenure-line assistant professor at Iowa State University. *The Journal of Popular Culture* will publish my essay on "Where are you going, where have you been?" in its winter issue. Self-doubt (a legacy of my nightmarish childhood?) surfaced as I proofed the galleys for this essay, called "An Unfilmable Conclusion: Joyce Carol Oates at the Movies" (the short story has since been made into a 1986 movie called "Smooth Talk"). I wondered whether readers would think my essay about rape and murder too positive. Perhaps I tried so hard to emphasize how Oates transforms an act of violence into a story of survival—a woman writer's survival—that I distorted my thesis: that violence against women will not stop until our society undergoes a spiritual transformation. I wonder did my personal background once again misshape my writing? Or is it the conventions of academic discourse that inhibit my search for an authentic shape for my truth? I don't know.

In the meantime, despite self-doubt, I continue to write, thinking of Joyce Carol Oates as my friend. I imagine her as part of my story—she could be an older sister, for example—and Oates has imagined me as part of her story. Because I wrote to her about her fiction, about sexual abuse particularly, she generously made me a character in her novel *Bellefleur*. I am Yolande, an older sister who rescues her young sister Germaine (born a hermaphrodite) from sexual abuse. Just as Oates makes Elaine Showalter a character in *A Bloodsmoor Romance* (Miss Elaine Cottler who ran for president of the United States), Oates creates a space for me in her fiction. And in that space, I imagine myself into being. I see myself as having many lives to live, many stories to tell.

Note

An earlier draft of this paper was presented at the Center of Advanced Feminist Studies, University of Minnesota, Spring 1987, where I was a "fellow."

References

Daly, Brenda O. "An Unfilmable Conclusion: Joyce Carol Oates at the Movies." *Journal of Popular Culture* 23:3 (Winter 1989): 101–14.

Gallop, Jane. "The Father's Seduction." *Daughters and Fathers*. Lynda E. Boose and Betty S. Flowers, eds. Baltimore: Johns Hopkins University Press, 1989. 97–110.

Froula, Christina. "The Daughter's Seduction: Sexual Violence and Literary History." *Daughters and Fathers*. Lynda E. Boose and Betty S. Flowers, eds. Baltimore: Johns Hopkins University Press, 1989. 111–35.

Jehlen, Myra. "Archimedes and the Paradox of Feminist Criticism." *Feminist Theory: A Critique of Ideology*. Nannerl O. Keohane, Michelle Z. Rosaldo, and Barbara G. Gelpi, eds. Chicago: University of Chicago Press, 1981, 1982. 189–215.

Oates, Joyce Carol. *A Garden of Earthly Delights*. New York: Vanguard Press, 1966.

———. *The Edge of Impossibility: Tragic Forms in Literature*. New York: Vanguard Press, 1972.

———. *Marya, A Life*. New York: E. P. Dutton, 1988.

———. "Stories That Define Me." *New York Times Book Review*. July 11, 1982, 1, 15.

———. "Where are you going, where have you been?" *Where are you going, where have you been? Stories of Young America*. Greenwich, Conn.: Fawcett, 1974.

———. "Why Is Your Writing So Violent?" *New York Times Book Review*. March 29, 1981, 15, 35.

"The Pied Piper of Tucson." *Life*. March 4, 1966, 18+.

Showalter, Elaine. "My Friend, Joyce Carol Oates." *Ms*. March 1966, 44+.

Sprengnether, Madelon. Remarks as Respondent to the Session, "Telling the Truth of the Body: Rereading Literary Representations of Father-Daughter Incest and Domestic Violence." Modern Language Association, Washington, D.C., December 29, 1989.

Somebody Must

Say These Things:

An Essay for

My Mother

*

Melody Graulich

This essay begins with a digression, with a personal rather than a literary experience. I have spent several years seeking the conclusion to this experience, so it is apt that I wander toward my thesis. The real story often emerges in a narrative digression, as I learned from my grandfather, who may have learned it from Twain's Jim Blaine. Born in the Badlands of South Dakota, or so he said, my tall, handsome grandfather was a western drifter who rode buffalo, sang songs about a girl named Duckfoot Sue, and was descended from Geronimo—or, on alternate days, Sitting Bull. Rambling with me in the western mountains, Gramps taught me through his "prevarications" the freedom of self-definition that comes in storytelling. Informing me daily that *he* had wanted to name me Rebel, he let me know that I could do anything I set my mind to.

Gramps himself had a lot more control over his tall tales than over his life. As I grew older and recognized some of his failings, such as alcoholism, my view of him was shaped by the name he had intended for me: I saw him as a flawed visionary, an outlaw from a seedy, conformist society, a man who would "go to hell" before he'd compromise his values. In my own stories, he became the quintessential American hero. His rebellious, freedom-seeking footsteps led me directly to American studies, and I began a dissertation on male writers and their narrative escapades about the West.

A few years after his death, I was confronted with some unwelcome

implications of the rebellious western myth my grandfather had personi-
fied for me. One night my mother described for me a scene that had
occurred many times throughout her childhood: my grandfather beating
up on my grandmother. Recalling details of thirty-five years earlier, details she had never before talked about—"he yanked her from the car by
her hair"—she recounted how she had felt powerless, embarrassed,
responsible. In retrospect I find it surprising that I didn't protest the truth
of the story she was telling me about the man I knew to be affectionate
and loving, the man who had twice cried through *The Incredible Journey*
with me, but somehow I could see the beatings happening, as if I shared
my mother's eyes. Although parts of myself seemed to have been yanked
raggedly apart, settling into new, uncomfortable relations, I accepted this
information about my grandfather calmly, meanwhile gathering all my
unconscious psychological strategies to hold onto my feelings about him.
When I saw my still-living grandmother the next day, I was appalled to
discover that I could not identify with her suffering, that I wanted to keep
my distance from her. Her experience recalled for me only the dark side
of my beloved grandfather, whom I had to find a way to explain and
excuse.

As a literary critic, I naturally turned to literature about violence
against women in an effort to understand my mother's story and what it
meant. I discovered, however, that feminist critics can be resisting readers
of female as well as male texts and that there are parts of our mothers'
stories that we sometimes evade hearing. I have opened this essay with a
convention long established in feminist criticism, the personal voice, not
simply to establish my relationship to my subject but because the engagement between critic and subject and how it shapes both reader and text *is*
my subject. The revisions in thinking and in feeling I went through in
writing two essays about how violence affects women testify that women
often cannot understand the significance of their own experience until
they see it mirrored in literature, that the dialogue we establish with
women writers as we read and write about their works inevitably alters
our perceptions, and that our best reading, like psychoanalysis, leads to an
examined life. It leads also to an acknowledgment of our connections to
other women and to an awareness of how those connections shape our
insights and conclusions.

As abuse of women has been until recently invisible within our society,
an embarrassing "abnormality" to be concealed, so has it been absent
from our literary canon. None of the books on my graduate school
reading lists touched the subject. In fact, the American studies tradition,

as Nina Baym has shown, has been dominated by a fascination with "melodramas of beset manhood," fantasies in which men escape into the wilderness in search of their own moral values, their relations to women presented in only the barest and most romanticized ways.[1] This tradition provided the story, the melodrama, in which I made my grandfather the star. It was at least two years after my mother told me her secrets before I came across a book little known outside of western history circles, Mari Sandoz's *Old Jules* (1935), ostensibly the biography of her father, Jules Sandoz, a "prophet" who came west seeking his "promised land": "free land, far from law and convention," where he could "live as he liked."[2] In his daughter's eyes, Jules is a "big man," the typical visionary frontiersman who pervades our literature and history. He possesses the heroic virtues of the romanticized masculine West: a desire for absolute free will and self-determination.

Yet hidden within this biography of her father, Sandoz wrote a woman's history of the West, focusing on the wide-spread physical and emotional abuse of women, suggesting that the "promised land" did not pay off on its promises to women, that women were often the victims of the frontier's celebrated freedom. Her portrayal of the frontiersman's attitudes toward women and marriage dominates her father's biography. Married four times, Jules beat each of his wives. When his first wife disobeys an order, "Jules closed her mouth with the flat of his long muscular hand" (5). When his second wife asks why he does nothing, "his hand shot out, and the woman slumped against the bench. . . . [Later] he pretended not to notice [her] swollen lip, the dark bruises on her temple, and the tear-wearied eyes" (102). Sandoz concentrates on his relationship to his fourth wife, her mother Mary, and on the power dynamics in their marriage:

Mary avoided crossing him or bothering him for help in anything she could possibly do alone. But there were times when she must have his help, as when the roof leaked or the calves had to be castrated. It took weeks of diplomatic approach to get him to look after the two bull calves before they were too big for her to handle at all. And when she couldn't hold the larger one from kicking, Jules, gray-white above his beard, threw his knife into the manure and loped to the back door. "I learn the goddamn balky woman to obey me when I say 'hold him.' " He tore a handful of four-foot wire stays from the bundle in the corner of the shop and was gone towards the corral, the frightened grandmother and the children huddled at the back window.

They heard the banging of the gate. Jules's bellow of curses. Then Mary ran through the door, past the children and straight to the poison drawer. It stuck, came free . . . the blood dripping from her face and her hand where she had been struck with the wire whip, the woman snatched up a bottle, struggled with the cork, pulling at it with her teeth. The grandmother was upon her, begging, pleading, clutching at the red bottle with the crossbones.

Jules burst in. "Wo's the goddamned woman? I learn her to obey me if I got to kill her!"

"You!" the grandmother cried, shaking her fist against him. "For you there is a place in hell!"

With the same movement of her arm she swung out, knocking the open bottle from the woman's mouth. . . . Then she led Mary out of the house and to the brush along the river. (230–31)

But Jules is no more brutal than most other men in his community, as Sandoz demonstrates through repeated example until *Old Jules* becomes a catalog of male-caused tragedies in women's lives. One of the grisliest examples suggests that sons learn violence from their fathers: When Mrs. Blaska summons the nerve to leave her husband, he uses her love for her sons to "coax" her back. After she is found dead, "stripped naked, in the open chicken yard," her husband admits he whipped her. "She started to run away again and, handicapped by his crutch, he sent her sons to bring her back. They held her while he pounded her" (412). Although Sandoz respects her mother and other pioneer women, she presents their lives as violent and circumscribed and the frontier marriage as institutionalizing male power; Mr. Blaska considers his behavior "every husband's right." Sandoz never suggests that Jules or the other men are mentally ill, nor that their behavior is motivated by their personal lives. The causes for their brutality lie in their society's attitudes about women and marriage. The conflict between men and women is clearly unequal, and the women's physical victimization symbolizes the social and institutional power men hold over them. Sandoz implies that there were two Wests, her father's and her mother's, one characterized by the qualities of Frederick Jackson Turner's classic description of power, freedom, and vision, the other by powerlessness, fear, and accommodation.

As these few quotations suggest, *Old Jules* is a powerful and disturbing book. I was initially interested in Sandoz's book for its historical evocation of time and place: She was born the same year as my grandfather and grew up only a few hundred miles from his birthplace. I imagined my great-

grandfather as another Old Jules, training his sons to behave like the
Blaska boys and saw my grandfather's behavior as the inevitable consequence of the society in which he was reared. But I soon realized that
Sandoz's story was really about the teller, that she had not resolved her
feelings about her father and mother. For me, *Old Jules* came to be the
story of Sandoz's uncertainty about whether to identify with her father's
or her mother's West, her ambivalent attachment to, admiration for, and
fear of each parent shaping her narrative. I know now that I attended
carefully to Sandoz's conflicted feelings, overlooked by other critics, because I too had been unable to resolve my own feelings about my grandfather and grandmother. I didn't project my feelings onto her, but she
allowed me to externalize them, to examine them in another guise.

Throughout her book, Sandoz shows how she was forced during her
childhood to take on a woman's responsibilities while being confronted
with her community's attitudes about women. She recognizes that she is
identified with her mother and what womanhood will bring her when
Jules, unable to beat the pregnant Mary, turned to his daughter as substitute and "whipped [her] until he was breathless" (279). Yet Sandoz
eventually comes to blame her mother for attempting to make her into a
copy of her own victimized self. She characterizes Mary as resenting her
husband's behavior and her own powerlessness, but as expecting and even
forcing her daughter to accept her own burdened and unrespected role.
Mary Sandoz had an idea of what it meant to be a woman, and she tried to
pass it on to her daughter; Sandoz could not see that had Mary not done
so, she would have undermined her own life.

Yet it is easy to understand why the daughter rejects her mother's
powerlessness in search of her own self-esteem and identifies with her
father's West. She sees as the central difference between her parents that
her mother "preferred the smaller, the more familiar things, while her
Jules saw only the far, the large, the exalted canvas" (191). Recognizing
her kinship to her mother, she finds her life filled with situations to avoid,
not to aspire to. She presents pioneer women as heroic within their
obvious limitations, as making "the best of the situation," but their lives
are filled with drudgery.[3] Her "visionary" father's dying words to her
reveal what kind of esteem she can expect—from herself and others—so
long as she remains woman-identified: " 'There is nobody to carry on my
work. . . . If [Mari] was a man she might—as a woman she is not worth a
damn' " (418). Forced to see women as deficient, desiring her father's
freedom, his imagination, his defiant and stubborn self-confidence, his
reknown—all traits promised to the western male—Sandoz turns away

from women in her later histories to explore the classic masculine West and its themes, to what she calls "the romantic days."[4]

I had done this myself, though my dissertation's title suggests that I had already begun to see, as indeed Sandoz had, some of the problems with the masculine western myths: "The Frontier Self: Freedom and Its Limitations." Sandoz revealed to me my own rebellious feelings about being a woman, my desire to escape from what I unconsciously defined as a confined life. She and I followed the pattern of many other successful women writers, which Carolyn Heilbrun describes in *Reinventing Womanhood*: "those women who did have the courage, self-confidence and autonomy to make their way in the male-dominated world did so by identifying themselves with male ideals and role models . . . by not identifying themselves . . . as women."[5] I differed from Sandoz, however, in that I defined myself as a feminist, and I *thought* I was woman-identified. It seemed healthy and natural to resist victimization, so powerfully symbolized by physical abuse. Yet I didn't realize that I was resisting much more than that until I found myself profoundly moved and disturbed by a fine essay by another western feminist, "Eve among the Indians," in which Dawn Lander describes her own "liberated" childhood in the West:

> I did not identify myself with houses, churches, and fences. I loved to be outdoors. I loved the space, energy and passion of the landscape. . . . Repeatedly, however, I could find no place for myself and for my pleasure in the wilderness in the traditionally recorded images of women on the frontier. Tradition gives us the figure of a woman, strong, brave and often heroic, whose endurance and perseverance are legendary. It may seem strange that I find it difficult to identify with this much-praised figure. But I can almost hear her teeth grinding behind her tight-set lips; her stiff spine makes me tired and her clenched fists sad. Victimization and martyrdom are the bone and muscle of every statue, picture and word portrait of a pioneer woman. She is celebrated because she stoically transcended a situation she never would have freely chosen. She submits to the wilderness just as—supposedly—she submits to sex. But she needn't enjoy it, and her whole posture is in rigid opposition to the wilderness experience: to the land, to the Indians. Her glory, we are told, is that she carried the family, religion, fences, the warmth of the hearth and steaming washtubs inviolate to the middle of the American desert.[6]

Initially I felt as if Lander voiced my own feelings as a well-read western tomboy who had always felt ill at ease with party dresses and social engagements—my own versions of her "churches and fences." We had felt the same frustration with the Molly Woodses and Miss Watsons our literary tradition had given us as female models; naturally we had both hungered to be Huck. Our literary tradition, as Judith Fetterley has demonstrated, had demanded of us that we identify with a selfhood that defined itself in opposition to us, and we had responded by resisting the stereotype of the civilizing woman, by attempting to claim male territory as our own.[7] Our feminism had led us to seek—and discover—women writers who themselves resisted the stereotype.

Yet something always nagged at me about Lander's response. It had to do with that single phrase "the warmth of the hearth," which she uses so ironically. This was not an institutional image but one that inevitably recalled for me the female body and its capacity for nurturance and "warmth," which I couldn't help but link to female values by turning the phrase into "the warmth of the heart." Lander's irony pained me, and I gradually realized that it seemed to me self-hating, that she—and I, and Sandoz—had too readily accepted the denigration of female values inherent in the stereotypes of our western myths, that her anger at the stereotype, like Sandoz's rejection of her mother, suggested an unwillingness to acknowledge and seek to understand the limitations in our mothers' lives. Mary Sandoz and many other pioneer women did grind their teeth and clench their fists; if my own grandmother occasionally acted like a fearful victim, she had good cause.

When I got this far—not nearly far enough, as some of you will have noticed—I wrote the essay about Sandoz I have summarized.[8] My conclusions tied in nicely with what were then, and continue to be, central questions in western women's history: Did the frontier liberate women, as Turner and many other historians allege it liberated men? Sandoz and many other contemporary feminist historians would clearly answer no; several important books and essays have argued that the pioneer woman went West reluctantly and analyzed why.[9] These historians portray western women in terms of what Lander claims is a stereotype created by men; like Sandoz, they suggest that most women "made the best of the situation," that their heroism is characterized, largely, by endurance and innovation within constraints. My reading and my experience had taught me that many pioneer women had indeed been victims of men, of male violence, but I sought a different personal response than those of Sandoz and Lander. My rhetoric was pretty dramatic, I now see:

It is natural for feminist scholars who yearn, like Sandoz and Lander, for the freedom promised the frontiersman to search for women who share their feelings of rebellion because the promise of the frontier is, after all, a *human* fantasy. But as feminists we must not purchase our self-esteem—our freedom—at our mothers' expense, or, as [the passage I quoted from Nancy] Chodorow suggests, we will turn against our very selves.[10]

I hid my personal response in a universal "we," just as I stated my final declaration abstractly (even quoting an authority): *Old Jules* "reveals the difficulties of writing about women while aspiring to male freedom and the importance, in Heilbrun's words, of learning to aspire '*as women*, supporting other women, identifying with them, and imagining the achievement of women generally.'"[11] That sounds pretty good. But it *was* an abstract response and not an emotional one; I had intellectually acknowledged my—or rather "our"—affinities but I had not felt them. I could see the difficulties Sandoz had had, and I admitted that her confusion was shared by many female scholars, but I had not overcome my own difficulties. I could see how my experience, and particularly my literary tradition, had led me to be male-identified. I could empathize abstractly with women's victimization, but it would still take me a while to imagine and redefine the achievement of women.

Although I removed my personal story from my published essay, I manipulated essays with it when I presented my research at conferences, telling the story about my grandfather with which I began this essay, a story that inevitably charms the audience into smiling at the familiar image of this endearing American tale-teller and then smacks them with his violence. Sometimes I passed around a favorite photo of mine: with the bare California foothills in the background, I, aged one, sit atop a horse; my grandfather, tanned, shirtless, blue-jeaned and booted, ready to catch me if I fall. I was quite aware of the power of this manipulative story, and I milked it. Yet it is also an honest story, focused as it is on my grandfather and then on me and my response. It took me too long to realize that there was a silenced person in the story, someone who got left out, the person who told the truth: my mother.

But I'm getting ahead of myself. My mother's voice came to me a year later, as I typed the conclusion to another paper on violence, in a digression that started out as yet another retelling of the story about my grandfather. I didn't want to write another paper about violence; it was depressing and disturbing, and my grandparents were both dead. But I saw that Sandoz had turned away from the subject too readily, had escaped too quickly. Learning from her example, I began to think about other western books and to look for links. I realized that it was daughters who broke the silence, who wrote autobiographical narratives about their pioneer mothers' victimization. While researching the Sandoz paper, I had asked several social scientists, experts on violence against women, about studies on the effect of such violence on daughters, and received no suggestions. Not surprisingly, the research has until recently concentrated on men, on how sons of abusers become abusers themselves. Obviously this is useful research, but it does not address the psychological consequences for women who grow up watching their mothers be victimized. How would that affect a girl's self-esteem? Was Sandoz typical in her response? It did not occur to me to wonder if my mother was typical in *her* response.

My second essay, "Violence against Women in Literature of the Western Family," explores the autobiographical narratives of four western women: Sandoz's *Old Jules,* Agnes Smedley's *Daughter of Earth,* Tillie Olsen's *Yonnondio,* and Meridel Le Sueur's *The Girl.*[12] The conclusion of these writers that violence against women is the result of patriarchal definitions of gender and marriage rather than of individual pathology anticipates the analysis of the most recent feminist scholars, and the first part of my essay explores this point in detail. But I eventually focused on what the books themselves stress: the effect of the violence on the mothers' lives and how watching a mother become a victim of male aggression affects a daughter's complex identification with and resistance to her mother's life. The books reveal the struggles women face growing up female in a world where women are victimized and devalued.

Sandoz, Smedley, Olsen, and Le Sueur describe how daughters see their mothers' self-esteem, independence, and even identity sapped; vulnerable and intimidated, each woman is effectively silenced, her anger buried under compliance. Violent and sexual incidents reveal to the daughters what it is to be a woman and demonstrate their ties to their mothers. Often identifying for a time with their fathers, whom they see as colorful, daring, and creative, the daughters resist but finally come to understand themselves through their mothers' lives. To understand their conflicts, I turned to feminist theorists such as Adrienne Rich, Nancy Chodorow, and Carol Gilligan, who have explored the psychic connections between mothers and daughters. I cannot discuss the details here, but it seemed to me that some of the daughters suffered from what Rich calls "matrophobia": the fear "of becoming one's mother . . . the splitting of the self, in the desire to become purged once and for all of our mothers' bondage."[13] She argues that daughters often see their mothers as representing "the victim in ourselves," as "having taught compromise and self-hatred," as "the one through whom the restrictions and degradations of a female existence" are passed on (238, 237). Such a response is obviously exacerbated by the presence of such a dominating symbol of women's "restrictions and degradations" as physical violence. The need to escape that image of what it is to be a woman leads some daughters to self-hatred and to rejection of their own womanhood, like Smedley's heroine Marie Rogers who "hated [herself] most of all for having been born a woman" (137). "I would not be a woman," she thinks, "I would not" (148–49).

The struggle to free themselves from their mothers' role as victim also causes some daughters confusion about women's values. "Love and tenderness and duty belong to women and to weaklings in general. . . . Love and tenderness meant only pain and suffering and defeat," thinks Marie Rogers, planning to have "none of them" (136, 148). While I myself was struggling with these issues, Carol Gilligan published In a Different Voice, in which she demonstrates how those qualities which Marie believes make women victims are actually psychological strengths, deriving from a young girl's feeling of "attachment" to her mother.[14] She confirmed my feeling that the patterns I've described lead women to attempt to separate themselves not only from their mothers but also from "the warmth of the hearth" and what it implies. Like many other feminist writers, I began to see that in attempting to demonstrate how women had been victimized and to claim male territory as our own—the initial stages of feminist inquiry—feminists like myself had failed to do what Heilbrun suggests: to "imagin[e] the achievement of women generally." I paused to write an essay on Le Sueur, whose narrator in The Girl knows that she will discover truths about her own identity from her mother's experience. She goes to her mother, knowing the mother "would tell [her] something," and comes back a "different person": "I was into my mama's life for the first time, and knew how she all the time, chased like a pack of wolves, kept us alive, fierce and terrible. . . . Mama had a secret. She let me feel it, let me know it" (40, 45). The mother's "secret" is a "fierce" attachment to others; when the girl realizes that her own capacity for nurturance, for the "love and tenderness" Marie Rogers sees as leading inevitably to "pain and suffering and defeat," is her "treasure," she thinks, "I felt like mama" (134). In a visionary ending about the birth of a girl attended by several midwives, Le Sueur asserts that women's devalued strengths can and will prevail. Although I resisted then—and to some degree still resist—the optimism of this vision, Le Sueur helped me to see the importance of reclaiming the values Marie's experience taught her to reject. More personally, she forced me to think about the connections between my mother's feelings and my own—and to value them.[15]

This is a lesson all of the daughters learn, for ultimately they cannot—and will not—separate themselves from their mothers, whom they associate with life and with their very selfhood, as Olsen shows:

> The fingers stroked, spun a web, cocooned Mazie into happiness and intactness and selfness. Soft wove the bliss round hurt and fear and want and shame—the old worn fragile bliss, a new frail selfness bliss, healing, transforming. Up from the grasses, from the earth, from the broad tree trunk at their back, latent life streamed and seeded. The air and self shone boundless. Absently, her mother stroked; stroked unfolding, wingedness, boundlessness. (119)

Although she sees her mother's life as "so cruel . . . so ugly," Mazie comes to feel the beauty in the world through her mother's nurturing. And Olsen comes to write a famous story, "I Stand Here Ironing," in which a mother meditates about her love for her daughter and guilt over her inability to protect her from the pain of being a woman.

The authors come to various and often not wholly adequate solutions to the blurring of personality Rich describes, but they never resemble the daughters who find it "easier by far to hate and reject a mother outright than to see beyond her to the forces acting upon her" (237). Partially through naming these forces, each author bears testimony to her inability to separate herself from her mother and to her belief that her mother's life had value. Each carries a central painful image of her mother in her mind. "Her tears . . . they embittered my life!" says Marie Rogers (32). "Mama wept all night," says Le Sueur's narrator (31). Olsen's Mazie sees her mother's "head bent over her sewing in the attitude of a woman weeping" (16). Seeking to break out of the mold of the weeping woman, they find that they cannot ignore their mothers' stories. As another western woman writer, Mary Austin, said in describing "the unwiped tears on [her] mother's face" when a friend came in the night "with a great bloody bruise on her face": "Somebody must say these things."[16] No woman can speak fully and completely for another, but these daughters do the best they can to give voice to their mother's experiences. They attempt to end the silencing.

Reading these books gave me a different ending to my neat little story about how I learned about storytelling from my grandfather. The women writers, the daughters, showed me how I had missed the point. My mother told me the secrets she and my grandmother had kept for thirty-five years, yet I used these secrets not to understand their lives but to explore my continued identification with my grandfather, to evade the most painful identification a woman experiences. Like Smedley's Marie Rogers, I learned—at first and unconsciously—that because I am a woman there is "something wrong with me . . . something too deep even to cry about" (12). I did not conceal the story, but like Sandoz I thought it was about the man, and I could not see that the story was really about the teller, my mother, about her deep, abiding attachment to my grandmother and how it affected her feelings about herself. I could not see that that attachment and the feelings and values it expresses were the richest "secret" my mother had to give me, that her story was meant to let me know—finally—that a woman's strengths—nurturance, love, interdependence, vulnerability—make her, in Le Sueur's word, a "treasure." Although I am a feminist, I rendered my foremothers invisible and thoughtlessly covered up the real costs of abuse of women.

I can remember the pain I felt when I first wrote that final sentence two years ago. But confessions mean little in isolation, and although I was ready to "say these things," I was still attempting to distance myself from the emotional implications of what I had discovered. Preparing to present my paper at the Women's West conference that year, I told myself that, like my mother, I am a very private person, and I would not cry when I got to the paper's conclusion. I was determined to resist the image of the weeping woman. Yet as I neared the end of my talk, I saw a woman in the audience begin to cry, making no effort to wipe the tears that welled out of her large, brown eyes. Certain that her tears were in response to her own experience, that she had confronted violence in her own or her mother's life, I began to cry in response to her tears. In front of sixty-five people, I cried for her, for my mother, for my grandmother, for myself, and for what connected us all. (The brown-eyed woman later told me that she had never experienced violence, but cried because she identified with the pain of the women I discussed—and with my own.)

I made this public emotional acknowledgment of my failure to understand nearly two years ago, but I did not tell my mother about my tears or about my essay. Like her, I find secrets tempting to keep. I was afraid that she would feel I had exposed her, afraid of the anger I know she too often has been unable to express, afraid that she, who has often claimed not to understand my essays, would not understand. I thought I would wait until the essay, dedicated to her and my grandmother, was published, and when it was published I decided to wait until I saw her. I took it with me on the next trip—and I couldn't find the right moment. I was afraid, really, of acknowledging the connections between us. Finally a friend, Barbara White, told me that though she too thought it might upset my mother, it was clear that I was going to send it someday so I might as well send it now. Knowing that there are things that Barbara regrets having left unsaid to her own mother, now dead, I mailed the essay that same day.

A few days later my mother called from California. "I got your essay," she said neutrally. "It seemed from your note that you'd been afraid to send it to me. Why?"

"Oh, I was afraid you'd be upset that I'd told your secrets."

"I think it's important for somebody to say these things, and I really understood what you were saying," she said. "I spent the afternoon crying. I'm so proud of you. I only wish your grandmother were still alive."

Starting to cry, as she was, I said, "That means so much to me. I wanted you to know that you and Grandma were in my mind while I was writing it. I wanted you to know that I've tried to understand."

As I have written these essays on violence, I have often thought in terms of how much the work was costing me emotionally, but in reading a recent essay by Bell Gale Chevigny, I realized more fully that it was my resistance, and not my conclusions, that was costly and painful. "Our difficulty in knowing our mothers dominates us as daughters and, to some extent, blocks our growth and self-knowledge," she writes.[17] Unconsciously acknowledging this "costly ignorance," women choose a subject

that symbolically reflects their internalized relations with their mothers and that offers them an opportunity to re-create those relations. . . . [T]he act of daughters writing about (foremothers) is likely to be, on some level, an act of retrieval that is experienced as rescue. When the work is more intensely experienced as rescue, the fantasy of reciprocal reparations is likely to become an underlying impulse in it. That is, in the rescue—the reparative interpretation and re-creation—of a woman who was neglected or misunderstood, we may be seeking indirectly the reparative rescue of ourselves, in the sense of coming to understand and accept ourselves better. In writing about our foremothers, we can be prepared to experience the specific nature for each of us of the mother-daughter dynamic, but we cannot be fully forearmed. My own experience suggests that some of our deeper motives will emerge only when the work is done. (375–76)

Chevigny's description of the feminist writer's need to establish "reciprocal reparations" recalled for me the efforts of Mary Austin's mother to bandage her friend's bruised face, the efforts of battered mothers and daughters to salve each others' wounds. All women share such wounds, whether physical or emotional, literal or symbolic. As Chevigny implies, the act of reading and writing about women leads us to rediscover the bonds that allow us to rescue and repair our selves.

Yet Chevigny is right that we can never be fully forearmed, that our motives require continual reassessment. One day almost two weeks ago as I sat making lists about what I wanted to say in this essay, I thought about my mother's comment that she wished my grandmother were still alive to read the essay I dedicated to her. As my mind wandered inevitably back to my grandfather, I realized that still, after all this, *I* wished *he* were alive to read it, that still I needed to communicate with him. After a few painful hours of soul-searching, I decided that while it would be too bad to end where I began, with my grandfather, I would have to conclude my essay with this admission. Now, only a short time later, writing this essay has made me realize—emotionally and not merely intellectually—that he isn't my audience any longer. In telling my story I've tried to attend to and tell my mother's story, to claim and be proud of—and no longer keep secret—my connections to her. To you, Mom.

Notes

1. "Melodramas of Beset Manhood: How Theories of American Fiction Exclude Women Authors," *American Quarterly* (Summer 1981): 123–39. As this point suggests, stories, histories, and critical theories about this rebellious western male have often been claimed to reveal America's "collective" fantasies, fantasies in which women are forced to take the role of the implicit antagonists to the story's values. I focus on western literature in this essay largely because I was raised a westerner and identified myself with qualities in my grandfather that my culture had taught me to see as "western": these personal facts led me to do my research on western literature. Yet because this western story has received so much critical attention, because the Natty Bumppos, Davy Crocketts, Huck Finns, Butch Cassidys, John Waynes, and Ben Cartwrights have so dominated our cultural myths, it is a particularly apt myth to explore for its power in shaping gender attitudes. If the women I discuss are right, that abuse of women was generally accepted and widespread in the West, then we must question whether, if these men had been presented in fuller and more realistic relations to women, we might discover that they too took for granted a patriarchal authority that sanctioned abuse of women.

2. Sandoz, *Old Jules* (1935; reprint ed., Lincoln: University of Nebraska Press, 1962), pp. 406 and 4. Page numbers follow subsequent quotations in the text.

3. Sandoz, "Pioneer Women," an unpublished essay excerpted in Mari Sandoz, *Hos-*

tiles and Friendlies, ed. Virginia Faulkner (Lincoln: University of Nebraska Press, 1959), p. 60.

4. "Pioneer Women," p. 59.

5. Heilbrun, *Reinventing Womanhood* (New York: W.W. Norton, 1979), p. 31.

6. In *The Authority of Experience: Essays in Feminist Criticism,* ed. Arlyn Diamond and Lee R. Edwards (Amherst: University of Massachusetts Press, 1977), pp. 195–96.

7. Fetterley explores this point in *The Resisting Reader: A Feminist Approach to American Literature* (Bloomington: University of Indiana Press, 1978).

8. Graulich, "Every Husband's Right: Sex Roles in Mari Sandoz's *Old Jules,*" *Western American Literature* 18 (May 1983): 3–20.

9. For a fuller discussion of this point and a list of the relevant historians, see "Every Husband's Right."

10. "Every Husband's Right," p. 19, where I discuss Chodorow more fully; generally I quoted her to show the problems girls face in developing self-esteem in a society that forces them to devalue their mothers.

11. "Every Husband's Right," p. 20. The Heilbrun quote is from *Reinventing Womanhood,* p. 32.

12. In *Frontiers* 7, no. 3 (1984): 14–20. This essay is also forthcoming in *The Women's West,* ed. Susan Armitage and Elizabeth Jameson (University of Oklahoma Press). In summarizing some of the conclusions from this essay, I have been forced to simplify them and to leave out others altogether; naturally the complete essay provides fuller and more subtle analysis, interdisciplinary sources, and much more complete support. Page numbers are taken from the following editions: Smedley, *Daughter of Earth* (1929; reprint ed., New York: Feminist Press, 1976); Olsen, *Yonnondio: From the Thirties* (New York: Dell, 1974; written between 1932 and 1937); and Le Sueur, *The Girl* (Minneapolis: West End Press, 1978; written in 1939).

13. Rich, *Of Woman Born* (New York: Bantam, 1976), pp. 237–38. Page numbers follow subsequent quotations in the text.

14. Gilligan, *In a Different Voice* (Cambridge: Harvard University Press, 1982).

15. I presented my as-yet-unpublished essay on Le Sueur, " 'For What Is One Voice Alone': Separation and Connection in Meridel Le Sueur's *The Girl,*" to a session of the Western Literature Association in St. Paul, Minnesota, in October 1984. In it I discuss the relationship of the Demeter/Persephone myth, so widely discussed in feminist literary theory, to violence against women.

16. Austin, *Earth Horizon* (Boston: Houghton Mifflin, 1932), p. 142.

17. Chevigny, "Daughters Writing: Toward a Theory of Women's Biography," in *Between Women,* ed. Carol Ascher, Louise DeSalvo, and Sara Ruddick (Boston: Beacon Press, 1984), p. 372. Page numbers follow the other quotation in the text.

The Scarlet Brewer and the Voice of the Colonized

*

Shirley Geok-lin Lim

I was eleven when I had my first poetry reading. Sister Finigan read my poem to my absent mother aloud to the Standard Six class. Rumors went around that my essay on a day in the life of a cock had been read to the senior students, the Form Five class in the new building across the street. When I was twelve and a Form One student in one of the ground floor classrooms in the new building, I had a poem published in the *Malacca Times*. I received ten Malaysian dollars for it and immediately spent the entire sum on noodles, ice-cream, sour plums, and dried orange peel which I shared with my second brother who had mailed the poem for me. Do all writers find their beginnings in such minor triumphs, hedged by school-day tyrannies, poverty, and the almost palpable presence of a community?

At twelve, the inchoate desire to write poetry that probably characterizes the unhappy childhoods of many withdrawn insatiable readers focused itself on a book. Somewhere among the Convent School's mildewed books sent by missionary agents in Ireland was a red linen-bound copy of R. F. Brewer's *The Art of Versification and the Technicalities of Poetry*. In fact, in later life I had misremembered the book, confusing it with George Saintsbury's better known *Historical Manual of English Prosody*. Before writing this essay on intellectual memory, I walked along the library stacks in search of the 1910 edition of Saintsbury's *History*. Instead I found the unevenly aged scarlet cloth-cover of Brewer's book and recognized it immediately, despite the almost thirty-five intervening years.

Published in 1931, this University of California copy is almost an exact replica of the one the twelve-year-old child took to bed with her. I remember the heavy yellowing paper with its uneven cut edges, the ornate character of the large print, the skinnier italics, and the plainer appearance of the reduced print used for the verse selections. Especially, I remember the magisterial categorization. Under "Kinds of Poetry," Lyric divides into Ode, Ballad, Hymn and Song, and Elegy; then there are Epic or Heroic, Dramatic, Descriptive, Didactic, the Sonnet and the Epigram. Who would undertake today to lay before us such a simple and grand sweep of poetry, a sweep that ignores *vers libre*, the major domain of the idiosyncratic and of the American transatlantic speaking voice? No wonder as a university woman I had suppressed memory of Brewer and chose instead to reconstruct the more liberal Saintsbury as my saint of poetic form.

Yet Saintsbury was himself influenced by Brewer, whose work he lists in his bibliography. This scarlet book of my childhood had first been issued in 1869 as *Manual of English Poetry* (the only book in Saintsbury's bibliography with the word "Manual" in its title, indicating perhaps its prominent influence on Saintsbury's later historical study, *Historical Manual of English Prosody*). Brewer's *Manual* was enlarged and reissued as *Orthometry* in 1893, and it was this late nineteenth-century version, essentially the same except in a new scarlet suit, that had enthralled me in my precocious preadolescence.

Remembering the many books that have found a permanent home in my life, I suddenly see myself as a basket case. Reliquaries held sacred by British imperialists are scattered like altar figures in a shambling cavern, one lit by faith as much as by skepticism. Shakespeare's plays, every single one of them, published in tissue-thin paper in a collected edition that somehow found its way to the school library. I remember best the poems that filled the back of the volume, although to an Asian child in the tropics, "When icicles hang on the wall / And Dick the shepherd blows his nail" must remain at best exotic words on the page. For me, English words, lines of English poetry, seemed to glow in the brain even in the brightest of languid steamy afternoons.

There were also, in a book-poor community, numerous copies of Everyman's Classics and Oxford University Press World Classics, among them Oliver Goldsmith's *The Deserted Village, The Poetical Works of Gray and Collins,* and Lord Alfred Tennyson's *Selected Poems.* These were required Senior Cambridge Examination texts in the 1940s and 1950s, part of that British literature canon schoolchildren in every British colony would have to master if they hoped to succeed in the colonial administration. Ibo and

Yoruba, Ghanaian and Egyptian, Tamil, Punjabi, Bengali, Ceylonese, Burmese, Malay, and Chinese studied this canon in order to get on in the British Empire. We studied mysterious volumes in which alien humans wandered through mossy churchyards, stood under strange trees called elms and yewtrees, suffered from dark, cold, gloom, and chills, and hailed "the splendour of the sun" (*Poems of Lord Alfred Tennyson* 242). Pacing the walled garden of the Buddhist temple to which I escaped from the disheveled two bedroom shack in which my five brothers and I barely breathed, in the near ninety degree glare of the equatorial sun from which there was no escape until swift night at 6 P.M., I somehow made out the sturdy figures of the English language under the encrustments of Victorian ethnocentric sentimentality.

That is, thinking hard now through layers of early colonized consciousness—the girl-child saw something in the poems beyond the cultural differences that eluded her imagination. This something was what Brewer's *Orthometry* made manifest for me: the mysterious English poetry of the British imperialists was laid bare for me in this revolutionary red book as the bones of craft. Brewer's book of forms demythologized once and for all that literary culture the English taught colonized native children to memorize and fear. Through Brewer, Gray's stanzas written in a country churchyard lost their awesome alienness. Deconstructed as prosody, they reemerged as iambic pentameters in rhymed quatrains, or as Brewer categorizes them, "Four heroics rhyming alternately . . . [to] constitute the Elegiac stanza" (73).

The simple naming of craft as craft unweighted the imperialism in English poetry and sent it floating deliriously within my grasp. What Brewer's *Art of Versification* proved to me was that the English language was not a natural possession of the English people; like me, like every governed subject of King George V, English was also a language that the English had to learn. English poets learned from other poets; there were versions, variations, imitations, parodies; they borrowed the rondel, the rondeau, and the sestina from the French and the Italians. English poems were not acts of inspired imagination issuing spontaneously from English genius and yielding their meaning only to like spirits. Instead they were mindful things constructed out of reading, observation, care, learning, and play with language and form. According to Brewer's late nineteenth-century primer, English poetry was socially constructed, not innately inherent in race and genius. The respect for craft that breathes in a book of forms, as in Karl Shapiro's *Prosody Handbook*, is also the respect for any reader who will study it.

The clarifying idea that an English poem can be understood because it is written as language using known traditions of expression was revolutionary in a time when literature teachers arriving fresh from Cambridge and Oxford warned students against studying English literature. Was it Mr. Piggott or Mr. Price and does it matter who said with helpful concern, "You haven't grown up in the British Isles—it's impossible for you to get the idioms of the Lake District to appreciate Wordsworth." Or Scottish dialect to understand Burns. Midlands speech for Hardy. British history for Shakespeare. English gentility for Austen. In short, although we were compelled to study this foreign literature and were judged civilized by our ability to write in this foreign language about this foreign literature, the iron bar Mr. Piggott, Mr. Price, and all the other colonial university teachers raised before us was that English literature was really only for the English people.

The triple bind of force-fed colonial literature, cultural imperialism, and denigration of ability has only begun to loosen in ex-British colonies. But iron and bondage will produce their own kind of revenge. Today, generations of colonial peoples are writing in English, warping it into their own instruments, producing other traditions, the way the Miltonic sonnet evolved from the Petrarchan Italian, the way that Marilyn Hacker's sonnets evolve from the English. Wole Soyinka, Chinua Achebe, Bessie Head, Narudin Farrah, R. K. Narayan, Salmon Rushdie, Bharati Mukherjee—these are the illustrious non-English names that appear in English-language literature from Africa, India, Pakistan. But the postcolonial canon is more than those admitted by Anglos into their mainstream. It is the numerous nodes of writing in English produced by local national writers, read perhaps only by their local national audiences, the entire rhizomous planet of minorities, as Deleuze and Guattari would argue, replacing the hegemonic and hierarchical world view of the imperialists.

To my young mind, Brewer's *Orthometry* displayed the human skeleton of poetry; it deflated the Occidental Mystique of English Culture and offered in its place a material body of social language, although one mediated through measures of syllables, interruptions of caesura, waverings between perfect and imperfect rhymes.

I can no longer read the scarlet Brewer with the intense pleasure of a child discovering the secret of adult power. Brewer's choice of lines and stanzas come too heavily freighted now with my own adult sense of power, the solid materially inclined intelligence occluding the mere sensory motions of sound and music. Brewer, I see all too clearly, was a Victorian patriarch. While he approached poetry seriously, it was for him a moral and emotional helpmate, a feminine sublime, the way repressed men want their wives to be: full of good feeling, good judgment, beautiful shape. His selected passages expressed narrowly prescribed ideals of elevated emotion and noble thought: "There is a pleasure in the pathless woods" [Byron, cited in Brewer 182]; "Small service is true service, while it lasts: / Of friends, however humble, scorn not one; / The daisy by the shadow that it casts, / Protects the lingering dewdrop from the sun" [Wordsworth, cited in Brewer 142]. Through bitter intelligence, I see how Brewer took strong poems and inevitably extracted their safest pulp. No wonder then that after twelve, I never returned to the book again.

Why have I picked this antiquarian volume as a foundational piece in my biography of mind? Probably to remind myself that a colonized childhood is composed of strange accidents of isolation and community; that, like Robinson Crusoe on a deserted island, a chest can wash to shore and we can find unexpected help—a book, published in Edinburgh in 1931 and read by the loneliest child in Malacca (or so I imagined myself to be), and leading her to believe that the English language could be as much hers as anyone's. Claiming English as my own was my first step out of the iron cage and into a voice, and who is to say it is not my language and not my voice?

References

Brewer, R. F. *The Art of Versification and the Technicalities of Poetry.* Edinburgh: John Grant, 1931.

Deleuze, Gilles, and Felix Guattari. "What is a Minor Literature?" *Mississippi Review* 11, no. 3 (1983): 13–33.

Gray, Thomas. *The Poetical Works of Gray and Collins.* Ed. Austin Lane Poole. London: Oxford University Press, 1950.

Saintsbury, George. *Historical Manual of English Prosody.* 1st pub. 1910. New York: Schocken, 1966.

Shapiro, Karl, and Robert Beum. *A Prosody Handbook.* New York: Harper & Row, 1965.

Tennyson, Alfred. *Poems of Lord Alfred Tennyson.* Oxford: London, 1950.

Dividing

Fences

*

Carol S. Taylor

Growing up Jim Crow

One of the most haunting images of my childhood memories involves two brick buildings: a school for the black students and one for the whites situated within viewing distances diagonally across the street from each other. I remember that during recess time, I could hear the faint voices of the white children at play and occasionally wondered what they were like. Seldom did our paths cross in the small rural, predominantly black community of Meridian, Oklahoma. The few white families that lived in the township (most lived in the outlying countryside) appeared to maintain some position of power. Indeed the bank, post office, and general store were managed by whites and many of the black kids were taught "to put their best foot forward" when entering these places.

Territorial boundaries were clearly demarcated in those days. Seldom did the two schools intrude upon each other's space. On several occasions the blacks played the whites in a game of softball. The statement, "We gone play the white kids today!" expressed our nervous anticipation about entering their boundaries. The game was played on their turf, never ours. Indeed, they were polite under the circumstances. But when one little black child enrolled in their school due to a dispute his grandparents had had with one of the black teachers, he was called a "nigger" and forced to experience a morally degrading isolation that no child should ever have to endure.

Today in my hometown, the two buildings no longer are used for educational purposes; the children are bused to the schools of an adjacent community. Years have passed since those days of de jure segregation. Yet blacks and whites remain conscious of racial boundaries, the fences that continue to divide us.

Although the concept of race as applied to humans no longer has a biological basis,[1] the term is loaded with social and political ramifications. For African Americans the historical notion, "Be a credit to your race" continues to be preached by the elders to the youths. This saying, connected with notions of progress in a white world, assumes that every individual achievement by a black American connotes racial advancement. Race is a metaphor for supposed difference and otherness, as well as "insiderness" and membership. The statements, "You know how they are," and "never let white people know what you're thinking" denote otherness. Conversely the sayings, "you know how my people are," and "we try to keep each other down" indicate sameness and group affiliation. Race serves as a frame for meaningful experience and determines the structure of various texts.

Zora Neale Hurston recalls her examination room in a white doctor's office in Brooklyn as being a closet where the soiled linen was picked up for laundering. The elegant decor that captures Hurston's eye when she initially enters the premises of the office serves as a backdrop for the desultory examination that quickly follows (163). The title of this autobiographical essay, "My Most Humiliating Jim Crow Experience," suggests that Hurston had encountered similar affronts. For Richard Wright in "The Ethics of Living Jim Crow," the ultimate violation of this system, particularly for black males, is the demeaning, "Uncle-Tomish masks" they are forced to wear when they encounter whites, the smiles that must exude from their faces when the black woman is being harassed by white men, and the taciturn, invisible, seen-and-not-heard posture they are expected to maintain.

For me, the most painful incidents of Jim Crowism took place in the white hospital, the only medical facility nearby. When I was about nine years old, I had my tonsils removed and became very ill after the operation. Consequently, I remained in the hospital a day or two longer than normally required. My devoted mother who spent the nights by my bedside sleeping in the chair, came down with a cold when my bed was moved from my room to an extremely cold and drafty part of the hall. We spent a very uncomfortable night in this makeshift space so that a white woman who had been moved in my room could enjoy its comforts.

Mother developed serious bronchial problems thereafter and was ill for a long time. I felt responsible.

The ultimate example of injustice occurred in 1958 when my brother was bleeding internally and dying from stab wounds that were inflicted unexpectedly by another youth. Burning up with fever, he began to hallucinate and attempted to remove his clothes. The attending white physician, while calling him disparaging names, would have stricken him with his fist, but my father in a very calm and gentle manner reasoned with the doctor and made him come to his senses. Being a minister, my father's persuasive powers at the time must have been most convincing. I was a child when my father relayed this story to me. Yet today, I sometimes have nightmares about my dying brother's last attempts to hold onto life in the midst of undeniably hostile circumstances.

Standing in the Shadows

During my recent fieldwork activities in the Low Country area of South Carolina, I visited two of the many plantation homes that are listed with the National Register. Although the tours were conducted on separate occasions by different companies, I remember the unsettling feeling that remained with me while both guides presented their text on slavery. Indeed the juxtaposition of power between the slave master and slave was made real for me as I stood inside the big "white house" listening about the grand life of the privileged. What was most disturbing was that little, if anything, was said about the slaves they owned. The side doors that the servants once used to go about the place serving their masters were pointed out to the group. The slave quarters of both plantations were yet standing but hardly acknowledged by the guides. Not one had been restored to the point where tourists could view it from the inside. Entry into the slaves' world was precluded, and I was left with a bitter taste in my mouth.

After one of the tours was completed, two other black women in the group and I were so shaken by this omission that we felt compelled to leave the master's mansion and walk over to the servants' quarters. We peeked through the cracks of the boarded up windows, thereby getting a glimpse into the past to see what slave life might have been like. At the other plantation home, the servants' wing area was closed off; tourists could view it at a distance only from the balcony of the big house.

For me, the tourist industry's silencing of the slave voice is indicative of the disconcerting shadow of the Old South that yet emerges in various forms. For example on the top level of a two-story building located in the old historic district of Charleston is a sign that reads "The Daughters of the Confederacy" in exaggerated letters looming against a black background. The purpose of this part of the building was unclear to me given that the entrance into the place was locked. I was told that the building had sustained substantial damage from Hurricane Hugo. The lower level of the building, however, was a mini mall with various types of gift shops. Life here appeared to be business as usual. In one of the stores of Santee Village, just off I-95 South, are numerous mammy and sambo dolls, figurines, and flower pots. While outside the store, I asked two black women from the area, "Why do the blacks allow such disparaging stereotypes to be on display here?" They could not give me an answer.

Today, many communities in the low country area continue to be designated by specific plantation names, even those newly constructed posh dwellings on man-made islands where northerners have come to retire. The word "plantation" in this sense has a romantic, "Gone-With-the-Wind" appeal that is far from the harsh reality of hard work and hard times many blacks associate with the term. Artifacts from sea island culture lay unprotected amid the sand in the backyards of many new residents as a reminder of the indigenous population that is being uprooted.[2]

On one hand, I was elated to have the opportunity to research the traditions and history of those blacks who have given us the Brer Rabbit stories and countless other tales and lore. Conversely, I experienced anger, frustration, and despair for having to come face to face with a system that made little or no attempt to honor and preserve the voices of the slave, ex-slave, and their descendants.

Failure to acknowledge the black ancestral voices can be seen at other institutional levels. For example, the public school system in many parts of the country has been resistant to integrating black history and literature into its curriculum. Students, black and white, are completely unaware that a black canon exists. The study of black people remains a peripheral exercise to be conducted, if at all, only during black history month. The students that I get at the college level, many of whom are from all-white, small towns, are unaccustomed to even mentioning the word "race" in the classroom and thus are understandably resistant to the notion of writing and thinking about it in analytical terms. Tensions can emerge in a class such as freshman composition that historically contains only mainstream, hence "racially neutral," subject matter. An instructor who departs from the status quo may be jeopardizing her status among the students to the point of receiving some unfavorable evaluations.

The above scenario epitomizes the challenge that exists for those like myself who are engaged in reclaiming the legacy of what James Weldon Johnson refers to as those "Black and Unknown Bards." The actual difficulty of my task was made exceedingly clear when I spent numerous hours in the Charleston Historical Society trying to locate possibly relevant material for my project while mulling over cryptic journal entries written by planters. Someone of European descent would come in inquiring about an ancestor who migrated to America as early as the seventeenth century, and invariably there would be the needed resource material on the shelf. Because my ancestors were denied access to the written word, few were privileged enough to write about themselves or to even relate their story to some sympathetic soul (usually an abolitionist). A few of us may know a little about our slave or free-born ancestors, but for the majority of us, our past, particularly family histories, remains unwritten and inaccessible. Those old enough to remember being told about the ways of ex-slaves must contend with a younger generation who in an "integrated" school system is too embarrassed to be interested in their past and is either caught up in "making it" and "blending in" with white society or too full of despair and too degraded to even try. Hence, on one level, there is this imposed silence on the part of African Americans that could potentially erase the past from the collective memory. In an inimical world that automatically relegates the story of black Americans to a bastard position, the discovery of even the smallest shred of evidence concerning the lives and traditions of black folk, particularly those of black women, is nothing short of a triumph.

I am interested in texts created by black people and other marginalized groups. I use the term "created" rather than "written" because as a folklorist, many of the texts that I read are/were part of an oral tradition even though some of the materials may be included in a printed collection. For me, the traditional text primarily is generated as a group's response to a certain set of historical, social, psychological, and economic conditions that have some degree of impact upon the group. More specifically, a fundamental assumption for me when I read a text as a black female scholar is that oppressive systems such as slavery, institutionalized racism, sexism, and classism have had a significant impact upon the black psyche as well as white society. These forces have affected black women differently than they have black men. I am concerned with how these evils help to shape and mold the black creative imagination both collectively and individually. Given that blacks were taken from their native land, forced to learn a foreign tongue, and forced to endure the brutal sting of the slave whip, forced to submit to the capricious dictates of the slave master and mistress, the creative resources that emerged in the black community, aside from other influences, must have been as W. E. B. DuBois and James Weldon Johnson state the product of an indomitable spirit, a creative genius. Knowledge of the unwritten legacy my foremothers and forefathers left in the folktales, folksongs, family stories, proverbs, and superstitions can provide that historical link with the past so needed to make us whole.

"The Lord Will Make a Way Outa No Way"

Throughout the black community, at home, and at church, I would hear this saying or some variant form stated in a song, sermon, testimony, or just in a casual conversation. It was often used to console those experiencing unmitigated circumstances that seemed unbearable and/or to affirm one's personal faith in self, community, and God. My father, a Pentecostal minister who depended upon farming as a means of survival, would from time to time declare from the pulpit, "I am glad I'm poor." When a particular crop would fail to yield the needed income, or unfavorable weather conditions would cause him to get behind in his work, he would experience serious financial consequences. In order to legitimate his existence and way of life, he associated hard times with spiritual maturation and humility. "One who is poor will pray harder and look to God to make a way outa no way."

The meaning of this formula became clearer to me while doing my fieldwork in the South Carolina Sea Islands among the Gullah-speaking blacks. As I collected a number of stories about hardship, survival, and the supernatural, a common notion that emerged was how hard work had been central to the lives of many of the island women and that mastering techniques of survival was indeed essential to maintain even the most basic existence. Some, however, went mad in the process and gave up the struggle. One informant related to me a memory from her childhood. She once knew an old neighbor woman who was an ex-slave. The neighbor was so preoccupied with her past life as a slave that any time of the day you visited her, she randomly spoke about getting to the field before the master came. In her mind, she was not able to leave the plantation even though her people had been freed for over fifty years.

Mule work is synonymous with the black female experience. In her compelling life story, *You May Plow Here,* Sara Brooks, reflecting on her southern childhood, recalls the hard work that she, her girl cousins, and the male children in the family did in the field: "But we never was lazy cause we used to really work. We used to work like mens. Oh, fight sometime, fuss sometimes, but worked on" (39). In Zora Neale Hurston's *Their Eyes Were Watching God*, Nanny, an ex-slave, has come to accept the disproportionate distribution of power between white and black, male and female. In trying to convince her granddaughter, Janie, that she should marry boring Logan Killicks for protection and not love, she states vehemently:

> Honey, de white man is de ruler of everything as fur as Ah been able tuh find out. Maybe it's some place way off in de ocean where de black man is in power, but we don't know nothin' but what we see. So de white man throw down de load and tell de Nigger man tuh pick it up. He pick it up because he have to, but he don't tote it. He hand it to his women-folks. De nigger woman is de mule uh de world so far as Ah can see. (29)

The black woman has had to take care of everybody's children including her own, scrub and clean the floors of white women, as well as please and support the black man who was/has been denigrated by white society and denied equal employment opportunities. Few black women, whether they wanted the protection or not, have had the option of being placed on the pedestal, taken care of and protected. Many native Sea Island women have worked a number of low-paying jobs in their lifetime in order to raise a large number of children with or without a husband.

Since the geographically isolated, swampy region of the Sea Islands is surrounded by marshlands and massive rivers, giant tidal waves and hurricanes have claimed the lives of many. In the past when agriculture was the way of life, the women and children along with the men worked the fields of the masters during slavery. Once the union soldiers sieged Beaufort and other coastal slaveholding areas, the planters had to abandon their land, and much of it was sold to pay the taxes. Many newly freed slaves, women included, became landowners. The acquisition of land was not without the price of hard labor. One woman, in explaining to me how she and her descendants acquired the property they live on today, told the following story: "Grandma was a rebel at Bunker Hill; she was a slave. She came to the island four year after freedom. When she came, she buy this land for plant cotton and ginned it with her foot."

After slavery, those women who did not depend solely on agriculture for economic survival turned to domestic labor and other unskilled jobs for employment. Even today, many young mothers get up at the crack of dawn to be transported miles away to another island to clean a hotel, to cook for a private club, or some such job, only to earn minimum wages. With high poverty levels reported among native black islanders, it is not uncommon for elderly women to work to supplement meager incomes.

Miss Carrie, the protagonist in the story below, was born in 1897 and lived on Johns Island afflicted with arthritis. Noted for her baking, this woman was devoted to her faith, family, and husband. According to Franklin Smith, a native Sea Island black who has collected narratives from five generations of his family, she became the matriarch of her family, the symbol of a "warrior woman engaged in a struggle for socio-economic and spiritual integrity" (11).

Missy Ann Put Money in Me Hand

Ya see I was in me early seventies and couldn't keep up wit the farm work, though I keep me a row or two of okra and beans. I learnt through the church that Missy Ann, she want a woman to work around the house. I go to see her, she had know about me name and I go to work around the house. Well, I done all the work around her house and see to her children. Done this about five years. Now she never pay much, and she work me way hard, but I had for to do cause I need to help out, to get the medicine for me husband who sick all the time. . . . This day me pressure work'n real bad and I had to work for Missy Ann. When I get to the house, she tell me to clean the big window to the porch. Well I cleaning and the first thing I know, I done fell through the window. . . . Missy Ann too worried, say I must go to the hospital. I tell her 'no, I fine,' but she take me to hospital. Doctor say me pressure way high, can't work no more. Hear'n this, Missy Ann take me home and put money in me hand. For a while, she come to the house every week, see about me and put money in me hand. I tell her no call, but she keep putt'n money in me hand. This go on and on, even when she stop comin' to the house, she'd see some of mine or them that know me and sent money to put in me hand. I wonder if Missy Ann think I going to see the lawyer, for me falling through the window.

Under the old plantation and sharecropping systems, southern blacks had no legal recourse. They were accustomed to getting some protection from benevolent whites; however, this paternalistic relationship assumed Anglo superiority. In order for blacks to benefit under this model, they had to wear the disparaging masks that Wright bitterly despises. With the civil rights legislation, black and white relations were transformed to some extent. People such as Miss Carrie could use the court system to achieve a certain degree of socioeconomic integrity.

Folk narratives (though not exclusively) may often exhibit an imagination that dismantles the power of white society, making it look ridiculous. For example, the understated tone of Carrie's last sentence reveals a woman who has more control over her circumstances than the image of the overworked, victimized, female suggested in the earlier part of the story. Whether her white employer has genuine concern for her well-being is unclear in the story; however, unlike the stereotype of the faithful loving mammy, Carrie remains somewhat skeptical about her employer's intentions. Language, a potential vehicle for self-expression, is used to mask black peoples' real selves, those feelings of hurt, despair, and defiance.

Like numerous other black writers and scholars, my work is aimed at legitimizing the black experience and documenting an affirming black presence. My reading of a text is political as I attempt to comprehend the magnitude of slavery, the possibilities of selfhood for a slave woman and man. How does that legacy continue to manifest itself as black men and women struggle to position themselves in an inherently hostile world? How does this legacy affect the relationships between blacks and whites, including those of black women and white women, white women and black men, etc.? More importantly, how can we break the bonds of slavery without disrupting the ties with our ancestors? Reading folk narratives reaffirms my identity with the black community by providing me the opportunity to acknowledge the strengths and vulnerabilities of my ancestors and to pass this knowledge on to future generations.

Notes

1. For a discussion of biological diversity in modern human populations see Stephen Molar, *Human Variation: Race, Types, and Ethnic Groups,* Englewood Cliffs, NJ: Prentice-Hall, 1983. Molar refutes the old but popular notion of biological determinism.

2. For an in-depth study of Sea Island culture, see Patricia Jones-Jackson, *When Roots Die: Endangered Traditions on the Sea Islands* (Athens: University of Georgia Press, 1987). Jackson discusses the transitions native Sea Islanders are experiencing due to development, modernization, and other forces and examines linguistic parallels between the Gullah Oral Tradition and some oral traditions in Nigerian dialects. In addition, see Mary A. Twining and Keith E. Baird, eds., *Sea Island Roots: African Presence in the Carolinas and Georgia* (Trenton: Africa World Press, Inc., 1991).

References

Hurston, Zora Neale. "My Most Humiliating Jim Crow Experience." *I Love Myself When I am Laughing*. Ed. Alice Walker. New York: Feminists Press, 1979. 163–64.

————. *Their Eyes Were Watching God*. Urbana: University of Illinois Press, 1937.

Simonsen, Thordis, ed. *You May Plow Here: The Narrative of Sara Brooks*. New York: Simon & Schuster, 1986.

Smith, Franklin O. "The Gullah: A People Painted by Oak Soldiers, Dirt and Spiritualism." American Anthropological Association. Phoenix, Nov. 19, 1988.

Wright, Richard. "The Ethics of Living Jim Crow." *Uncle Tom's Children*. New York: Harper & Row, 1936. 3–15.

What Do Women

REALLY *Mean? Thoughts*

on Women's Diaries

and Lives

*

Suzanne Bunkers

Dear Abby:
I have kept a diary—never missed a day—since Jan. 1, 1933. I'll be sixty-nine this year and have been sorting my belongings and dividing them for my three children.

My problem is what to do with all these diaries. There are some things I wrote that could hurt some feelings, but it is also a record of my thoughts and the activities of my life and the lives of family members. Much of it could even be boring to them.

Should I burn them all? Or give them to my eldest? I am still writing every day—it's a habit. Now, what should be done with more than 50 diaries?
                              —Mrs. G. in St. Joseph, Missouri

Dear Mrs. G:
Don't burn them! Regardless of what they contain, they are a part of history. But why should the eldest inherit them all? Perhaps the youngest or middle child would have more interest in them. Discuss it with all your children, and then decide.
                              —Abby (from "Dear Abby," July 2, 1987)

When I came across this "Dear Abby" column in the local newspaper, I immediately clipped it out. What Mrs. G. and Abby had to say intrigued me, not only because I have been keeping diaries and journals for over twenty-five years but also because their brief exchange echoed so clearly the kinds of conversations I've had with other women who do diary and journal writing.[1] Should they carefully wrap up their diaries and journals, pack them away in the attic, and mark the cardboard boxes "For Posterity"? Or should they sit down some winter evening with a large cup of strong black coffee, read through all the old volumes, then toss them, one by one, into the crackling fire?

In journal-writing classes that I've taught, women often speak with deep regret and sorrow about burning their girlhood diaries—those repositories of adolescent fantasy and agony—or about bundling up their (or their mothers' or grandmothers') old journals and setting them out with the trash. "I just never thought they were worth anything," is a common sentiment, expressed with a curious blend of embarrassment and pride, by many of these women.

I understand. When I found my adolescent diaries in my mother's attic several years ago, I sneaked them downstairs and locked myself in the bathroom, where I spent hours poring over the entries I had made. My first diary was my favorite. It had a blue cover with a teenaged girl and boy strolling arm in arm past what looked to me like a stadium. The boy carried a tennis racquet, and the girl bounced a tennis ball. They smiled at each other, serenely in love, I imagined. As a girl, I found this cover sketch particularly romantic and exotic, for I lived in a tiny Iowa town of four hundred, where there were no tennis courts, let alone a stadium.

My first diary was a one-year diary, about 4″ × 6″, with one lined page per day *and* a genuine lock and key. I received it on Christmas Eve 1960. My younger sister Linda received an identical diary, only in red. That very night I made my first entry in the diary:

> December 24, 1960. Dear Diary, Am very happy with all my gifts. Some are Diary, Barbie Doll, nightgown, slippers, scarf, Bad Minten set, pencil sharpener, candy from Dad's patrons on the mailroute. & perfume. All for now.
>
> —Susie

I resolved to write regularly in my diary, and I did, although I often did not have a full page's worth of events to report. So, my first diary became a more-than-one-year diary. I "reformatted" it, writing in it periodically over more than seven years. I wrote about my family's activities, my schoolwork, the birth of my youngest brother, and my first (and second, and third) true love(s).

At the back of the diary were several pages labeled "Memoranda." Here I recorded my secrets. I was surprised to find, sitting in my mother's bathroom and rereading this first diary, that I had written a note to my future children in "Memoranda." I hadn't remembered that I'd even thought about having children at that point in my life:

To my children,
I started writing in this diary at the age of 10. I am 12 now and the date is Dec. 15, 1962. Some of the things I have written are crazy, but I was then too.

Suzanne (Suzy)
Bunkers (now
but not forever)

Not all of the entries in this first diary were so lighthearted. When I was twelve, one of my uncles died. At first everyone in the family was told that he had had a heart attack; later we learned that he had killed himself, distraught, the family legend went, over his wife's suspected infidelity. I was heartsick. On the final "Memoranda" page I wrote about my uncle's heart attack; and, after I had learned the truth from my mother, I wrote a second entry, which I buried deep within the diary's pages. Looking back at that entry now, I realize how taboo it was in our staunchly Catholic family to think about, much less write about, the subject of suicide. I couldn't even discuss it with my sister; my mother had warned me to keep silent: "So now I will try and get everyone to pray for him so he can go to heaven. I wish I could ask Mom more, but I'm afraid to. No one, not even Linda, is supposed to know how Dick died."

When I received a five-year diary for Christmas later that same year, I vowed to continue my diligent diary keeping, and I did. I wrote four lines per day every day for the next five years, until I ran out of pages midway through my senior year of high school. The four-line-per-day restriction meant that I recorded mostly brief accounts of each day's events; however, I discovered ways of incorporating forbidden topics into the text. For instance, I encoded monthly menstrual periods by marking dates with circles, stars, triangles, or squares.

Only on occasion did I write about how I was feeling. On January 4, 1967, I wrote: "Hi there. Boy am I depressed. Help Help. I need help. Send the Coast Guard, the Marines, Batman, ANYONE!!! That's a joke son." As I look back, more than twenty years later, it's difficult for me to remember what I felt depressed about or how seriously or long the mood lasted. I know that, like many adolescent girls, I cloaked my admission in humor, just in case anyone happened to open my diary and read what I had written. (I usually kept the diary locked and hidden in my underwear drawer, but I suspected that my sister Linda had from time to time discovered it lying on the bed and read part of it. Many years later, when I confessed to her that I had sometimes locked myself in the bathroom to read her diary, she confirmed my suspicions.)

After I'd finished keeping that diary, I started one more five-year diary, which I kept conscientiously until the day I arrived at college. Then I stopped writing in it, perhaps because I got busy with studies and social life, perhaps because during those years I felt little need to write down what I did.

I resumed my diary keeping when I was a junior in college. But I decided to switch to a more open-ended format: a 6″ × 9″ hardbound lined journal. It started out as a commonplace book of lines from my favorite poems, but its pages eventually gave way to lengthier introspective journal entries. I've continued my journal writing without interruption ever since, and I now have approximately forty-five volumes filled with journal entries from 1970 to the present. I keep these journals in a large cardboard box in my attic study.

Although I have always been interested in keeping my own diaries and journals, I started thinking about their roles in women's lives on a much larger scale when I began writing a book on the history of my family in 1980. I was disappointed that I could find no diaries, letters, or reminiscences by any of my great-grandmothers. My desire to imagine and reconstruct my foremothers' lives led me to search in historical society archives for first-person accounts by other nineteenth-century Midwestern American women.

I wasn't prepared for what I found: hundreds of diaries and journals by women, texts written from the 1840s to the early 1900s. Nothing in my literary training had prepared me for how to approach these autobiographical writings. Like other scholars of women's history and women's autobiography, I've kept feeling my way along, opening diary after dusty diary, squinting to decipher spidery nineteenth-century script in faded ink, poring over tiny marginal notations, being puzzled by blank and ripped-out pages, studying carefully the many kinds of formats used by the writers.

This essay represents my ongoing efforts to make sense of what I have been doing. It reflects my interest in studying women's diaries and journals as one form of autobiography. In fact, I like to think that the diary might be considered the most authentic form of autobiography because it reflects life as process rather than as product. This essay also entertains possible ways in which a variety of critical approaches can usefully be applied to the study of such texts. It builds upon the work of many other scholars, all of whom share a commitment to the rediscovery, reexamination, and revisioning of women's writings. Finally, it emphasizes my belief in the necessity for a self-reflexive approach to my research. Such an approach is grounded in my attempt to name and understand the ways in which my own presuppositions, biases, and hidden agendas might influence the ways in which I read and interpret nineteenth-century women's diaries and journals.

This essay reflects my understanding of the diary or journal—and of my own research—as process rather than as product. For this reason, I think of the ideas in this essay as speculative and provisional rather than as dogmatic and unyielding. One of the most fascinating aspects of the work which I'm doing is my recognition of the day-to-day changes that occur in my approach to reading and interpreting women's "private" texts, many of which were written as collaborative and/or family texts rather than as secretive and intensely personal accounts.

A second intriguing component to my work has to do with my analysis of my own regular journal writing. Developing a self-reflexive attitude concerning the dynamics of my writing process gives me valuable insights into my readings of other women's diaries and journals.[2] I think a good deal about what I don't write in my journal as well as about what I do write, for I know that my silences reveal as much as my words do. I consider who my intended audience for each journal entry might be. I used to think that I was writing only to myself. But after my daughter Rachel was born in 1985, I became more acutely aware that I was writing to and for her as well as to and for myself.

Conversely, my reading of other women's "private" texts sparks insights and observations which find their way into my own journals. Thus, in a sometimes startling and delightful way, my own journal writing bears the marks of a collaborative effort with the many nineteenth-century women whose hundreds of diaries and journals I have read closely and empathetically.

I'd like to share with you some observations about one of the most intriguing collections of women's diaries that I've studied—the numerous one-year and five-year diaries kept by Louise Bailey, who lived in Prairie du Sac, Wisconsin, during the late 1800s and early 1900s.[3] The poem "Mile Stones" is printed on the inside cover of the diary which Louise began in 1931:

Mile Stones

What an easy thing to write
Just a few lines every night!
Tell about the fun you had,
And how sweetheart made you glad.

Write about the party gay,
In the sail-boat down the bay;
The motor-trip, that perfect dance;
The week-end at the country manse.

Courtship—then the wedding time,
Honeymoon in southern clime;
Home again in circles gay,
Till "Little Stranger" came your way.

So day by day the story grows,
As onward your life-journey goes.
Lights and shadows—memories dear,
These are *Mile Stones* of your career.

Louise Bailey had been keeping diaries since 1893, when, at the age of twenty-three, she wrote her first entry: "One of my New Year's resolutions is to keep a diary of each days doings. May its pages be records of that which is good, is my hope and prayer. The day is very quiet and uneventful, am at my boarding place, will go to church to-night. My first New Years from home."

Louise, who attended the Whitewater, Wisconsin, Normal School, had a lengthy career as a teacher in Wisconsin and Minnesota. Her thirty-seven one-year diaries (spanning 1893–1930) are a series of small (3" × 5") leatherbound American or Standard diaries. At the front of each volume are printed such bits of information as yearly calendars, lists of postage rates, populations of major cities, and tide tables. At the back of each volume are places for names and addresses as well as "Memoranda" pages. Many of these tiny diaries have three-fold leather covers, with small pockets at the back of volumes for the insertion of loose papers. Some of the diaries allocate the diarist one-half page per day, others a full page per day.

Louise's four five-year diaries cover the period from 1931–50. Four lines are allotted for each day's entry; additional pages at the back of the diary are labeled "Memoranda," "Christmas Cards Sent," "Birthdays," "Anniversaries," and "Important Events." Three of the four five-year diaries have a lock and key, the presence of which appears to be a distinctly twentieth-century phenomenon. On the title page of the 1936–40 diary are printed these lines:

> Memory is Elusive—Capture It. FIVE YEAR DIARY. The Mind is a wonderful machine. It need but be just refreshed and incidents can again be revived in their former clarity. A line each day, whether it be of the weather or of more important substances, will in time to come bring back those vague memories, worth remembering, to almost actual reality.

On the inside of the 1946–50 diary is a Gimbel's price tag reading $1.69. Louise Bailey wrote in her diaries faithfully over the course of fifty-seven years, penning daily entries, spilling words into the margins, and rarely leaving blank lines in any of the forty-one volumes.

I was astounded when I first opened the huge Hollinger boxes containing Louise's diaries. How could anyone have written *so many* diaries? My first impulse was to shut the boxes and walk away. My second impulse was to search for the earliest diary and leaf through its pages randomly, reading entries and hoping to glean some first impressions of Louise. I opened that diary to May 24, 1893, and read: "I think my diary must be without spice if variety constitutes spice. It is merely a daily account of the weather and a few, oh, how few, other details. I must be living a quiet life judging from these pages. Had a new scholar to-day, who I think is the most lively child I ever dealt with."

My appetite was whetted. This early entry reflected its writer's emerging self-reflexivity about her diary-writing process and, by extension, about her life. Did Louise feel that she needed to rationalize her keeping a diary? Did she need to justify her life as an unmarried schoolteacher? After all, on January 17, 1893, she had written: "I haven't been blessed with a great deal of patience to-day, it has been difficult to keep from being cross. It is my birthday to day, too, am twenty four years old, that is getting to be very nearly an "old maid." A year ago to-day I was at Harry Drew's house. It is my third birthday from home."

Although I couldn't be certain what Louise felt, I was drawn to her diaries because I knew that from them I could speculate, muse, imagine, then reconstruct (from my own perspective) the story of her life. I spent three eight-hour days reading each entry in her thirty-seven one-year diaries and four five-year diaries. I examined how some of her earliest observations about what diary writing meant to her might be reflected in diaries that spanned her life from age twenty-three to age eighty-one. I had ample opportunity to consider the "Mile Stones" in Louise's life.

Louise's first diary entry for 1894 showed that she saw her diaries as her "life's story" and that she planned to reread her entries at year's end: "My dear friend Mrs. Daniels has been so kind as to make me a present of this diary, in which I hope to write day by day my life's story for another year. God grant that at the end of the year I may read the good with smiles, and blot the bad with tears." Such revelations ran counter to almost everything I had read by critics who discounted diaries and journals as autobiography, who viewed such texts as haphazard, nonselective, and ultimately boring accounts of their writers' daily lives.

I also discovered that Louise Bailey used her diaries to shape a life story that would be both "private" and "public": "private" in the sense that it was not meant for publication, and "public" in the sense that she chose to "publicize" or "valorize" certain details of her life by recording them in writing, for her own rereading and perhaps for that of others. Moreover, her decision to save all of her diaries and donate them to historical society archives is a strong indication that she had a larger purpose and intended audience than herself alone in mind. While I cannot determine with certainty what her purpose and intended audience might have been, I can reasonably speculate that her preservation of her diaries and her commitment of them to the "public" realm lend credence to her designation of her diaries as her autobiography.

Louise Bailey's life did not enact the "Mile Stones" poem printed on the title page of her 1931–35 diary. She did not write about suitors, parties, marriages, births of children, or life as a homemaker. Rather, she wrote about her daily struggles as a teacher, about her efforts toward furthering her education, and about her fears of growing old. Contrary to the notion that diarists write only about the "private," Louise was keenly aware of what was happening in the world around her. At the back of her later diaries, on pages labeled "Important Events," she listed details of world wars, economic depressions, local disasters, political upheavals.

Louise Bailey made her final diary entry on December 31, 1950:

> Once more we come to the end of the year. It has been a good year in most ways; but one can not help but wonder what the new year will bring. Threats of war make one apprehensive.

We can only hope and pray for Divine Guidance to meet whatever comes. Went to church. Communion service.

John and Cora Buckles & Donald Hufford & wife joined the church.

The diaries of Louise Bailey convincingly disprove the assertion that women's "private" writings are not autobiography. They dispel the notion that diaries and journals are shapeless texts comprised of haphazard, fragmented jottings. They provide evidence that a woman might use her diary to rewrite what it meant to be female by creating her own "Mile Stones," whether or not they agreed with culturally defined concepts of what a woman's life ought to be.[4]

My study of other nineteenth-century Midwestern American women's diaries and journals reinforces my observations gleaned from a careful analysis of the diaries of Louise Bailey. Many such women kept diaries and journals throughout their lifetimes; the very existence of so many of these texts requires that we reexamine the past male heroic paradigm that has served as the basis for the way in which the generic boundaries of autobiography have been defined. The hero's quest is not always the central framework for the autobiographer's story, particularly not when the autobiographer is female and when she writes her story in the form of a diary or journal.[5]

Realizing this, we need to search for paradigms that work when applied to women's autobiography and for forms that affirm rather than deny female existence. The diary or journal is one such form. Women's diaries are "handmade"; they are not "finished," nor are they "made up." As other scholars of diaries and journals have noted, the dailiness of the diary is analogous to the dailiness of living in one's female body, and the cyclical yet progressive nature of such writing is analogous to female physiological (and perhaps psychological) cycles.

The diary or journal is not a shapeless entity; it bears the marks of its writer's examination, selection, and shaping of detail. Yet it is often characterized by a unique expression of that shaping process. Perhaps the artistry of the diary or journal as a form of women's autobiography resides in its writer's creation of the *appearance* of randomness and aimlessness through intricate semantic, syntactic, and formal shaping.

Another challenge facing us as we search for alternative paradigms for women's autobiography has to do with language. Terms such as *fragmented, disjointed,* and *discontinuous* have all been used to characterize the diary or journal and hence to deny it inclusion in the genre of autobiography. Such terms are culture-bound reflections of a binary system that

valorizes only what it has defined as *coherent, cohesive,* and *continuous* and
that labels all other texts as marginal, deviant, and unworthy of serious
attention. Such terms are insidious—they minimalize or altogether deny
the processes that characterize the ways in which meaning is encoded into
the diary or journal and the way in which the overall text takes shape.

Essential to my study of women's diaries is an exploration of alterna-
tives to dependence on a binary system of language, with all of its connotations and implications. I'm intrigued by the possibilities inherent in
redefining words and, by extension, the thoughts and actions which they
connote.

> A knowledge of piecing, the technique of assembling fragments into
> an intricate and ingenious design, can provide the contexts in which
> we can interpret and understand the forms, meanings, and narrative
> traditions of American women's writing.—Elaine Showalter, "Piec-
> ing and Writing"

> Invisible mending is delicate, necessary, skilled labor, mending and
> preserving the fabric of society. The measure of a woman's skill is
> the degree to which the work can't be seen.—Jane Marcus, "Invis-
> ible Mending"

> And so our mothers and grandmothers have, more often than not
> anonymously, handed on the creative spark, the seed of the flower
> they themselves never hoped to see: or like a sealed letter they could
> not plainly read.—Alice Walker, "In Search of Our Mothers' Gar-
> dens"

Elaine Showalter, Jane Marcus, and Alice Walker, among others, have
explored the notion of women's "private" writings as analogous to wom-
en's sewing, weaving, piecing, quilting, and gardening. All are acts of
economic necessity, rarely done in complete isolation, seldom done at
one's leisure. As Showalter puts it, all are acts of "scarcity, ingenuity,
conservation and order" (228). All are delicate forms of skilled labor that
function to preserve the fabric of women's experiences, regardless of
whether the artistry of the creator's work is visible.

Women's diaries, journals, daybooks, deathbooks, letters—all part of
the fabric of women's experiences—are forms in which their writers'
painstaking, careful work can't always be seen. This does not mean,
however, that selection, shaping, stitching, and structuring have played
no role in the creation of such texts. On the contrary, many are so
skillfully "invisibly mended" that only a very close reading can reveal

what Showalter has called "ragged edges"—those bits and pieces that defy tidy inclusion in standard literary schema (245). I have begun to look more closely at diary entries that refuse to stay within the four tiny lines allotted them, at necrology entries that both affirm and subvert nineteenth-century ideals of true womanhood, at sentences in letters that reflect a writer's consciousness of creating a specific self for a particular reader.

I have begun to ask myself what such "ragged edges" can tell me about the writer, about her writing process, about her intended audience, about her text. I need to pay attention to these "ragged edges." They invite me to sit down with the writer, to piece and stitch, to plant and weed with her, to admire the artistry of the work which she has created.

I have begun to reexamine the uses of language. I no longer start from the assumption that I am working with "odds and ends," "fragments," "bits and pieces" of women's experiences—everything that has traditionally been relegated to the dustbin of *man*kind's experiences. I'm beginning to recognize that, as I read and interpret forms of women's "private" writing, I choose interpretive pieces; and I cut and shape them—arranging them into intricate, carefully wrought designs, both consciously and unconsciously. In so doing, I am reenacting the process in which the writers of diaries, journals, daybooks, deathbooks, and letters engaged.

My reexamination of language and of the processes which that language describes is a crucial part of my self-reflexivity about my study of women's diaries and about my own journal writing. Naming and examining the presuppositions and purposes which underlie my research is essential to my own creative process as a writer.

What are some of these presuppositions and purposes? I've recognized that I write in my own journal as one way of shaping the story of my life. I do not intend to create a false story; yet, like anyone, I see things from my own perspective. I have a large stake in telling my story as I want it told. I'm also conscious of wanting to leave a record behind, primarily for my young daughter, but also for women who years from now will want to learn more about what it was like to be a middle-class white woman in the Midwestern United States during the latter half of the twentieth century. I've always known (even back when I encoded my menstrual periods in my five-year diary) that I write selectively in my journal. I'm aware, too, of just how careful I can be—and of how careful I need to be—about what I say and don't say on my journal's pages. Who knows who might be reading my journals someday?

My musings on this last question took a serious turn in late 1988, when

Rachel and I returned to Minnesota after living for six months in Brussels, Belgium, where I had been on a Fulbright Research Fellowship. I had never married Rachel's father, and I had separated from him before she and I left for Europe. Upon our return, he filed papers for sole custody of Rachel. He asked the court to order that the numerous journals I had kept during the past four years be handed over to him and his attorney. Those journals, he argued, would reveal just how unfit a mother I was.

My attorney and I counterargued that, if my journals were handed over to Rachel's father, the privacy of persons mentioned in the journals would be violated and their and my confidentiality would be broken. My attorney suggested that the judge handling the case read the journals in his chambers to determine whether any passages were relevant to the custody case. Only those passages deemed relevant would then be xeroxed and handed over. My attorney explained to the judge that I was a prolific journal writer and that there would be hundreds and hundreds of pages for him to read if he chose to take the journals into his chambers. Not surprisingly, he ruled that my journals were not relevant to the case and that they would remain my private property.

I'd be lying if I said that my journal writing was unaffected by these attempts to intimidate me. Of course, I became more discriminating about what I did and didn't write in my journal. At one point during the year-long custody struggle, I wrote this about my feelings of personal violation: "I feel that I have to dig deeper and deeper inside myself, searching for some more strength—whether it's there, who can say? So far, it has been, but I wonder how much deeper I can go? I fear losing Rachel—I fear the exposure of myself—like being stripped naked."

The custody struggle was resolved in my favor out of court, just days before the trial was to begin. Afterward I wrote this in my journal:

> When I told Rachel that it had been decided that she'd continue to live with me, she hugged me & smiled—"Oh, Mommy, I'm so happy!" Then, "I love you better than Daddy." I said, "Honey, it's OK to love both your mom and your dad. I'm glad you are going to stay living with me." Then I got tearful & so did Rachel. She asked, "Why are you crying?" I said, "Because I'm happy that we will be staying together." "Me, too," she replied.

My daughter continues to live with me, and she visits her father regularly. It hasn't been too hard for me to write these statements down as part of this essay. It is still too painful for me to reread very many of the journal entries that I wrote during the custody struggle; and it would be unwise for me to quote any more of them here, since in Minnesota the issue of custody can be reevaluated every two years at the request of either parent. I'll simply say that my experiences over the past several years have given me a good deal to ponder vis-à-vis issues of self-reflexivity in my journal writing and in my study of other women's "private" writings.

Years ago, the second wave of the American women's movement defined the personal as the political. Although this definition has come to sound like an outworn cliché, it has a sound basis. My work on women's "private" diaries and journals does not take place in a vacuum. It occurs within the context of my own daily journal keeping, my own letter writing. It occurs within the context of enduring and not-so-enduring relationships, changes in daily responsibilities, alternations in mind-set and habit. It occurs within the context of my attempts to choose, piece, and sew the garment of "self"—whether or not that garment is in vogue, according to the whims of current critical fashion.

My study of nineteenth-century Midwestern American women's diaries and journals is exhausting and exhilarating precisely because I am reassessing timeworn and culturally bound perceptions of how to envision women's lives and of how to understand the generation and survival of the remaining written records of these lives. In being self-reflexive not only about what I observe in these "private" texts but also about the emotional and critical "baggage" which I bring to my research, I like to envision myself taking off the musty, smothering cloak of scholarly objectivity. Then I imagine myself opening the door and walking out into the fresh (and sometimes chilly) critical air, uncloaked but hardly naked.

Postscript

Thank you to the National Endowment for the Humanities, the American Council of Learned Societies, and Mankato State University for funding which has made my research possible.

Thank you to the Women's Studies Research Center at the University of Wisconsin-Madison, the Center for Advanced Feminist Studies at the University of Minnesota-Minneapolis, and the Departments of English and Women's Studies at Mankato State University for encouraging my work. Thank you to Kira Edmunds for helping me put the text of this essay into its final form.

Thank you to these scholars and writers, whose work has inspired and influenced my own: Ilene Alexander, William Andrews, Gloria Anzaldua, Bettina Aptheker, Susan Armitage, Virginia Beauchamp, Linda Bergmann, Lynn Z. Bloom, Carol Bly, Jeanne Braham, Germaine Brée, Margo Culley, Rachel Blau de Plessis, Susanna Egan, Carol Fairbanks, Robert Fothergill, Gelya Frank, Penelope Franklin, Susan Stanford Friedman, Joanna Bowen Gillespie, Dure Jo Gillikin, Patricia Hampl, Elizabeth Hampsten, Carolyn Heilbrun, Rebecca Hogan, Cynthia Huff, Gloria Hull, Estelle Jelinek, Suzanne Juhasz, Annette Kolodny, Susan Lanser, Patti Lather, Janet Le-Compte, Judy Nolte Lensink, Meridel Le Sueur, Rashmi Luthra, Thomas Mallon, Nellie McKay, Jane Marcus, Mary Mason, Nancy K. Miller, Mary Jane Moffat, Marilyn Ferris Motz, Cherry Muhanji, Barbara Myerhoff, James Olney, Charlotte Painter, Janis Pallister, Roy Pascal, Daphne Patai, Annis Pratt, Glenda Riley, Paul Rosenblatt, Jay Ruby, Jo O'Brien Schaefer, Lillian Schlissel, Elaine Showalter, Carroll Smith-Rosenberg, Domna Stanton, Brenda Stevenson, Trudelle Thomas, and Alice Walker.

A special thank-you to my grandmothers, Lillian Welter Bunkers (who taught me to piece quilts) and Frances Kokenge Klein (who taught me to sew); to my mother, Verna Klein Bunkers (who knew my first diaries were worth saving); to my sister, Linda Bunkers Kennedy (who knew my diaries were worth reading); and to my daughter, Rachel Susanna Bunkers (who inspires me to write in them).

Notes

This essay is for Rachel Susanna.

1. I use the terms *diary* and *journal* interchangeably because I have found few texts that can clearly be defined as either a diary *or* a journal. Most incorporate characteristics usually attributed to the diary (e.g., brief descriptive entries, daily reports on events) as well as to the journal (e.g., lengthy introspective entries, narratives, and commentaries).

2. Barbara Myerhoff and Jay Ruby's work on reflexivity has greatly influenced my understanding of the concept and my belief in its centrality to my work.

3. The manuscript diaries of Louise Bailey are housed in the Wisconsin State Historical Society archives in Madison, Wis.

4. Scholars such as Lynn Bloom, Margo Culley, Elizabeth Hampsten, Rebecca Hogan, Cynthia Huff, Gloria Hull, Judy Lensink, Brenda Stevenson, and Trudelle Thomas have explored the ways in which women have shaped diaries, creating patterns that, on the surface, may appear random and haphazard but that are actually carefully constructed texts. My work builds on the work of these scholars.

5. The work of Gloria Anzaldúa, Germaine Brée, Susanna Egan, Susan Friedman, Nellie McKay, Annis Pratt, Domna Stanton, and Elaine Showalter has helped me reassess the model of the male heroic quest and the notion of the heroic self, noting the ways in which this paradigm does not work when applied to forms of women's autobiography.

References

Marcus, Jane. "Invisible Mending." *Between Women.* Boston: Beacon Press, 1984.

Showalter, Elaine. "Piecing and Writing." *The Poetics of Gender.* New York: Columbia University Press, 1987.

Walker, Alice. "In Search of Our Mothers' Gardens." *In Search of Our Mothers' Gardens: Womanist Prose.* New York: Harcourt Brace Jovanovich, 1983.

PART III

Autobiographical Literary

Criticism

*

The master's tools will

never dismantle the master's house.

—Audre Lorde, SISTER

OUTSIDER

Not to be able to come to one's

truth or not to use it in one's

writing, even when telling the

truth having to "tell it slant," robs

one of drive, of conviction,

limits potential stature.

—Tillie Olsen, SILENCES

Between the Medusa

and the Abyss:

Reading JANE EYRE,

Reading Myself

*

Ellen Brown

"*The Dark continent is neither dark nor unexplorable.*—It is still unexplored only because we've been made to believe that it was too dark to be explorable. And because [men] want to make us believe that what interests us is the white continent, with its monuments to Lack. And we believed. They riveted us between two horrifying myths: between the Medusa and the abyss."—Helene Cixous, "The Laugh of the Medusa"

I've been reading *Jane Eyre* since I was about twelve. That means that for the last eighteen years I've been trying to integrate Bronte's novel into my life, putting it down, but always coming back to it, finding another reason to read it, another way to absorb its mysteries and myth, another way to identify with the plain and penniless heroine. I keep rereading *Jane Eyre* and revising myself.

I

During my third year of college I am transported to the University of Aarhus in Denmark where I take my first women's literature class. As an English major at a small, private, liberal arts college, I have read very few female authors in my classes and have had only two female professors, neither of whom is in my chosen department. Suddenly, in a land where women do not shave their legs and where they refer to Marilyn French's *The Women's Room* as the Bible, I am learning why, according to Joanna

Russ, women can't write and am taking a course taught by a woman where most of my classmates are female and we read only women authors.

Here I read Charlotte Bronte again (for the third—fourth?—time), this time not in the company of male authors or patriarchal periods of historicity, but in the company of Jane Austen, George Eliot, and Emily Bronte and in the context of women's place in literary history. I am told that, compared to Emma, Jane Eyre is a prig and that, compared to her sister's novel, Charlotte's is not nearly so complex. I disagree passionately with both of these pronouncements. I am not certain why it is so important for me that *Jane Eyre* be validated as a novel and Jane Eyre as a character, but, like Jane, I rebel. I write a paper comparing Jane's Mr. Rochester to Emma's Mr. Knightley and vindicate my heroine's choices over those of her arrogant, meddling counterpart. Even if Jane is not beautiful (like Emma), she is smart; if Jane is not, for most of her story, a woman of independent means, she is an independent woman; if Jane has no social standing, she knows how to stand up to social codes that repress women; if she has no social graces, she does have spunk; if Jane is an orphan, she is not selfish; if she does marry a vulcanian cripple twice her age, she does not marry a gentleman far too polite, patient, and obedient to be real or interesting.

Years later I will rewrite my paper on Rochester and Knightley to analyze Jane and Sue Bridehead as examples of the New Woman; after that I will revise the paper again to submit as the "star" paper for admission to my Ph.D. program. Right now I am working on an essay about Henry James's appropriation of Jane Eyre *in his story* The Turn of the Screw. *I must somehow keep revising my relationship to* Jane Eyre.

What I did not realize when I was in Denmark but do realize now is that I have identified strongly with Jane through the years: her station, her personality, her choices. At different times in my life I have identified with different parts of Jane's story. When I went to Denmark, I was like Jane when she chose to leave her childhood at Lowood and claim "liberty" (or "at least a new servitude") at Thornfield: I thrust myself into a new and frightening situation, a foreign land, where my desire for liberty would be qualified by my "servitude" as a student. I was like Jane in other ways, too: "orphaned" because I was alone; placed in a position of responsibility as a young woman on my own for a semester in a strange country; tested by mysteries and customs I did not understand. I, too, had the opportunity to prove my maturity. I, too, had nightmares: dreams of being imprisoned in a room from which only one person could set me free: her name was Louisiana, and I was she.

Years later my mother told me that after she had put me on the airplane, she had returned to the car, rested her head on the steering wheel, and wept. Did she cry because I would be alone? because I was so young? because I was grown up? because this flight somehow symbolized the inevitable act of separating myself from her? Did anyone cry when Jane set out for the foreign land of Thornfield?

When I was younger, I also resembled Jane. Perhaps the first few times I read the novel I identified with Jane as the displaced one. As a child, I also liked to sit in out-of-the-way places and read books undisturbed. Jane was separated from her cousins Reed by her social station. I was separated from my siblings by a leap of six, nine, eleven years: like Bronte's characters, we were related, yet it often seemed we had little in common but sibling rivalry.

Years later, I found (as Jane did) that I had a family after all. My brother and two sisters (resembling St. John, Dianna, and Mary Rivers in gender and number) became my friends. Though we had always loved each other, I had had to grow up for us to find each other, to see our common heritage, to appreciate each other's differences without the petty jealousies of childish competition. When I began to realize recently that my mother is getting old and that she will die, my sister expressed surprise that I had not allowed myself to imagine what Christmas would be like after my mother's death. I responded testily that it is easy for her to think of such things: she is married; she has another entire family to share holidays with. She reassured me that we would always come together with our other siblings for Christmas. "You're my sister, Ellen."

When I was older, I found myself attracted to dark men of mystery, to older men, to married men; I was disappointed when they didn't respond with the passion of Rochester, when they didn't find it as natural as he did to treat their lover as an equal being, when they didn't offer me the complete adoration that was Jane's. (My life, it seems, is not a novel.) I saw Bertha as only an evil hindrance and could not understand why Jane has to leave Rochester. I was always moved by the moment when, on the brink of surrendering to St. John, Jane hears her lover's voice in the wind and hurries to find him.

Although, as I grow up, I am never told that I am plain, I am rarely told that I am beautiful. Instead, I am smart. (Jane was smart.) So I hone "smart." I polish it up as the me I'll present to dissertation committees, to interviewers, to students, to colleagues. (At my graduate school there is a rumor that a powerful female professor once said to an attractive female graduate student, "Pretty girls don't get Ph.D.s.") I polish "smart" up so shiny (like burnished wood) that it reflects more of those who look at me than it does of myself. Even so, I'm still patronized, spoken around rather than to, or made to feel like I'm twelve years old by many male colleagues: even those who like me, even those who can speak the discourse of feminism, even those who know better, often see me as a threat.

Now that I am older still, I admire Jane's rebelliousness, her disdain for Helen's doctrine of endurance, her loyalty to those she loved, her practicality (often mistaken for "plainness" or "conventionality"), her adamance in requiring Rochester to treat her as an equal, and her strength in leaving him. (One of my students dubs Jane "Cinderella with an attitude.") Having read Jean Rhys's *Wide Sargasso Sea,* I gain more sympathy for Bertha. I try to pass that on to my women's studies students when we read *Jane Eyre.* We talk about being "Other" and the need for rage.

When I discover that none of my women's studies students read Jane Eyre *as a child, I wonder silently as I look at them, "How did you grow up female without Jane Eyre?"*

II

I've read *Jane Eyre* so many times I don't even remember exactly how old I was when I first read it, but I know I had read it at least twice before I was eighteen and my mother gave me her copy of it that had belonged to her mother before. When my grandfather died of bone cancer in my first year of college, my mother stayed on at the ranch to help my grandmother clean up and move out. Fifty years' worth of living had accumulated in the rambling, two-story, white frame house that had belonged to my grandfather's family before he moved into it with his new wife and newer baby. And much of the unwanted from those fifty years had ended up in the so-called "bee room" in the back of the second floor.

The only room to remain unfinished when my grandparents redecorated, the bee room came to serve as a kind of small and select attic where things were casually tossed—unboxed, often broken, inevitably dusty—because my grandmother (nicknamed "the squirrel" by her brothers) couldn't bear to throw anything away, including used butcher paper and string. The bee room contained relics of a past life: the excess, unused, obsolete, outgrown, defunct; the residue of old memories, forgotten pastimes, long-lost friends, other lives; things which reminded one of the life one had outgrown or wanted to forget. (In a letter, my mother writes, "Anytime Nana didn't know what to do with something, she'd say, 'Take it upstairs and put it in the Bee Room.' It was just easier to shove it in there than to determine what to do with it.") For a period of time my grandparents tried, on different occasions, to clean out the bee room, but in the end they only rearranged things, so finally they just gave up.

Costumes, used wrapping paper, broken lamps without shades, games with missing pieces, homemade decorations from holidays past, books, napkins left over from church dinners, vacant bird cages, antique dressers and washstands, out-of-style clothes, empty candy boxes, remnants of sewing material—any or all of these things could come crashing down if you ventured to open the door. ("Never knowing when she would have money to buy things, Nana saved every scrap against that time when it could be created into something lovely. She could make something beautiful out of nothing.") No one outside the immediate family was allowed inside the room: my grandmother's embarrassment, my grandmother's shame.

Rummaging around once in this refuse of other lives, I found my mother's college yearbook, a picture of the graduating Neva Sohl labeled "Practical"—a title I at first saw as unglamorous but in later years came to appreciate and venerate as a skill, a gift, a source of help for friends and of reliance on oneself: a word often used to describe my mother's daughter. From this attic room (both "treasure trove" and "disaster area")—closed up and locked off, but not forbidden to curious children who opened the door with breathless awe, suspicious eyes, and desire for mystery—from this attic room my mother retrieved her discarded copy of *Jane Eyre,* the maroon cover marred, the pages yellow and tired but still intact.

As I think about the bee room from which my mother rescued Jane Eyre *("It was heartbreaking to clean out the room; I had to burn most of the things myself"), I can't help but think of Bertha Mason, in a bee room of her own, madwoman in the attic at the top of the stairs. ("It was mostly a women's room," my mother writes. "Daddy had places outside to store his junk.") Bertha Mason (brain defunct), discarded, unused refuse; outgrown wife; relic of a past life; reminder of the self her husband no longer will claim. One of my students points out that Bertha only strikes out at the men who have used her: trying to burn her husband in the bed from which she has been rejected; attacking her brother, whose silent complicity in his family's deception of Rochester makes him responsible, too, for a marriage that brings the family money the color of blood. Bertha could hurt Jane but instead vents her wrath on Jane's bridal veil as if to say, Beware the wedding day.*

My mother tells me that she was scared as a child to enter the bee room because bees nested in the chimney of the room. Uninsulated, the room was hot in the summer and cold in the winter. No screens on the windows, so the windows were never opened. Bees would escape from the chimney or sneak into the room through cracks in the windows or loose boards in the frame and roam aimlessly, apparently unable to get back out. My grandmother told my mother that if she opened the door to the bee room she must shut it again quickly or else the bees would get out into the house. My mother was scared of the bee room because she never knew when the bees would attack her. After many years of attempted extermination (my grandfather's efforts failing again and again), the insects were finally disposed of by a professional county agent who put the fearsome bees to sleep.

Again I think of Bertha Mason, bees in her bonnet creeping in through the cracks in the edifice of her brain. Bertha, trapped first in a marriage, then in a room from which she could not escape except on those rare occasions when someone was careless enough to leave the door open too long. Bertha, a secret to all but the immediate household. Bertha, one-time beauty, maker of honey; now frightening, face like a vampire, black hair tangled and swirled around her head like writhing snakes. Biting like a bee stings—out of fear, out of revenge, out of rage—liable to attack those who would enter her world. Bertha, trapped in the bee room where she is the excess, the unwanted, the rejected remnant of Rochester's past life; where she is stored in a small space—uninsulated, suffocating. (I can't open the windows: can't breathe, can't see, can't escape, can't jump!) *Bertha, trapped in the bee room of her mind.*

On the inside cover of the maroon book under "Elsie Weik" in pencil lies "Neva Sohl" in pen. I add my name and later wonder to whom I will pass on this treasure.

III

Disturbed by a break in continuity when she is reading Bronte's novel, Virginia Woolf concludes that "the woman who wrote those pages had more genius in her than Jane Austen; but if one reads them over and marks that jerk in them, that indignation, one sees that she will never get her genius expressed whole and entire. Her books will be deformed and twisted." Woolf is referring to the famous passage in *Jane Eyre* where Jane is philosophizing to herself about how women "are supposed to be very calm generally," but that they "feel just as men feel; they need exercise for their faculties and a field for their efforts as much as their brothers do," and that men are wrong to "condemn" women or "laugh" at them when "they seek to do more or learn more than custom has pronounced necessary for their sex." At this point Jane is interrupted by Bertha's laugh. Woolf finds this juxtaposition, this break, "awkward" and attributes this "upsetting" discontinuity to Bronte's writing "in a rage where she should write calmly." "She will write foolishly," Woolf insists, "where she should write wisely. She will write of herself where she should write of her characters. She is at war with her lot. How could she help but die young, cramped and thwarted?"

As I read this passage in *A Room of One's Own,* appreciating so many other things that the book does to make us sympathize with women writers, I take issue with Woolf. The interruption seems to me very appropriate. At the point when Jane is thinking her rage rationally, silently, philosophically, she hears the laugh of Bertha, the one who expresses rage out loud, violently, passionately. Bertha's laugh breaks Jane's silence, speaks Jane's rage.

Cixous: "You only have to look at the Medusa straight on to see her. And she's not deadly. She's beautiful and she's laughing."

Laughter is appropriate here because laughter is power. Laughter interrupts; laughter explodes. With laughter I express pleasure or amusement; with laughter I express disdain or anger. Laughter disrupts propriety, and I am the proprietor of my own laughter: I choose to let it spill out or to suppress it. Laughing is a choice: whether I do it, when I do it, how I do it, with whom I share it. Laughter is my own. Bertha's unleashed laughter is unleashed potency, sexuality, rage.

Medusa: Gorgon with huge teeth, sharp claws, snake hair; monster turning to stone those who glance at her. Medusa: beautiful woman, hair her glory; jealous Minerva, transforms wavy locks to writhing serpents. Medusa: a sight to behold changed to a frightful sight: "scared stiff" to look upon her. Perseus creeps up while Medusa sleeps, directs his gaze away from her (reflecting her face in his shield to help guide his sword), slices her head off. Medusa, still powerful in spite of death, turns even mighty Atlas to stone when he looks upon her face. From her drops of blood springs Pegasus, winged horse. From her drops of blood grows flaming coral (medusa: free-swimming sexual stage in the life cycle of coelenterate—jellyfish, hydras, sea anemones, corals). "She could make something beautiful out of nothing." Bertha.

Why does Woolf dismiss Bronte's rage, her "indignation," as a "flaw in the centre"? "Now, in the passages I have quoted from *Jane Eyre*," she writes, "it is clear that anger was tampering with the integrity of Charlotte Bronte the novelist. She left her story, to which her entire devotion was due, to attend to some personal grievance. . . . [W]e constantly feel an acidity which is the result of oppression, a buried suffering smouldering beneath her passion, a rancour which contracts [her] books, splendid as they are, with a spasm of pain." If even Virginia Woolf, who made room for a certain tradition of women writers, disallows rage in women's writing, where are we to put it? If Bronte's rage is too much, how much is acceptable? Must we always rein it in? Must we be forever wedded to a narrative in which the author must always kill off Bertha Mason (the "evil" one—Jane's anger, excess, laughter, madness) so that Jane—the "good" one—can contain her rage and return to sanity? Will there ever be room for a woman's excess, a woman's rage?

I used to think that Bertha's death was a kind of betrayal by Bronte. I understood the reasons—legal, symbolic—that Bertha's death was necessary for the resolution of the plot, but I saw in Bertha the monster Bertha the victim as well: an innocent abused by her family, her marriage, and, ultimately, a gene pool of insanity which she cannot control. A woman whose lack of control over her own life represented the horror of women's place in history.

Lately, I've seen Bertha's end as triumphant, an escape from the patriarchal bonds that have made the room of her own a prison. Tired of the bee room in which she has been thrust for life, she gets out into the house one last time, lets loose her rage, and sets the place on fire. ("It was heartbreaking; I had to burn everything myself.")

Eyewitness report: "[Rochester] went back to get his mad wife out of her cell. And then they called out to him that she was on the roof; where she was standing, waving her arms, above the battlements, and shouting out till they could hear her a mile off; I saw her and heard her with my own eyes. She was a big woman, and had long black hair: we could see it streaming against the flames as she stood. I witnessed, and several more witnessed Mr. Rochester ascend through the skylight on to the roof; we heard him call 'Bertha!' We saw him approach her; and then, ma'am, she yelled, and gave a spring, and the next minute she lay smashed on the pavement."

Dark mass of hair flying behind her—coiled snakes ready to spring— she dances over the rooftop, the laughter of her woman's excess rage spilling out over the logical structure of Thornfield's beam and stone. Perched on the edge of the wall, she looks down into the abyss before her and sees death, chaos, hell, void. Looking behind her she sees Rochester bearing down on her: oppression, bondage, imprisonment, suffocation. Knowing that "Much madness is divinest sense, / To a discerning eye," she chooses to jump, taking Rochester's undiscerning eye along with her. Leaping to death, she leaps to freedom.

Discerning eyes reported that a winged horse sprang from the wall with her; flaming coral grew from her blood splattered on the stones.

Shakespeare's sister comments:

> Full fathom five thy mother lies;
> Of her bones are coral made;
> Those are pearls that were her eyes;

Nothing of her that doth fade
But doth suffer a sea change
Into something rich and strange.

IV

As I write this essay in my study, I am wearing the sweat shirt I bought during my last year of graduate school. On one side it says, "Defend or die"; on the other, "Publish or perish." In between these warnings I sit. I wonder where I will publish such an article as this. PMLA? Hardly.

Doubts. I am not doing close readings of specific passages; I am analyzing Jane Eyre *less than I am my relation to it. Am I getting too far away from the text? Where is my thesis? Where is the marshaling of evidence from the book? What kind of organization do I have here (do I have an organization here?) This is very personal: do I want to say these things in public? Who cares what I thought about* Jane Eyre *when I was fifteen, how I felt when I went to Denmark, whether I will have a place to go for Christmas after my mother dies? Am I writing of myself when I should be writing about characters? Am I writing foolishly and emotionally when I should be writing wisely, calmly? Is the personal truly political?*

The fact is, I'm doing here what I can't do elsewhere: I am speaking in my own voice(s). I am admitting that it is not Bronte's narrative complexity or linguistic skill that attracts me to her book again and again. I am confessing that one of the reasons I keep reading *Jane Eyre,* one of the reasons I like it, one of the reasons I teach it is that it has continued to speak so powerfully to me as a girl, as a woman, as a teacher—in spite of all the changes in American society and in my life.

Every time we write, it is a political act.

In *A Room of One's Own,* Virginia Woolf reminds us of the "effect of sex upon the novelist": how women writers have had to struggle against the angel in the house; how they often could not even afford the paper to write on; how they wrote without rooms or time of their own. But what about the effect of gender upon the reader? I have taught *Jane Eyre* to a "Masterpieces" class filled with males and females, and many of the men liked it. I have taught *Jane Eyre* to a room full of women and talked about PMS and what it's like to grow up female. In both cases I wanted my students to greet the novel as more than just a "good read"—something that equates it with the transcience and superficiality of a "good lay." I want them to see paradigms of how to live and not to live; I want them to see choices; I want them to identify with the characters and learn from them. Choosing to teach *Jane Eyre* is a political act.

Every time we teach, it is a political act.

I have no children to teach, but I do have two nieces. Sara and I have a special bond because she and I are both the youngest: we have learned how to assert ourselves, how to rebel. I also have a unique bond with the older niece Kay because I was still young when she was born and I spent a lot of time with her for the four years before her little sister came along. The bond we created then is still strong now, even though I only see her once a year. Kay needs to read *Jane Eyre* more than Sara does.

For Kay's fifteenth birthday I sent her the battered copy of *Jane Eyre* rescued from the bee room, inviting her to add her name to those of her foremothers, to claim her heritage. I hoped she would read *Jane Eyre* and like it and learn from it as I have. I hoped she would find some of herself in Jane's story.

What we choose to read is a political act.

Later, Kay told me she read half of it. Again I wonder how one can grow up female without reading *Jane Eyre*. As Kay gets older and approaches the time when she'll leave for college, I want to help her make the leap into freedom, I want to see her choose to jump as Bertha does. Kay is sixteen, smart, sweet and obedient, indecisive. When I think of her now, I think, "Jump."

Just jump.

V

When I started writing this paper, I knew that I would be writing in several voices: my adolescent self, my older self; myself as student, myself as teacher; myself as daughter, granddaughter, sister; my personal self and my professional self. What I did not know was that speaking in my own voice(s) also meant being silent so that other voices could speak through me: my mother, Virginia Woolf, my grandmother, my teachers, Charlotte Bronte, my sister, Bertha. I began this paper thinking it was about Jane Eyre. I now realize it is at least as much about beautiful and wild Bertha Mason as it is about its homely and sane protagonist: the Medusa and the plain Jane in all of us.

When I began this paper, I wasn't exactly sure where it was going. Now I see it is telling me that, ultimately, *Jane Eyre* teaches us about choices. Jane's choice to talk back to Mrs. Reed, Jane's choice for liberty or a new servitude, Jane's choice to leave Rochester, to reject St. John, to return to Rochester, to be useful. But perhaps more importantly, this novel is about dark Bertha, the unexplored continent of women's rage:

Bertha's choice to laugh, Bertha's choice to escape the bee room, Bertha's choice to jump into the abyss. What *Jane Eyre* teaches us is that, though we may be between the Medusa and the abyss, the Medusa is beautiful and she's laughing. And between the Medusa and the abyss is choice.

Just jump.

Rereading

MIDDLEMARCH,

Rereading Myself

*

Peter Carlton

This past spring, I reread *Middlemarch,* I believe for the fifth time. This time through, the following episode caught my attention. Dorothea Brooke, now Casaubon, has just returned from her so-called honeymoon in Rome, where her new husband spent most of his time holed up in the Vatican Library, while she spent most of hers plunged in grief, her emotions, but not yet her understanding, having caught the full extent of her dreadful mistake: "How was it that in the weeks since her marriage, Dorothea had not distinctly observed but felt with a stifling depression, that the large vistas and wide fresh air which she had dreamed of finding in her husband's mind were replaced by anterooms and winding passages which seemed to lead nowhither?" (136; all citations refer to the Norton Critical Edition, ed. Bert Hornback). We are told nothing about the journey home, but I imagine her during the trip in that state of minor ecstasy we all know from experience: a little beside herself, outside herself, whether caught up in observing the sights along the way, or lost in thought, or, prodded by her overactive sense of wifely duty, self-projected into her husband's concerns. But now she has come home again, to her new Lowick home, and as I watch her enter her boudoir, I can sense her taking that tiny, invisible backward step by which we all come back home to ourselves.

Dorothea hasn't been in this room since before the wedding, back when she was so happy because so well deceived. Now, under the pressure of the emotional sea-change she has undergone since that first visit, she *rereads* her boudoir; and her rereading carries her toward conscious awareness of what her feelings have known for weeks:

> . . . in the morning, when Dorothea passed from her dressing-room into the blue-green boudoir that we know of, she saw the long avenue of limes lifting their trunks from a white earth, and spreading white branches against the dun and motionless sky. The distant flat shrank in uniform whiteness and low-hanging uniformity of cloud. The very furniture in the room seemed to have shrunk since she saw it before: the stag in the tapestry looked more like a ghost in his ghostly blue-green world; the volumes of polite literature in the bookcase looked more like immovable imitations of books. (188–89)

Throughout the novel, Eliot shows how her characters—and surely she intends us to understand that this holds good for her readers too—exist as collections of signs to be read and misread by their neighbors. Here, Dorothea's rereading of her boudoir implies as well a rereading of her husband—whom she had so tragically misread and married on the basis of that misreading—and of her own sadly changed situation: grayness, motionlessness, shrunkenness, ghostliness all characterize Casaubon as well as Dorothea's new life.

She continues to gaze about her, her own hawk-eyed, partly blind, multi-hooked contraption of a self looking for an object that will give back to her something other than the letters that spell her own emptiness and despair:

> Each remembered thing in the room was disenchanted, was deadened as an unlit transparency, till her wandering gaze came to the group of miniatures, and there at last she saw something which had gathered new breath and meaning: it was the miniature of Mr Casaubon's aunt Julia, who had made the unfortunate marriage. . . . She felt a new companionship with it, as if it had an ear for her and could see how she was looking at it. Here was a woman who had known some difficulty about marriage. (190)

This was the passage that seized my attention: since the last time I had read *Middlemarch,* I too had known some difficulty about marriage. The "picture" of Dorothea's suffering caught my eye and heart, just as the picture of Aunt Julia caught Dorothea's. Taking the obvious next step, I realized that this passage figures for me the very act of rereading *Middlemarch.* Every rereading is like returning to a familiar room and finding it changed. I take the tiny backward step that brings me back home to myself, and I begin to look around, half-curious and half-fearful to discover who or what will emerge from the disenchanted background, gather new breath and meaning, and tell me something about myself that I may or may not want to know.

Then, too, since I have reread the same copy of the novel every time, and since I keep writing myself into the novel in my copious underlinings and marginalia, each rereading is both a new self-inscription and a rereading of previously inscribed versions of myself, more or less continuous with the self I currently know myself to be. This process keeps becoming more emotionally charged. One whole set of comments reveals to me the time I read myself into Fred Vincy and my fiancée into Mary Garth, hoping to find in their happy marriage the prefiguring of our own; and as I reread the novel this time, on the far side of that relationship, the poignancy of identifying with Dorothea identifying with Aunt Julia took on an extra intensity because of the marginal afterlife of this earlier self, now ten years old but made present again in the inscriptions he left behind. Another set of inscriptions from another reading tells me about an even earlier self who read the entire novel with a reductive *idée fixe* about sexuality and sublimation. I found myself wanting to ridicule and reject this prior self, to disclaim all acquaintance with him; but there he was, saying, "I too have been you, and probably to some extent still am." He challenges my capacity to accept myself.

Which brings me back to Dorothea in her boudoir. As she continues gazing at Aunt Julia's portrait, it metamorphoses into a picture of Will Ladislaw, the man she will in fact one day marry after the joyful event of her husband's death. Eliot tells us that "the vivid presentation came like a pleasant glow to Dorothea" (190). Clearly, Dorothea is lost in fantasy about the man she really wants. But she cannot admit this desire to herself, so she rejects it, just as I would like to reject some aspects of myself that come out to greet me every time I open my haunted copy of the novel. Her memory cooperates with her self-rejecting impulse by serving up Ladislaw's harsh characterization of Casaubon's futile research: "Oh, it was cruel to speak so!" she says to herself. "How sad—how dreadful!" The next moment, she is rushing away from her boudoir—this scene of rereading that has told her more about herself than she wants to know—and from herself as well: "She rose quickly and went out of the room, hurrying along the corridor, with the irresistible impulse to go and see her husband and inquire if she could do anything for him" (190). An irresistible impulse pushes her back out of herself: this is not an act of self-renunciation, but of self-abandonment.

Dorothea by this time has already given plenty of evidence that she is all too ready and willing to abandon herself. The whole course of her prematrimonial acquaintance with Casaubon is nothing but a series of self-abnegation and idol-worship. She is utterly incapable of staying inside herself and seeing him even a little bit objectively. Instead, she assumes that whenever something about him seems wrong, she herself must be at fault: "His efforts at exact courtesy and formal tenderness had no defect for her. She filled up all blanks with unmanifested perfections, interpreting him as she interpreted the works of Providence, and accounting for seeming discords by her own deafness to the higher harmonies" (49). So caught up is Dorothea in her fantasy of Casaubon's perfections (and her own inadequacies) that she doesn't notice that the style of his proposal letter reveals a man totally disconnected from his own heart; and worse, she fails to detect his obvious self-centeredness: "A consciousness of need in my own life," he writes her, "ha[s] arisen contemporaneously with the possibility of my becoming acquainted with you" (27). Why is Dorothea so apt to discount, negate, abandon herself? Eliot tells us next to nothing about her girlhood, but we do know that she lost both her parents when she was twelve (2); and modern psychotherapy teaches us that children who lose their parents experience the loss as abandonment, that abandonment generates shame (understood as a profound conviction of one's worthlessness, a conviction normally unavailable to consciousness but revealed through behavior), and that one of the ways shame expresses itself is through repeated acts of self-abandonment that perpetuate the original trauma.

Here, too, I read myself in my latest rereading of Dorothea; but rather than rehearse the many ways in which I have abandoned myself, I want to focus on the particular habit of self-abandonment that bears relevance to the act I am engaged in this very minute. When I was in graduate school, and through the first years of my academic career, I was praised and rewarded for practicing a kind of literary criticism that aspired to objectivity, validity, and inclusiveness. My goal was to detach myself as completely as possible from the critical act, to gather up as many strands of the text as I could possibly manage, and to weave and reweave them until I had come up with *the* all-comprehensive synthesis of that text's meaning. In other words, I strove to *master* and *control* the literary text. At the root of this so-called intellectual activity, I now plainly see, was shame: unconsciously convinced that I was less than or beneath, I struggled to produce critical work that would incarnate a version of myself who was greater than and above. Moreover, I felt deeply threatened—at the time,

I didn't know why—by poststructuralist critical theories that announced the uncontrollability of textual meanings. Am I alone in this response? It's been estimated that 95 percent of the U.S. population has grown up in shame-based and therefore shame-generating families. Even if we take such a statistic with the biggest grain of salt we can find, might there not be reason to suspect that at least some of the outrage and fear poststructuralism has occasioned originates in the threat its theories pose to the critic's shame-based need to control textual meaning?

I'm not at all convinced, however, that embracing a version of poststructuralist critical practice is the answer. There's more than one way for the critic to abandon him- or herself in the critical act. One way is through the kind of scientistic impersonalism I aspired to. Another might well be through buying into the disappearance of the self announced by Foucault or the "decentering" of the self occasioned by theories that make the self merely an "effect" of language or ideology. Of course, a person might simply be *convinced* that poststructuralist theory is right and do his or her critical practice accordingly. But I remember how tenaciously I used to defend Hirschian validity among my departmental colleagues, and I'm now convinced that my tenacity had less to do with the merits of his argument than with my need to control textual meaning, though a few years ago I would have repudiated that truth. Since then I've learned never to underestimate the power of shame to infiltrate and subvert my best arguments. In fact, the more watertight the argument, the more likely that my shame is motivating it. I speak, of course, strictly for myself, but I also invite you to wonder whether I speak for you too.

Part of me would like to go back to doing the kind of criticism I used to do. I feel awkward and exposed, and it would be easier, in one way, to hide again behind the implied author I know so well how to invent: magisterial, elegant, controlled and controlling. There are plenty of good reasons for me not to do so. For one thing, that kind of criticism reinforces the spirit of patriarchy, and that would be just as true if I were a woman rather than a man. For another, the kind of criticism I used to do shamed my students. Its persistent underlying message was, "See how large and inclusive and coherent my interpretation is? Doesn't really leave you much to say, does it?" I thought I was giving my students these wonderful gifts of insight and understanding, and what they told me in return, in their various ways, was that I was systematically (if indirectly and unintentionally) silencing and shaming them. Besides, doing that kind of criticism shames me as well. It's a way of telling myself that to respond humanly to something another human being has written isn't enough, that I must hack and claw my way up above it, master it, control it; and then and only then will what I have to say be worth anything.

As compelling as are all these reasons, I don't know that they would have been enough without the self-rereading occasioned by my latest rereading of *Middlemarch*. For it was with a growing sense of dread and even horror that I discerned in Casaubon the outlines of an all-too-possible future self. Casaubon represents the tragedy of the shame-based academic interpreter of texts, with his grandiose ambition of producing The Key To All Mythologies, his intellectual vanity, his need always to sound like the most intelligent person in the room, his anxiety over what "Carp and company" at Brasenose College will say about his latest monograph, and his resentment of Dorothea's even suggesting that it might be time for him to stop taking notes and start writing his book: "Instead of getting a soft fence against the cold, shadowy, unapplausive audience of his life, had he only given it a more substantial presence?" (140). Casaubon doesn't want a wife. To assuage the pain of his shame, he wants a worshipper. Dorothea, because of her own shame, had presented herself to him as precisely that, so no wonder Casaubon feels betrayed here. In any event, when I read myself in Casaubon, when I saw in him the worst-case scenario for the self that I could easily become, I realized that the days of literary-critical business-as-usual were over for me. The profession has modestly rewarded me for abandoning myself and playing the shame-based game of "my interpretation is bigger than your interpretation"—one of many versions of a more general comparison game played by males. But it's a game I can no longer afford to play.

What's the alternative? Imagine attending a professional conference where, instead of listening to hyperintellectualized, alienating papers, we talked with each other as much about ourselves as about literature—about how reading this poem or that novel or this play had helped us to reread ourselves, perhaps even about how a given work had served for us as an occasion of grief or outrage or joy. Our profession contains communities of colleagues for whom something like this imagined scene is or at least has been the case: feminists, gays and lesbians, people of color. (I say "is or at least has been" because we all face the permanent temptation of abandoning ourselves and succumbing to the dominant alienating style. Our profession doesn't exactly encourage simplicity.) But do we have to belong to an oppressed minority in order to admit that we're in pain, that we need to grieve and to recover? Perhaps we're afraid that if we dared to talk like real human beings having real human responses—direct, emotional, personal—to literature, we would lose our professional stature. I mean, couldn't just anybody do that? How would we justify ourselves as a legitimate discipline? (Fine word, "legitimate.") There could be a lot at stake. But what's at stake—at least for some of us, and I would bet a good many of us—if we insist on continuing to practice a self-abandoning style of criticism?

I want to conclude these exploratory remarks by returning to Dorothea's boudoir, as she herself does more than once. Just as her visit there after the failed honeymoon figures for me my most recent rereading of *Middlemarch,* so her revisitations figure the whole history of my repeated rereadings. What implications might those revisitings have for the kind of critical practice I am at once suggesting and trying to exemplify?

Eliot makes Dorothea's boudoir the setting of two more crucial scenes, both for Dorothea and for what I take Eliot to be trying to teach her readers about how to live. The first brings to a climax an episode that begins with Casaubon's cold and silent rejection of his wife's tender concern (he has just found out that he is suffering from a serious heart condition). Dorothea seeks out her room, and there, in "the reaction of a rebellious anger stronger than any she had felt since her marriage," she reflects on what her life with Casaubon has been and what it has done to her, "she who waited on his glances with trembling, and shut her best soul in prison, paying it only hidden visits, that she might be petty enough to please him. In such a crisis as this, some women begin to hate" (294–95). But not Dorothea. Like "a man who begins with a movement toward striking and ends with conquering his desire to strike," she renounces anger, renounces hate, renounces revenge.

> It cost her a litany of pictured sorrows and of silent cries that she might be the mercy for those sorrows—but the resolved submission did come; and when the house was still, and she knew that it was near the time when Mr Casaubon habitually went to rest, she opened her door gently and stood outside in the darkness waiting for his coming up-stairs with a light in his hand. If he did not come soon she thought that she would go down and even risk incurring another pang. She would never again expect anything else. (295)

The second scene may be more briefly recapitulated. After Dorothea has seen Ladislaw and Rosamond Lydgate apparently enjoying a romantic tête-à-tête in Lydgate's absence, she passes a sleepless night on the floor of her room, sobbing out her grief, but finally triumphing over herself in what must be the novel's most famous speech: "What should I do—how should I act now, this very day, if I could clutch my own pain, and compel it to silence, and think of those three?" (544).

I confess I cannot read that speech without getting tears in my eyes. And on every previous reading of the novel, I felt no doubt that I was witnessing the very essence of moral beauty, a living incarnation of Christ's teachings about self-denial and love. But this time, I'm not so sure. Is Dorothea really capable of self-renunciation? For some—I would say many—people, nothing could be more subtly self-abusive than attempting to square one's life with the Sermon on the Mount. Read it over, and then consider this translation of Christ's words from a shame-based perspective: "You are not to have any boundaries; you are not to protect yourself from harm in any way. You must allow anyone who wants to, to walk over you with hobnailed boots. If someone treats you abusively, say 'thank you' and smile. No matter how shamelessly someone is exploiting you, just keep giving that person whatever he or she wants, no matter what. And not only must you accept every kind of abuse without complaint, but you must love your abusers and be kind to them. Finally, you must constantly strive for perfection: until you're as perfect as God himself, you're not good enough." While I do believe that this sermon articulates a profound spiritual teaching, I suspect that relatively few people are capable of living by that teaching in a non-self-harming way. The rest of us must first heal our shame—must first know in our bones that we are beautiful, valuable, deserving of respect. Does Dorothea possess that knowledge? If she does, then when she says to herself that she will never expect anything more from Casaubon than the pain he causes her, or when she forces herself to "think of those three," she is performing a sublime act of self-renunciation. But if she doesn't, then despite the seeming difference between her flight from herself in the first "boudoir scene" and the conquest of herself in the second and third, her self-renunciation is really self-abandonment.

And what about me? When I reread *Middlemarch,* when I revisit that dearly loved room, I never transcend myself as Dorothea at least seems to do. Instead, I always end up rereading myself again. Does that mean I'm stuck? Unable or unwilling to renounce self, and by so renouncing to practice lit. crit. in the usual, more impersonal style? Or am I being true to myself, refusing to abandon myself through a pseudo-self-renunciation? Are Dorothea's self-renouncing moments premature? Are mine in danger of never happening? Just where, between the two of us, is the truer wisdom, the truer love of self and neighbor? These are questions to live with, in the silence after words.

The Crippling

of the Third World:

Shiva Naipaul's

Heritage

*

Rosanne Kanhai-Brunton

The figure of the invalid haunts Shiva Naipaul's "Unfinished Journey." It first appears as the Legless Man With Crutch who "with practised agility and assurance, plunges into the stream of traffic, dodging this way and that" (75) making for the writer/traveler as he arrives in Sri Lanka. But Legless Man With Crutch is not persistent and Naipaul dismisses him as one of the manifestations of the Third World in its capital cities.[1] The second time the invalid appears as "a shrivelled tangle of flesh and bone," the "limpet-like creature" that clings to the writer, digs fingers into his flesh, and then, having received alms, reappears "suddenly agile, suddenly no longer a cripple" (104). The third time his proximity is even more threatening. Naipaul, on a minibus, en route to the home of a frustrated artist/intellectual, reports: "A yellow-skinned man, his head swathed in towelling, shared my seat. Eyes half-closed and glazed with vacancy, he was moaning softly and trembling. A spasm of coughing convulsed his frail body. When the bus jerked and shuddered into motion, he collapsed against me in a fiery invertebrate heap" (119). Significantly he collapses on Naipaul in a grotesque huddle of brotherhood that horrifies the writer. The dilapidation and disease of the human condition are overpowering. Naipaul's final encounter with crippling is ambiguous—we cannot be sure if the invalid makes a physical appearance or if he has become a specter that inhabits the consciousness of the writer. "As in a dream, I saw the invalid. He floated spectrally across the luminous face of the doorway.

For a moment he seemed to hang there, suspended in the glare of light and heat, before finally disappearing from view" (126).

Who is this invalid and why does he haunt the writer's imagination? In fact, why does he haunt my imagination? I read Naipaul because I hope to find echoes of my own experiences of dispossession and displacement. Naipaul traveled to other Third World countries looking for answers to his own identity. I read his accounts and am traumatized by the references to degradation and dehumanization.

My own crippling is more intellectual than it is physical. It comes from being the descendant of Indian indentured laborers for whom mere survival was barely possible and the nurturing of the intellect had to be neglected. Like Naipaul's, my ancestors were brought from India to the West Indies to work the sugar plantations after Emancipation. Exacting plantation labor, barrack-like living conditions, and inadequate diet are my inheritance. Indentureship ended in 1920, and my grandparents began the slow task of picking themselves up out of the canefields and rice paddies. They could improve their physical conditions through sheer hard work, but intellectual enrichment was beyond their reach. There were few schools available and certainly no libraries, nor any other sources of books. By my parent's generation the situation had improved for there were elementary schools in the villages. The catch was that most were managed and supported by Christian churches, so Indian-ness had to be sacrificed for literacy. In the case of my mother, she was given enough schooling to sign her name and do simple arithmetic. Then she was kept at home where her virtue could be protected and where she could be trained in the skills of homemaking and housekeeping. My father's gender worked to his advantage for, not only did he finish elementary school, he was, at the urging of the school principal, sent to a secondary school in the city. He was the first in the village to have a secondary education and was determined that his children would get even more. He defied the traditions of my family who could, by now, see the value of educating sons but still kept daughters at home for an education more pertinent to womanhood. I found myself at Christian-type, British-oriented schools.

As Naipaul's cripple dug his fingers into Naipaul, himself a representative of First World sophistication, so too I dug my mind into the knowledge made available to me. My inquiring mind sought answers in geography, history, and the sciences, all presented from Western perspectives. My starved imagination could not get enough of Shakespeare, Dickens, Austen, and Poe. I consumed these texts eagerly because they offered an escape from my own stunted reality. My mother's life promised me drudgery, these books offered opportunities for adventure.

In addition I could see that education equaled economic well-being. Fortunately for me, the University of the West Indies was established in the late 1960s, and I was able to study for a B.A. and an M.Phil. The more I read, however, the more I could see the enforcement of underdevelopment in societies such as mine. I learned of international and political systems that drained resources from the Third World into the First. I became aware of the cultural hegemony of the West, led by the United States, and was convinced that to empower myself I would have to make my way to the centers of power.

The cripple found his way to Naipaul—harbinger and symbol of Western power—and clung there. So too I have found my way to the United States, first as a graduate student in Pennsylvania and now as an assistant professor in Washington. My presence at professional meetings, forums, and conferences are attempts to articulate my plight—to seek alms. I refuse to be left behind in my own limited society, and I maneuver my way into the bus marked "Women's Studies," "Ethnic Studies," or "Multiculturalism," where there will be passengers with whom I can huddle. Whatever prompted them to get on this bus, I am here too and I refuse to be ignored. Maybe there will be disgust at my frailty and repulsion at my vulnerability, but I must be tolerated at least for the duration of the ride.

The last time Naipaul sees the cripple is at an inn after they have left the bus. Here the luminous face of the cripple haunts the writer as it appears suspended in the light of the doorway. I wonder if I, too, must remain outside, and if I must, is my presence there more powerful because it haunts the mind even as physical confrontation is avoided?

Naipaul moves from physical to cultural crippling as he describes the Tamil woman whom he meets on an airplane. I see her through Naipaul's eyes as she caresses her fur coat with bejeweled fingers, stumbling between French and English, explaining that she is married to a Frenchman and is on her way to visit her Sri Lankan family. She flirts, giggles, drinks champagne with a grimace, and then coos herself to sleep hugging a pink-faced doll with blue eyes. Naipaul comments: "I was alarmed because I felt I understood this bizarre child-woman, overwhelmed by the absurdity of an absurd existence. Like me, the plaything of another ocean, she was compounded out of scraps, this *tres coquette*, Brahminical traditionalist who loved *aperitifs*; who had ceased, even, to possess a language. How could she help but be crazed?" (72). Crazed is the word to which I respond, for this woman shares with me the horror of crippling as a cultural heritage. My identity is an incoherent collage of cultures. My knowledge of my ancestry is limited to the vague notion of "India," for I cannot identify province, town, or village. I can not even claim a family name—the only grandmother that I remember gave me a garbled version of name changes and advised me to forget about my genealogy. My home functioned according to Hindu values—semi-vegetarianism, arranged marriages, extended family structure, and religious rituals—that are etched in my memory even though Western values often ridiculed the vestiges of Hindu culture to which I clung. In an effort to gain acceptance in the wider society my brothers and sisters were all given "Christian" names and encouraged to hide the household words by which we named our relatives, the food we ate, the rituals we practiced. For the sake of progress we were thrown into urban grammar schools with the richer, more sophisticated and, to a large extent, Christian students. In my case, most students were of African origin, but had rid themselves of any semblance of lower class Afro-Trinidadian life. Without being told I knew I had to be silent about my home culture at school and vice versa. With my Afro-Trinidadian sisters, I was disadvantaged by the qualities of passivity and humility in which I had been trained. At home I was accused of disrespect, ingratitude, and betrayal when I displayed mannerisms and attitudes I had learned at school.

The schizophrenia increases as I live in the United States where scraps of American values stick to me. Here I learn to be focused and ambitious, to expect efficiency and order, to function in a society that is secure in its dominance. Western feminism encourages me to be independent and successful. When I am weary of this life, I return to Trinidad. I find myself appreciative of the intimacy of family life but resentful of the lack of privacy. I enjoy the slower pace of life but am impatient at the inefficiency and the chaos that underlie most Third World societies. I am frustrated when I see that progress is being defined in Western terms, the very progress that is obstructed by Western institutions. I shuttle to and fro in the absurdity of my double-diaspora experience. The effort to understand my disorientation and compensate for my dispossession has made me an eternal traveler.

Naipaul does nothing to ease my anxiety as he continues to describe his journey through the Sri Lankan countryside:

> The countryside repeated itself. The road, winding narrowly, took us past the same bungalows with tiled roofs and little verandas, the same lanes debouching from the hinterland, the same unending

stream of pedestrians and unsteady bicyclists. The driver never stopped honking his horn, though often the effect was precisely the opposite of what—presumably—was intended: the cyclists, touched with apprehension, would swerve and sway even more alarmingly. We halted frequently, losing and gaining passengers. (124)

I feel a strong sense of identification with the passengers who are lost and gained haphazardly—their incoherent journeying echoes my own—and with the bicyclists who are "touched with apprehension." I join the composite mass of frustrated Third World citizens for whom the road winds endlessly and for whom the landscape is "nameless," "straggling," "grey," and "bleak" (124). Naipaul's emphasis on repetition and on monotony underscores the fact that for people who have been displaced by colonialism the journeying never stops.

The motif of the cripple combines with that of the traveler to make a statement about the impotence of the Third World intellectuals[2] who roam the world unsuccessfully trying to make sense of their condition. Indeed it has been the pattern for West Indian scholars, artists, and writers to go to England—a location from which they hoped to exploit the resources of their "common" wealth. In more recent times, as imperialistic power has relocated itself in the United States, it has been unnecessary to cross the Atlantic. As representatives of the U.S. oligarchy use cultural and economic repression together with military aggression to plunder the resources of the so-called Third World, Naipaul's "unfinished journey" proves, if anything, the internationalization of monetary relations which perpetuate the asymmetrical balance of resources between the Third World and the First.

Naipaul never finished his journey, so I am left on my own to make sense of my own choice of relocation in a U.S. academy and to examine the options available to me here.[3] My previous recollections of U.S. intervention in Third World affairs tell me that the attempt at self-realization, separate from the United States, is not allowed. If separation is not feasible, then we have to find some way of negotiating with the First World that will be to our benefit—negotiation that must take place where the cultures meet, at the point of encounter, in the liminal areas of intersection between the Third World and the First.

One such meeting place is on First World soil itself, within its very institutions. As the First World appropriates our capital, we, the dispossessed, make our way to its urban settlements in search of employ-

ment, providing cheap labor, sending money home if we can, hoping to
return, but in fact developing a precarious existence that is fraught with
fragmentation. Indeed, there are millions of Third World citizens involved
in menial labor in the First World, but, since most form a lower class of
laborers, their political influence has been marginal or nonexistent. In
recent years, however, there has been a significant increase in the number
of professionals gaining access to the technological and intellectual resources of the First World. Obviously this area of intersection provides
certain privileges even to the crippled. The question is, how can I, with
my heritage of crippling, influence a rearrangement of power relations to
my benefit.

To gain entry to the U.S. academy, I must first make the case for the inclusion of postcolonial or Third World studies within established canons.
Barbara Harlow speaks for me in her *Resistance Literature,* explaining that
the struggle for nationalization and the process of decolonization has
produced a body of literature that (a) reflects the political, ideological,
and cultural parameters of the struggle, that (b) challenges the values of
Western civilization, in particular the codes and canons of the theory and
practice of literature and criticism as these have developed in the West,
and that (c) calls into the question the issue of national literatures and the
hegemonic structures that nationalism brings (xvi). The assumption is
that we are reconstructing our relationship with the First World. We demand access to its culture; what we want is to relocate ourselves within it.

In addition to bringing our own perspectives on the decolonization
process, we, as Third World scholars, have the responsibility of correcting
the distortions that First World scholars have developed about our cultures of origin. Ifi Amadiume, in her study *Male Daughters, Female Husbands:
Gender and Sex in an African Society,* challenges the claim of Western anthro-
pologists that in all traditional African societies women were relegated to
subordinate positions. She prefaces her study by expressing her anger and
disbelief at the racism that has masqueraded as research in the eighteenth
and nineteenth centuries, explaining that anthropology has been the
"handmaiden of colonialism" and that the portrayal of non-Western
cultures as "primitive," "barbaric," "savage," etc. were in fact justifica-
tions for economic rape. Amadiume also denounces the contemporary
activities of Western feminists of the late 1960s and 1970s (continuing
until now) who take on issues of androcentricism and sexism in African
communities, according to their own definitions, ignoring and ignorant of
the conventions within which gender relations occur in the communities
under study. Amadiume makes a case for postcolonial studies to be done

by the postcolonial peoples themselves who are without such biases and who are better able to access information from their own cultures. Again the emphasis is on empowerment, on alleviation of the crippled condition, to be done only by those who are themselves crippled.

An evaluation is also needed on the environment within which we, as scholars, must function, and the tools which are available to us. The question of using the master's tools to dismantle the master's house becomes particularly significant. Can we extend the metaphor to say that the master's tools are designed to perpetuate our own crippling? Actually, we need to avoid a discourse that assigns a "master" position and instead to discover the insecurity of a group that devises desperate machinations of oppression. Henry Louis Gates discusses the potential for crippling that is packaged with Eurocentric theories that form part of the politics of pedagogy in the United States in his commentary on the deconstructionist/postmodernist trend of devalorizing subject and privileging multiplicity and relativity. He says:

> Consider the irony: precisely when we (and other Third World peoples) obtain the complex wherewithal to define our black subjectivity in the republic of western letters, our theoretical colleagues declare that there is no such thing as a subject; so why should we be concerned with that? Long after white American literature has been anthologized and canonized and recanonized, our attempts to define a black canon are often decried as racist, separatist, nationalist, or essentialist. . . . What is wrong with you people? our friends ask with genuine passion and concern. After all, aren't we all just citizens of literature? (25)

The double irony is that the tendency of postmodernism toward multiplicity is what allows us cracks through which we can work. But it does seem that theories are being devised or manipulated to subvert our efforts at empowerment and that we must be wary lest we be led down garden paths that prove to be cul-de-sacs.

Since many of us gain access to U.S. institutions through Affirmative Action policies, we also need to scrutinize the motivations for these policies, as they may themselves carry viruses of crippling. Chandra Mohanty discusses the recruitment of minority faculty as "a management of race"—the managing being done by those already in power. Speaking of the insertion of "Third World" or "multicultural" courses within traditional departments, she suggests that in order to manage the disruptions being caused by the oppression of Western civilization over the years, the dominant group now attempts to harmonize race relations by co-opting people of color to join its ranks and by instituting courses sufficient only to ensure the smooth running of its organizations. The management of persons, she says is symptomatic of capitalism—it is one of those cost efficient strategies that have been developed. The question is are we doing more harm than good by allowing ourselves to be co-opted into an intrinsically racist system?

Compounding these feelings of being used, we also struggle with consciences which remind us that the Third World needs our skills. Are we in fact selling out to the physical benefits of the First World and, in so doing, losing touch with the issues which impelled us here in the first place? When and where does co-option stop being a necessary evil and become a privileged loss? Gayatri Spivak, an Indian scholar who has been functioning within U.S. institutions for many years, addresses this aspect of crippling. She calls it double displacement—from the academic environment in which she works and from the one which she has left. Trained in the Western academy, is her own turning toward the East itself a Eurocentric desire? How far has she displaced her own desire? Can she unlearn her own privileged discourse so that she can be heard by people that are not within the academy? Spivak, identified as a postcolonial, Marxist, feminist critic says: "When I think of the masses, I think of a woman belonging to that 84% of women's work in India, which is unorganized peasant labor. Now if I could speak in such a way that such a person would actually listen to me and not dismiss me as yet another of those many colonial missionaries, that would embody the project of unlearning about which I have spoken" (56). In spite of her anxieties of displacement, Spivak sees her role within the academy as one of negotiation. She says:

> I really believe that given our historical position that we have to learn to negotiate within the structures of violence, rather than taking the impossible elitist position of turning our backs on everything. In order to be able to talk to you, in order to be able to teach within the bosom of the super power . . . I have to learn myself and to teach my students to negotiate with colonialism itself. (101)

Spivak speaks for all of us when she talks of negotiation, but what does she mean by the phrase "structures of violence?" My own experience in writing this paper involved a violent encounter with the colonial education which trained me to make associations with canonized anglo writers. As I read Shiva Naipaul, I found myself connecting his descriptions of cripples with T. S. Eliot's Prufrock, his "carbuncular young man," and his

Sweeney. So I reread Eliot, all the time wondering why. In graduate school I had been peeved at being forced to read him, now here I was, unable to avoid him. Then I realized that such was the violence that was being done to my mind and that I had to negotiate my way through it. In order to address the crippling of the Third World, I had first to submit to the very culture responsible for it and to somehow make my way through its structures. I was inside the culture, yet it was necessary for me to circumnavigate it as if from the outside.

Thinking of Eliot while reading Naipaul seems to be the ultimate stance of defeat, so does writing about the Third World in the First. But it is from this position of crippling that I must negotiate, for I need to make a deal with the power structure which dominates me. I take the first step when I replace Eliot's cripples with a disempowered character from West Indian literature who also makes a deal with white culture—Derek Walcott's Ti-Jean.

As the story goes, Ti Jean is the youngest of three brothers who live with their mother. The family is dying of poverty so the devil sends his messenger to make a deal with them. If any of the brothers can make him feel the human emotion of anger, he will reward the family with all they need. If the brother gets angry, instead, he will be killed. Gros Jean, the oldest, goes out to meet the challenge, confident that his strong arm will serve him well. The devil appears in the guise of the white planter who sets Gros Jean the tasks of counting the leaves of the sugar cane and of catching fireflies. Gros Jean performs the tasks successfully, but the devil goads him into anger by refusing to remember his name. The next brother is Mi-Jean—the intellectual. Mi-Jean depends on his ability to reason to save him from anger. He gets the task of repeatedly catching the devil's goat and tying it up. When he tries to rationalize his frustration, the devil compares his articulations to the bleating of the goat. Mi-Jean loses his temper and the devil claims him. Finally, there is Ti-Jean. With neither physical strength nor booklearning, he is his mother's pet. He goes out to meet the devil and is issued the same challenges. He catches the devil off guard by castrating the goat and making himself curried goat seed for supper. Then he incites the devil's workers to burn down the canefields. For good measure he sets fire to the planter's house. The devil/planter loses his temper and Ti-Jean confronts him with the deal they had made.

Of course the planter does not keep his word. For when has white civilization ever negotiated in good faith? Has not the history of race relations been a crippling of Third World peoples through broken treaties, denied contracts, manipulative loans, schemes and scams of all sorts. Ti-

Jean's skills were those of the archetypal trickster—rank disobedience, presence of mind, common sense, and cunning. To begin to trust would be to give up those skills.

If we look at Naipaul's invalid, we see similar trickster strategies. Legless Man With Crutch "with practised agility and assurance plunges into the stream of traffic, dodging this way and that." And again, the limpet-like creature cons Naipaul into giving him alms, disappears and then reappears "suddenly agile, no longer a cripple." Then there is the yellow-skinned invalid who "floated spectrally . . . suspended in the glare of the light and the heat." Here we have maybe the most valuable means of empowerment for the crippled: agility, persistence, and cunning, in fact, the ability to cling precariously but obstinately to the structures of power.

Such is the heritage of crippling.

Notes

1. For the moment I am going to ignore the implications of the terms Third World and First World. Third World will be taken to mean economically underdeveloped countries, previously under the yoke of colonialism. First World will be taken to mean economically viable countries that have benefited from colonization.

2. The word intellectual is also being used cautiously, keeping in mind the snob appeal sometimes associated with intellectualism. Here the word is simply taken to mean professionals whose skills are reading, writing, and thinking.

3. Naipaul died before he could write the book that was to be about his trip to Sri Lanka and Australia. *An Unfinished Journey* is a collection of his essays put together by Douglas Stuart, his father-in-law.

References

Amadiume, Ifi. *Male Daughters, Female Husbands: Gender and Sex in an African Society.* London: Zed Books, 1987.

Eliot, T. S. *Collected Poems: 1909–1935.* New York: Harcourt Brace, 1934.

Gates, Henry Louis. "On the Rhetoric of Racism in the Profession" in Betty Jean Graige, *Literature, Language, and Politics.* Athens: University of Georgia Press, 1988.

Harlow, Barbara. *Resistance Literature.* New York: Methuen, 1987.

Mohanty, Chandra. "Challenging Eurocentrism: Curriculum and Pedagogical Imperatives." Plenary, GLCA Women's Studies Conference, Nov. 4, 1990.

Naipaul, Shiva. "An Unfinished Journey." *An Unfinished Journey.* New York: Penguin, 1986.

Spivak, Gayatri Chakravorty. *The Post Colonial Critic: Interviews, Strategies and Dialogues.* New York: Routledge, 1990.

Walcott, Derek. "Ti-Jean and His Brothers." *Dream on Monkey Mountain and Other Plays.* New York: Farrar, Straus & Giroux, 1970.

Penelope's

Web

*

Gail Griffin

I

October 1988

For the past five weeks I have been at sea—the Winedark Sea, that is. I
have been reading the *Odyssey*—and rereading it, annotating it, reading
about it, musing about it, leading class discussions about it, thinking up
paper topics about it and then reading the papers on it, firing frantic
questions about it at various colleagues and boring others with my theories
about it. I feel a sense of discovery, as one tends to do at the charged point
of intensely personal intersection with a world-renowned text, in this case
a very long poem written a very long time ago by a mysterious entity or
entities whose name may or may not be Homer. Its plot itself is curious to
me: a voyage home on the part of the man who won the day at Troy with
the nifty idea of a giant wooden horse. The *Odyssey* is about the adventure
after the adventure, the transition from the nightmare of war to the even
realer nightmares of the winedark sea: cyclopses, sirens, sorceresses,
possessive and paralyzing nymphs, angry sun-gods and even angrier sea-
gods, men turning into pigs (which may have been what prompted one of
my students to ask hopefully if there were any chance that Homer was a
woman), and the dynamic (and hungry) duo of Scylla and Charybdis—the
latter a voracious whirlpool, the former a six-headed horror who gobbles
up Odysseus' crewmen, as one of my students put it, like shrimp cocktail.

No wonder that when Odysseus finally crashes on the shore of Ithaka, he doesn't know where he is.

That would seem to be enough for one epic. But as we in the literary criticism game know, the story is never the whole story. "How many odysseys are there in the *Odyssey*?" asks Italo Calvino.[1] In fact, Homer's poem is as plural as he himself may have been. Not only are there many voyages in the poem, but many versions of the voyages, as Odysseus and others tell and retell his and others' stories. Odysseus, the master of disguise, even invents alternate *Odysseys* when called to account for himself. In many ways the *Odyssey* is a verbal voyage, a quest for the real story.

And the story most of my student questers were interested in finding was not that of Odysseus at all, but that of Penelope, his wife. "Penelope, who really cried," in the words of Edna St. Vincent Millay.[2] Penelope, for whom "long-suffering" is a pitiful euphemism but, according to my students, no less a qualification for heroism.

As someone whose intellectual quest usually centers on finding the lost, buried, mistranslated, obscured, cryptic stories of women, I could sympathize. And we are not alone, my students and I, in our fascination with Penelope. Generations of readers have wondered about Penelope. In popular conception she is usually the prototypical (not to mention stereo-typical) Good and Faithful Wife, who waits patiently for twenty miserable years for her illustrious husband's return. Static endurance and doglike fidelity—that's Penelope.

Hardly. In fact, what the *Odyssey* reveals is another epic pushing to get out: that contradiction in terms, the domestic epic, the saga of a woman awesomely powerful and desperately powerless, fighting a lone battle to retain her self and her sanity against horrific odds. After fifteen years or so of Odysseus' absence, the good male citizens of Ithaca decide to redefine Penelope—without her consent, of course. Instead of the noble wife of their absent lord, she becomes a rich widow and thus eligible prey. So that horde of 108 move into the house, draping themselves all over the great hall downstairs, eating and drinking Penelope and Odysseus out of house and home, and making pigs of themselves without Circe's help in a sort of gluttonous sit-down strike: when Penelope picks one of them, they swear, they'll go in peace.

This, then, is Penelope's predicament: she is either Odysseus' wife (in which case the orgy of male bonding downstairs goes on indefinitely, keeping her captive in the "women's quarters" of her own house), or she is somebody else's wife (in which case she is torn from her roots and transplanted to another man's house). The choice is sharpened by the fact that unless she concedes and chooses a new husband, her son, Tele-machos, can never come into his own in his father's house. Her resistance, in effect, impedes his manhood. Hers is the very human reality of the terrible choice between Scylla and Charybdis with which her husband wrestles: either way, she is devoured. Her husband's repeated encounters with cannibalistic creatures become dreamlike shadows of the domestic reality, the rapacious hunger surrounding Penelope.

One of the suitors refers to her as "the beauty that we came here laying siege to" (21: 177).[3] The metaphor is more than apt, for the parallel between Penelope's situation and the siege of Troy from which Odysseus is returning was surely part of Homer's strategy. Now Odysseus won the Trojan War by means not of heroic military prowess but of the quality by which Homer constantly defines him: his cleverness. Penelope, having no army behind her and no physical or legal power, must by default turn to her wits. Fortunately, Odysseus married his match: fortunately, those wits are pretty sharp. As Odysseus is called the "master tactician," Penelope is repeatedly referred to as the "deep-minded queen." Her mind is her own winedark sea, and her voyage an inward one. Odysseus invents his famous horse; Penelope invents her own secret strategic weapon.

It comes straight from those women's quarters she inhabits, where the constant activity of the women is spinning and weaving. Enmeshed in the human web the suitors have spun around her, she spins a web of her own. The story is told and retold in the *Odyssey*; here is the first telling, from the mouth of one of the brashest, angriest suitors. In a classic bit of buckpass-ing, reminiscent of Adam in the Garden of Eden, he tells young Tele-machos that the source of the evil in his home is not the suitors; "It is your own dear, incomparably cunning mother" (2: 94). And then he recounts the story:

> she had her great loom standing in the hall
> and the fine warp of some vast fabric on it;
> we were attending her, and she said to us:
> "Young men, my suitors, now my lord is dead,
> let me finish my weaving before I marry,
> or else my thread will have been spun in vain.
> It is a shroud for Laertes,
> when cold death comes to lay him on his bier.
> The country wives would hold me in dishonor
> If he, with all his fortune, lay unshrouded."
> We have men's hearts; she touched them; we agreed.

So every day she wove on the great loom—
but every night by torchlight she unwove it;
and so for three years she deceived the [suitors].
(2: 101–18)

Incomparably cunning indeed.

II

And here I want to stop the *Odyssey*. Let Odysseus dally with Calypso and Telemachos's anguish about his manhood; here I want to follow Penelope to the loom. I want to stand there for a while this morning and read over her shoulder the story emerging from the threads. For the untold story is in the text on the loom.

How often do we refer to storytelling as "spinning a yarn"? Homer constantly refers to the gods and the fates as spinning or weaving human lives, human stories. In her weaving, Penelope is only trying for a little authority over her own life, a little authorship of her own story, a little creative control in this epic production. But she seizes it from characteristically female sources. Like women historically—like oppressed people generally—she uses conventional tools to unconventional purposes. She uses weaving, above reproach as an appropriate female occupation; and she uses the role of dutiful daughter-in-law, which again can only incur approbation. In such quiet, unheroic, and apparently submissive endeavors do female subversion and resistance often lurk. Similarly, the story of black American resistance to slavery is the explosive subtext of "spirituals" that superficially seem to speak of resignation to a better world yet to come, when in fact they are songs of liberation and strategy for escape. Some of our culture's greatest epics, I think, come down to us in code. If we can decipher them, we find enough outright defiance and sacrifice to satisfy our craving for heroics; but we also find the less glamorous substratum, where survival and endurance look like triumph and redefine courage.

The suitors, like most power gluttons, recognize this brand of subversion. When they discover Penelope's ruse, they are furious. With scantily veiled resentment at being outwitted by a woman, one of them says threateningly, "she may rely too long on Athena's gifts, / talent in handicraft and a clever mind" (2: 124–25). Since reliance upon Athena, who particularly cherishes Odysseus' family, is the means by which they are reunited, this warning seems misguided, if not blasphemous. Acknowledging that I'm working with a translation, I'm still fascinated by this suitor's terminology: "talent in handicraft" is the diminutive term for traditional female art, and "clever" is a less impressive synonym for "intelligent." What he is begrudgingly, backhandedly admiring in Penelope is her goddess-given artistry and intelligence. The admiration rightly takes the form of a warning, for these have been dangerous qualities for a woman to possess.

Yet they are also the qualities that can save her, and Penelope knows it. It is creativity, in the deepest sense, that she needs in order to navigate the winedark sea where hungry mouths wait to swallow her. Her creative intelligence and her bond with Athena are one and the same. For above all, the divine is *creative*. In enacting the divine by imitating Athena, Zeus' favorite child, who spins and weaves the stories of the *Odyssey* before our eyes, Penelope is both honoring the goddess and saving her own life. She is creating space and time for herself, concocting a little power where there was none, creating and recreating herself, Penelope, whole and undevoured, for as long as she can hold out. Hers is a desperate art, the art of crisis and emergency. Necessity mothers her invention. I think of the American woman who wrote in her journal, "We women made quilts as warm as we could, so our families wouldn't freeze, and we made them as beautiful as we could, so our hearts wouldn't break."

Yet Penelope's is a highly ephemeral art, too, unraveling by night to be rewoven by day. This metaphor explodes in many directions. I watch her work disintegrating in her hands before she retires to bed upstairs, "her mind turning at bay," we are told, "like a cornered lion" (4: 844), until Athena pays her nightly visit with the gifts of oblivion and powerful dreams. And then I see Penelope rise again in the rosy-fingered dawn to begin again, from scratch. And I see the centuries upon centuries of women whose creativity was bound on a wheel, moving in a vicious and exhausting circle: washing dishes and clothes so they could be dirtied again, scrubbing floors to clear the way for more muddy boots, changing babies who promptly required changing again, cooking meals that quickly disappear, bearing children only to watch them die and then bearing new ones—doing women's work, which traditionally amounts to remaking and reordering their worlds daily, ensuring that life goes on against and through constant destruction. As it happens, that's the gods' work too.

But now I move a few feet and look again at Penelope's web. From this vantage point I see all the artistry of women that in fact I cannot see—the music, the books, the paintings that are gone, vanished, unraveled by time and neglect, disrespect and despair. I think of the work of Sappho, so celebrated in its time, surviving only in unwoven shreds. I think of an English girl named Ellen Weeton, 150 years ago, who nourished a demon in her heart, a desire to write so relentless that finally, when her family absolutely forbade her to do so on grounds that such dangerous tendencies in a girl must be curbed, she took to finishing her lessons quickly so she could scribble guardedly on her slate, but then wiping it clean before her mother could discover it.[4]

Now I back away from the loom to get its bigger picture, and something occurs to me: what if Penelope's "creation" is a process and not merely its product? That is, what if the creation includes the destruction? Perhaps Penelope's is a dialectic imagination, involving a creative yet dangerous tension between forces of generation and disintegration. This is the Penelope who spoke to Katha Pollitt, the Penelope whose passion to order and preserve masks another, darker passion:

> No one imagines
> how almost lovingly,
> with what delight each night I make destruction.
> I rip and slash. My fingers bleed. And then
> I dream in my abandon
> I am tearing the whole house down.[5]

This is the Penelope in every woman I know who exists in that constant tension between, on the one hand, the woman's work of daily creation and recreation—bearing, raising, and educating children, nourishing and healing the human and natural life around her—and, on the other hand, the urge to rip apart the web entangling her. This is the Penelope in every woman who just barely manages to write a poem or knit a sweater instead of throwing a butcher knife or lighting a fire. This is the woman in whom love and rage collaborate, sustaining each other. When my friend Diane and I talk about our work—hers in psychotherapy, mine in teaching—we are always twin Penelopes describing the same daily handiwork: with the right hand we shape, soothe, plant, feed, summon, or bless; with the left we rip and slash, tearing the whole house down, pulling away the tough, sticky web of patriarchy that grips all of us, constricting our human potential. In this case, the right hand *does* know what the left hand is doing, for they do the same work, the project of renewal and transformation whose yin and yang are creation and destruction.

At this point Penelope's fingers are dizzying me. I have scanned her text so many times that it begins to blur. It unravels for the night, as does my train of thought. "Grey-eyed Athena / presently cast[s] a sweet sleep" on my eyes (21: 402–3).

And when dawn's rosy fingers prod me awake, lo and behold, Penelope is at it again. By now even I want to shout, with the suitors, "Will this woman never give up? For Zeus' sake, lady, pick the richest guy and be done with it!" But when I approach the loom this morning, the weaving has taken on a different aspect. Or is it my eyes that are different? Has Athena been working on me in my sleep? For suddenly the whole redundant, fruitless, futile enterprise makes clear sense. I see what Penelope has been up to all along: above all else, hers is the art of re-vision, of seeing again. If we do not revise what we have written—*and* revise what has been written for us—we begin not to see at all. Our eyes go dead. Lies become indistinguishable from truth, justice from injustice, ugliness from beauty. Fragments masquerade as complete sentences. We must in fact rewrite our stories daily, with new eyes. The story is never finished; the pattern in our weaving is ever-shifting. Penelope, silent and dogged at her loom, "her mind turning at bay like a cornered lion," reminds us all of the necessity to revise our truth constantly; but most particularly she weaves for those of us who are women and must be vigilant to keep our truth emanating from our own fingers, always authentic and newborn.

III

Eventually, Penelope's propensity for weaving webs pays off. Odysseus returns, disguised as a beggar. Only Telemachos knows his real identity. Penelope responds to his presence in a triumph of women's intuition— another interesting word, which means "to look at or contemplate"— another mode of vision, that is. Sent by Athena against 108 able-bodied and united enemies without one shred of a plan, Odysseus is rather up a creek. It is Penelope who resolves the *Odyssey,* by suddenly coming up with the test of the bow, which she unaccountably discloses to the beggar: whoever can shoot an arrow from her husband's massive hunting bow through the sockets of a row of twelve axe handles will win the grand prize, herself. Against opposition, she demands that the beggar be given his chance along with the rest. To this comes a retort from Telemachos, now revelling in his father's return and his newfound sense of manhood, which he exercises upon his mother:

Tend your spindle.
Tend your loom. Direct your maids at work.

> This question of the bow will be for men to settle,
> most of all for me. I am master here.
> (21: 394–97)

One wants to ask if he is quite sure about that last claim. Telemachos seems to forget that the test of the bow was Mom's idea and to ignore the fact that her insistence upon the beggar's participation clears the way for Dad to seize the day. But listen also to that dismissive "Tend your spindle. / Tend your loom." He consigns her to what he contemptuously regards as women's work. You and I, who have stood at her shoulder and read her multilayered epic as it unfolded, can stand aside and chuckle to ourselves: apparently Polyphemus the Cyclops is not the only one in this story who is seeing out of only one eye.

After he has massacred everybody in sight, Odysseus is revealed to his wife by Athena. Instead of open arms and gushing tears, he meets with one final test in his long journey home. He who specializes in testing others, he who has returned intent upon testing Penelope's faithfulness, finds the tables turned. She weaves one more strategic deception, a deliberate lie about their bed, designed to see if he knows the secret of that most symbolic article of furniture and thus, as she so tellingly puts it, "If he really is Odysseus, truly home" (23: 122). Penelope's quest has taught her the virtue of re-vision—seeing again, looking more deeply. Can we blame her? Everybody else does, calling her cold and suspicious. When Odysseus passes her test, she holds him in her arms and explains: "I could not / welcome you with love on sight! I armed myself / long ago against the frauds of men" (23: 241–43). No Trojan Horse will slip through her gates. In a work where the retelling of the tale is as important as the events it contains, Penelope is here tentatively beginning to recite her own epic, cast in the martial terms her husband will comprehend.

Later, when they are finally in bed after twenty years, they have first physical and then verbal intercourse. They lie "revelling in stories" (23: 337), in a kind of wonderfully reciprocal odyssey-swap. He tells his story "of what hard blows he had dealt out to others / and of what blows he had taken" (23: 344–45); she tells "hers of the siege her beauty stood at home" (23: 338). One of these odysseys we have heard in detail, recounted several times in progress and now repeated yet again in short form. The other odyssey we have had to imagine, to conjure, to discern in the rhythm of Penelope's hands, weaving, unweaving, reweaving. I have filled in the dark or bare places with my own life and the lives of other women. That is what myths are for. Only Odysseus has heard the whole story in that bed. Or has he? Who knows how much she has told him, how much she could translate into language he might understand, how much she has kept and pondered in her heart? But he seems to have felt something of the weight of her story, for when he wakes the next morning, the first words out of his mouth are these: "My lady, /what ordeals have we not endured!" (23: 393–94). He rolls over and finds not Calypso or Circe, but his own wife, and he recognizes a comrade—a fellow voyager, a fellow sufferer, a fellow warrior, another hero.

In a few moments, of course, he's up and out the door, for there's business to be done: he must visit his father and deal with the suitors' relatives, who are bound to be a little disturbed about yesterday's bloodbath. On his way out, he turns to Penelope (who is probably wondering how long he'll be gone this time) and commands her to take her women to the women's quarters and to "Stay there / with never a glance outside or a word to anyone" (23: 412–13). So much for liberation.

We find out in the final book of the *Odyssey* how Odysseus spent his day. Penelope we do not see again. But we know, don't we, how she passed those hours?

> In silence
> across the hall, beside a pillar, propped
> in a long chair, Telemachos' mother
> spun a fine wool yarn.
> (17: 120–23)

And probably said to herself, in Linda Pastan's words, "Only my weaving is real."[6]

Notes

1. Italo Calvino, "The Odysseys within the Odyssey," *The Uses of Literature* (N.Y.: Harcourt Brace Jovanovich, 1986), p. 135.

2. "An Ancient Gesture."

3. All quotations from the *Odyssey* are taken from the Robert Fitzgerald translation (N.Y.: Anchor Press, 1962).

4. Nancy Murray, *Strong-Minded Women and Other Lost Voices From Victorian England* (N.Y.: Pantheon, 1982), pp. 204–205.

5. "Penelope Writes."

6. "You Are Odysseus."

"Ain't Gonna Let

Nobody Turn Me Around":

Reading the NARRATIVE

of Frederick Douglass

*

Dolan Hubbard

Reading Frederick Douglass's *Narrative of the Life of Frederick Douglass, An American Slave, Written by Himself* (1845) is liberating and exhilarating for me. On numerous occasions his words have lifted my spirits such as when I was unexpectedly thrust into the spotlight as chair of the Faculty Senate at Winston-Salem (N.C.) State University, or when I felt worn down during the grind of a rigorous doctoral program as one of three African American students at the University of Illinois at Urbana-Champaign, or in those moments when I do a self-inventory regarding my position in the academy whose atmosphere, at times, can be lonely and indifferent. I use his narrative as a motivational tool to cope with the stress generated by questions such as: Do I belong? Can I do the work necessary for a productive and successful career? Can I handle the expectations of both community and academy? I draw sustenance from the achievements of this self taught man who rose from his position at the bottom of the social order to become one of the dominant voices in the nineteenth-century fight for freedom, social and economic justice, and women's suffrage.

I first encountered Frederick Douglass (1818–95) in church and elementary school in my Piedmont North Carolina hometown. The teachers at Granite Quarry Colored Elementary School filled the minds of my classmates and me with the exploits and accomplishments of Frederick Douglass, Harriet Tubman, Booker T. Washington, Paul Laurence Dunbar, James Weldon Johnson, Mary McLeod Bethune, and Langston

Hughes. Along with learning Bible verses, we had impressed upon our minds the heroic deeds of these magnificent seven. This ritual action was repeated in church on Sundays. With a quiet confidence bordering on messianic fervor, teacher and preacher encoded our fragile minds with models of success to offset the impact of life in a rigidly segregated American South. As I neared the completion of the eighth grade, another name was added to this list, W. E. B. Du Bois.

The black teachers under whom I studied through the ninth grade constantly reminded us that we cannot take our education for granted— that like Douglass and other blacks who had achieved we must draw upon all of our resources in order to succeed in a system that was designed to see us fail. They saw education as a weapon of liberation. Of all the teachers that I have ever had, no one ever put my classmates and me through the paces like our fourth grade teacher of Ghanaian descent Rosebud Aggrey (1910–1990). On the job training for success in life began the moment we opened the door to the classroom. Just as Douglass was inspired by the stirring words that denounced oppression in *The Columbian Orator* (1799), Miss Aggrey instilled in us the value of mastering the three r's—'reading, 'riting, and 'rithmetic—as the route to independence.

Among this group of teachers and writers, Douglass occupies a special place in my imagination because of the power of his pen and the power of his fists. With his pen, he deconstructed the ideology of slavery; with his fists, he demolished the demons of inferiority in his epic fight with Covey. He won his manhood on the battlefield of life. I now realize that the teachers and preacher held up Douglass and other black men and women of distinction so that we would not allow anybody to turn us around.[1]

An inescapable fact of my reading of Douglass's *Narrative* is the extent to which my personal history shapes and informs my reading of him. Three of my favorite passages from Douglass's *Narrative* are his learning to read, his fight with Covey, and his description of Col. Lloyd's garden. While I do not claim to speak for all Americans of African descent, I am sure many will hear in this brief record of my experiences an echo of their own.

Without a doubt the most celebrated passage, the defining moment, in Douglass's *Narrative* occurs in chapter 3 where he describes in riveting detail his accidental discovery of "the pathway from slavery to freedom" (59). The epiphanic moment occurs when Hugh Auld brusquely reproaches his wife Sophia for teaching Douglass how to read with the furious denunciation that "Learning would *spoil* the best nigger in the world" (58).[2]

The means by which Douglass creates an image of the heroic "self" is intrinsically linked to his ability to read and write. He (re)defines the terms of his humanity and challenges those who use the Bible to justify the enslavement of black people. Moreover, Douglass's encounter with reading and writing as a subversive activity resonates in the works of black writers such as Richard Wright, Maya Angelou, Peter Abrahams, and Malcolm X.

I remind students in my Major Black Writers class that Douglass learned to read and write between the age of eight and fourteen, and he went on to write a recognized masterpiece by the age of twenty-seven. In spite of the many accomplishments of Douglass as pacesetter—newspaper editor, entrepreneur, government official, and adviser to presidents—all roads lead back to the major epiphany in his life: his learning to read and write.

Occasionally, I bring to class the Benjamin Quarles edition of Douglass's *Narrative,* my favorite text—which I found while rummaging through the used-book section of the Goodwill Store in Winston-Salem, N.C., in late 1977 with my friend and mentor Joseph Patterson—and read some of my editorial comments on my favorite passages from its dog-eared pages. I remind my students that Douglass did not suffer and endure the indignities he chronicles in his *Narrative* in order for them to come here and complain about inadequate funds, insensitive teachers, and indifferent classmates—and be passably mediocre. He wants them, young, gifted, and bright, to give their best and be their best. The ritual action of his life would be refined by a black scholar of another generation into the concept of "the talented tenth."[3] To my words of uplift, some of my black students exclaim, "Ease up, Dr! That was then, this is now."

As near as I can gauge, the response of my white students to this rhetoric of uplift ranges from muted anger to let's make America a better place for all. In a society that favors them at every turn, many white students think that the world has turned upside down. Douglass unveils the ideology that we commonly refer to as the American Dream; he challenges us to think about what it means to be an American. Having said this, most students respond positively to Douglass for he jump starts their imagination. They admire him for his use of words, for his refusal to be defeated, and for his honesty. I remind my students that the best way they can honor the memory of Douglass is through the development of their critical thinking skills. For Douglass it was not enough to be free; we must be about the business of the development of the total self.

The development of the total self includes the right to defend oneself.

In a system designed to break the spirit of the enslaved black people, one thinks twice about defending oneself as Douglass makes clear with his telling of violent incidents he witnessed as a slave. Viewed from this perspective, the emotional center of his narrative occurs in chapter 10 where Douglass describes the epic fight he has with the notorious slave breaker Covey. The fight sets Douglass's narrative apart and gives it a special meaning for me. It triggers a rush of emotions which are almost indescribable, the prime one being the thrill of victory.

Although Douglass couches the fight in apocalyptic language as the triumph of good over evil, students intuitively respond to the larger reality that lies behind the meaning of his words. They tap into a funda-mental urge on the part of many blacks to avenge centuries of abuse directed at our community as a result of what Grier and Cobbs describe in *Black Rage* as "the unwillingness of white Americans to accept [black people] as fellow human beings" (1968: vii). Much of the rap music, as well as Spike Lee's movie *Do the Right Thing,* taps into this suppressed rage. Moreover, the fight enables Douglass to exorcise the demons of in-feriority, many of which are associated with his impotence in not being able to defend the black woman. Douglass argues, implicitly and cor-rectly, that a man without the essential element of force does not possess the ability to defend himself.

I want my students to see the fight with Covey as the logical culmina-tion of a process rooted in Douglass's ability to read and write. As a result of his mastery of the word, Douglass not only begins the process of rehabilitating his damaged self-consciousness, but he also sees that on a larger scale, "writing is fighting."[4] In another classic black American first-person narrative, Richard Wright makes a similar discovery in chapter 13 of *Black Boy* (1945). He discovers that H. L. Mencken "was fighting, fighting with words. He was using words as a weapon, using them as one would a club" (272). I experienced the rush that comes from using words as a weapon during my days as a staff writer on my college newspaper as one of eleven or twelve blacks on a campus of 1,200 students (1967–71). I was given plenty of ammunition about which to write: the Vietnam War, the assassination of Martin Luther King, and, of course, what it felt like to be one of a handful of black students on an overwhelmingly white campus during an angry decade.[5]

"Writing is fighting" is most apparent in chapters 2 and 3 in which Douglass describes the palatial splendor at Col. Lloyd's *Great House Farm.* With biting irony, Douglass describes "the home plantation of Colonel Lloyd [which] wore the appearance of a country village" (35) as "the seat of government for the whole twenty farms" (32). The opening paragraph of chapter 3 contains the centerpiece of Douglass's attack on wanton opulence:

> Colonel Lloyd kept a large and finely cultivated garden. . . . Its excellent fruit was quite a temptation to the hungry swarms of boys, as well as the older slaves, belonging to the colonel, few of whom had the virtue or the vice to resist it. Scarcely a day passed, during the summer, but that some slave had to take the lash for stealing fruit. The colonel had to resort to all kinds of stratagems to keep slaves out of the garden. The last and most successful one was that of tarring his fence all around; after which, if a slave was caught with any tar upon his person, it was deemed sufficient proof that he had either been into the garden, or had tried to get in. (39)

To be sure, many of us recognize in Douglass's description of Col. Lloyd's garden an alternative reading of America as the promised land, the Garden of Eden. I would suggest that for Douglass the garden is a metaphor for government's descent into institutional immorality, which is consistent with his view of slavery as a living hell. It is an extension of his view that the slave traders were nothing but "a band of successful robbers" (67) who had the Bible and government on their side. They rob the enslaved African Americans of their dignity and their labor. For those readers who may have missed his point, Douglass drives it home with his reference to the ubiquitous tar, which signifies on the relation of blacks to America as he unveils a fundamental paradox of life in America. Black people assist in the building and maintenance of many of the carefully coiffured "gardens" in America from courthouses to country clubs; yet they do not benefit in any meaningful way from the fruits of their labor.

Douglass's image of America as "a large and finely cultivated garden" registers strongly in the imagination of many of my students who have ambitions of being successful in the world of corporate America. If fraternity row represents the garden with a lowercase "g" and the country club represents the garden with an uppercase "g," then I ask my students: What does this mean in terms of the implications for public policy? Who lives where and why? How will this affect their opportunities for success? And to be successful, must my black students become Afro-Saxons, black on the outside and white on the inside? I tell them that these are questions we all have to work our way through.

As an African-American intellectual, I see the academy as a type of garden—a private preserve in which many of us are spoken *of* but rarely spoken *to*. By this I mean, we are often out of the loop in regard to meaningful academic discourse; many of us discover upon our arrival in the academy that we are *cultural elites* without portfolio. Consequently, our presence is tolerated in an atmosphere of benign neglect. This serves to create feelings of inadequacy and ambivalence; it thus raises an interesting question: Are we scholars who are black or blacks who are scholars? As I wrestle with this question, I am aware that those on the outside see us as having made it, while those on the inside see us as necessary but unwelcome interlopers.

I read Douglass's *Narrative* as an impressive hymn to the indefatigable human spirit. His autobiographical statement is his declaration of semantic independence. He measures his creation of a human and liberated self by the degree to which he is able to articulate imaginatively his experiences. As one who is the first in his family to graduate from college and whose life is now paying dividends on the promise so many people saw in me, Douglass's *Narrative* puts me in sync with my history and the possibility that lies beyond the restrictive categories of race and gender. That his narrative is so in tune with the spirits that move in the souls of black folk may be gauged by how quickly it assumed scriptural significance.

And like any sacred text, there is room in Douglass's narrative for those with divergent points of view to go "up from slavery," "stride toward freedom," or seek freedom and liberation "by any means necessary." The unmistakable optimism that infuses Douglass's vision makes it possible for all to say in unison, and "still [we] rise" (Washington, King, Malcolm X, Angelou). Frederick Douglass, the heroic voice of black America, challenges us to not let anybody turn us around.

Notes

1. One of the verses to this classic spiritual is:

> Ain't gonna let nobody turn me 'round,
> Turn me 'round, turn me 'round.
> Ain't gonna let nobody turn me 'round.
> Gonna keep on decidin'
> To keep on a-ridin'
> Ridin' to the Promised Land.
> (qtd. in Farmer 1985: 15, 185)

2. Subsequent references to Douglass's *Narrative,* edited by Benjamin Quarles and published by Harvard University Press (1960), will be designated parenthetically.

3. In his essay, "The Talented Tenth," originally published in the anthology *The Negro Problem* (1903), Du Bois argues that liberal arts education is essential for creating the

"aristocracy of talent and character" that will raise "the masses of Negro people" (1986: 847).

4. Ishmael Reed, one of the most productive black writers of his generation, titles a collection of his essays *Writin' is Fightin'*.

5. I attended Catawba College in Salisbury where I earned my B.A. in English. I had a very rewarding and productive four years at this institution affiliated with the United Church of Christ.

References

Abrahams, Peter. *Tell Freedom.* New York: Collier, 1970.

Angelou, Maya. *I Know Why the Caged Bird Sings.* New York: Bantam, 1970.

————. "Still I Rise." *Poems.* New York: Bantam, 1986. 154–55.

Bingham, Caleb. *The Columbian Orator: Containing a Variety of Original and Selected Pieces.* 2d ed. London, 1799.

Douglass, Frederick. *Narrative of the Life of Frederick Douglass, An American Slave, Written by Himself.* 1845. Ed. Benjamin Quarles. Cambridge: Harvard University Press, 1960.

Du Bois, W. E. B. "The Talented Tenth." 1903. *Writings.* New York: Library of America, 1986. 842–61.

Farmer, James. *Lay Bare the Heart: An Autobiography of the Civil Rights Movement.* New York: Plume, 1985.

Grier, William, and Price M. Cobbs. *Black Rage.* New York: Bantam, 1968.

King, Martin Luther, Jr. *Stride Toward Freedom: The Montgomery Story.* New York: Harper & Row, 1958.

Preston, Dickson J. *Young Frederick Douglass: The Maryland Years.* Baltimore: Johns Hopkins University Press, 1980. 83–96.

Reed, Ishmael. *Writin' Is Fightin': Thirty-Seven Years of Boxing on Paper.* New York: Atheneum, 1988.

Washington, Booker T. *Up from Slavery.* 1901. *Three Negro Classics.* Ed. John Hope Franklin. New York: Avon, 1965.

Wright, Richard. *Black Boy.* New York: Harper & Row, 1945.

X, Malcolm. *Autobiography.* With Alex Haley. New York: Ballantine, 1965.

————. *By Any Means Necessary.* Ed. George Breitman. New York: Pathfinder, 1970. 41.

Texas in July 1983. A heat wave year, 104 degrees F. Breathing is an act of courage, and the electric blue sky blares relentlessly over a baked land shimmering in its own glare. I have lived in the south most of my life, and never, never have I known such heat. Mid-morning, and I have made coffee for the grandmother, fixed a lunch for my eight-year-old and left it in the fridge; have put fresh water in the three dogs' bowls and a bucket by the back porch for the five cats; have scrawled a love note to the woman of my dreams who lives with us only on weekends; and I am driving back to Austin to continue my work.

I switch on the radio as I drive through yellowed hills of burnt grass, to variations on Handel's "See the Conquering Hero Comes." Tears choke my eyes. It will not always be this way, I think. Somewhere there is transcendence, beyond this heat, this yellow house with its fleas and fire ants, these endless miles of melting tarmac, the hours and hours of commuting to Austin through cowboy country, this dizziness. Some-where there is green, there is stability, a gentler way of life. Somewhere there is England.

Later today I will begin applying for grants, awards, whatever I can get that will take me to London. The London I want is not Thatcher's London, of course, which is having its own heat wave this summer, but the London of my fantasies: the London of Queen Anne and her gentle Abigail; of frantic theaters in Drury Lane and Lincoln's Inn Field; and of the curious Catharine Trotter Cockburn, whose life and works I am attempting to make sense of. She, too, knew what longing was.

At the age of fifty-nine, living in a small town in godforsaken Northumberland, having reared her houseful of children threadbare and in genteel poverty through thirty years of marriage to a dour clergyman, she wrote a letter to the young and successful Alexander Pope, in London: "You had but just begun to dawn upon the world, when I retired from it. Being married in 1708, I bid adieu to the muses, and so wholly gave myself up to the cares of a family, and the education of my children, that I scarce knew, whether there was any such thing as books, plays, or poems stirring in Great Britain" (*Works* 10, 1). This from a woman who'd set the London intelligentsia afire in 1696, who'd been toasted by the duke and duchess of Marlborough, had served as Farquhar's mentor, defended John Locke, corresponded with Leibnitz, dined with Congreve, and entertained the smirking attentions of a doddering Wycherley. She was so much a fixture of the fashionable scene that when she was caricatured on stage and in libelous novels as "Calista," everyone who was anyone in London knew that Calista was Catharine Trotter. A sparkling prodigy, dazzling London society with her witty poetry and plays, she was also the "favorite" of a certain lady about town. All this until, in 1708, she married and disappeared.

As Mrs. Patrick Cockburn she must have been known in small parish circles. She must have visited the ill, done her washing on Mondays, baked on Tuesdays, mended torn linen, wiped the runny noses of a succession of offspring. There she was, her blonde curls thinning to grey wisps, her breastfruits sagging down toward her waist, her hands knotting up with arthritis and her eyes growing dim, in Long Horseley, Northumberland.

So she made a third career. She began publishing again, as Mrs. Catharine Cockburn, philosopher-poet. She carried on paper debates with deans, published elaborate defenses of great men of her day, penned weighty proofs of what would later be called the "moral imperative." Her literary output between the ages of fifty and seventy was enough to fill one and a half of the two large volumes collected and published shortly before her death. What motivated her? I imagine that sometime during menopause, perhaps as her last child neared independence, she must have listened to "See the Conquering Hero Comes," perhaps on the church organ, and thought with determination, it will not always be this way. Somewhere there is transcendence.

Kendall, I lecture myself, you're projecting. This is the voice of your own longing you hear. Catharine Trotter Cockburn may have known a different thing. But her story, in the context of my own life's questions, obsesses me.

My eyes travel the horizon, the line of stunted and gnarled Texas oaks rooting desperately into a cracked earth in search of moisture, their parched leaves burnt at the edges, caked with dust. I remember Virginia Woolf's line, "who shall measure the heat and violence of the poet's heart when caught and tangled in a woman's body?" Weak, cramping and bleeding from my menses, my back and underclothes soaked with sweat, regrets, blood, and memories, I park the car and stumble toward the frigidly air-conditioned recesses of the Humanities Research Center to continue my quest for the truth about this curious woman who lived at least three apparently unrelated lives in Britain between 1679 and 1749.

What first drew me to Trotter was the pulsing, devoted, and unmistakably erotic energy between two heroines in Trotter's first play, *Agnes de Castro,* written when she was sixteen years old. The mottled pages of the text printed in 1696 set my whole life swirling in spirals around my chair. My sitting in that refrigerated library, holding *Agnes de Castro* in my hands, was subversive. The little play, exquisitely bound in gold-tooled leather by a nineteenth-century book collector, was never intended for the eyes of an irreverent leftist dyke. I knew, as I read, that Agnes was a lesbian heroine. I doubted my judgment, read again, knew, and still doubted.

Trotter's Agnes is indifferent to the Prince because she was not "made for Love" (p. 13) of any man but is passionately in love with the Princess, who loves her husband and Agnes equally and is torn between them.

In their first scene the Princess cries, "My Agnes! Art thou come! My Souls best Comfort, / Thou dear Relief to my oppressing Cares" (3). Instead of lusting for the Prince, Trotter's Cleopatra is jealous of him. She swears, "Gods! Is it just the Prince enjoy this Blessing, / Who knows not how to value the vast Treasure" (7). An observer reports, "They mingled Kisses with the tend'rest Words, / As if their Rivalship had made 'em dear" (20).

Driving home to a weekend with the dusky butch whose working-class humor puts my scholarship in proper perspective, I can't wait to tell her what I've found. She listens, seated in front of the fan with a beer and a cigarette, shaking her head. "They'll never believe you," she predicts. "They'll say you made it up. They'll say dykes didn't exist back then." She reaches for my hand, "How old did you say this kid was when she wrote it?"

"Sixteen."

"Possible," Mary muses, caressing my palm. "I knew when I was ten. I knew that I wasn't supposed to feel that way, but I didn't care." I picture the sixteen-year-old Trotter. Maybe she could be so daring precisely because she was so young and didn't care. *Agnes* came three years *after* Trotter's epistolary novel was published. That book, *Olinda's Adventures, or the Amours of a Young Lady,* appeared first in 1693, while Trotter was making a reputation for herself as a juvenile genius; it was reprinted the year after her success with *Agnes de Castro.* The novel reappeared again in 1718 and 1724, during the financially difficult years of her marriage.

I wondered why Thomas Birch, whose 1751 account of Trotter's life is the one authoritative source, never mentioned her novel. I was to find out why when I reached London, with my son in tow, in 1984. What I found in the British Museum manuscript collection was a scrap on which Birch had written this note to himself: "Ask if not better to omit mentioning the Atalantis etc.—Ask if not proper to give some reason for not publishing all Plays mention'd.—Also Life of Olinda" (Add. Ms. 4265, f. 43). That scrap of paper was one of my major finds that summer, because Birch *did* mention (and discredit) *Atalantis,* Delariviere Manley's key novel that depicts Trotter as promiscuous with both men and women; but he said little about *Agnes* and not a word about *Olinda.*

Olinda is a titillating little masterpiece by a girl whose dream was to dazzle a collection of suitors but outwit them all and avoid the marriage market by becoming independently wealthy. Olinda has no romantic notions about love, marriage, and the fulfillment of motherhood. Her relations with men are uniformly shallow and manipulative; she weighs their proposals in terms of pounds sterling. When she gives her heart, it is to another young woman. She writes that Clarinda is "the only Woman that I ever trusted, not with any Secret, for you see I then had none of consequence; but with my Love, and in that she betray'd me" (149).

After this betrayal, Olinda dedicates herself to a lifetime of platonic friendships. Her mother wrings her hands, "What do you mean Child, to receive with equal indifference all the Proposals that are made to you? Do you resolve to lead a single Life? I should approve of the choice in one of a better Fortune, but you must conform your self to yours, and consider that I am not able to maintain you" (189). Olinda, ever realistic, yields to her mother's pressure to marry: "I had no Aversion for him, and since my Circumstances would oblige me to Marry, and that I knew I could never love any Man; I thought it might as well be he as any other" (189). At the last moment, a dashing, wealthy, married nobleman provides a handsome income for her in return for her promise to wait for his "condition" to change (i.e., for his young and perfectly healthy wife to die).

I went back to her line, "And that I knew I could never love any Man." That line was to be echoed memorably by Agnes, swearing she "was not made for Love." What could it mean, but that Trotter was a lesbian, whether or not she had a word for it? And yet. *Was* she what we now call a lesbian? Her one-time friend and playwriting cohort Delariviere Manley claimed in *The New Atalantis* that Trotter was part of that "cabel," of ladies who "seek their Diversion in themselves" according to "the devices of old Rome riviv'd" (43). But Delariviere Manley said many things, and she had her reasons for wanting to take Catharine Trotter down a peg.

My second great find, that summer of 1984, was a volume of fantastic, panting letters from Lady Sarah Piers to Catharine Trotter, parts of them razored out or torn off, and the parts that remain as circuitous as they are heated. Take this one, written to a coy and flirting nineteen-year-old Trotter: "I am too Charmingly convinc'd what additional joys your Letters will bring, not to deny my Self the perfection of all my pleasures, and thus break through all opposition to send you my softest wishes, and remind you how much t'is in your power to oblige me." Two years later Sarah Piers was still running on these themes, "not dareing to give my self the liberty of thinking on a subject too tender for my senses," and commenting that, as often happens with lesbian couples, their menstrual periods are occurring at the same time: "I can't omit my malicious pleasure in finding you indispos'd at the same time with me, hopeing it a sympathy that demonstrates our unity" (Add. Ms. 4264, f. 291).

It would require an effort of incredible denial to believe Trotter was having only an affair of the mind with the Lady Sarah, and given these letters, added to the portraits of Agnes and Olinda, I became convinced that I had indeed found a proto-lesbian playwright. Hurrying down Oxford Street to meet my brave boy at Trafalgar Square, where he spent the afternoon counting Ferraris while I pored over manuscripts, I was bursting with my discovery, with what it might mean to women who always knew what kind they were, but had no sense of the history of tradition of their kind.

Given my choices, I think there's no question Trotter would have lived as a lesbian; she certainly had the imagination of a woman whose tenderest feelings are for other women, who is indifferent to male desire, and who rebels against male power. Not just in *Agnes* but in all her plays, she creates female characters who are morally and intellectually superior to the men around them and who regard marriage merely as a financial necessity. Her women wear breeches, debate with Archbishops, tease and flatter men, and reveal their true spirits only to other women. Heterosexual passion is the downfall of both heroes and heroines, while friend-ship—between women, between men—is nobler than love. This was the classical tradition, of course, and in some ways she was writing for her market, creating plots to bear out the beliefs of her time. But Dryden, Pix, Congreve, Centlivre—most of her contemporaries—allow heterosexual love to triumph now and then. She didn't. What does this say about her vision? Given the options available to her, maybe it would be more honest to call her—what? bisexual?

I would never call myself bisexual, but I wouldn't swear I "could never love any man," which argues more for calling her a lesbian. I did, in fact, love several men, my son's father prime among them. Wasn't he gorgeous as he kneeled over me that morning in New Orleans, listening to Handel's "Love in Bath," the sunlight golden on his lean body, a fire in his eyes and traces of apple butter on his lips? I could never have, with him, what I've had with women—that true intimacy, that understanding borne of years of conditioning in common, that heat in the blood surpassing all others. He was very nice, in his way; I would say I loved him. But we could get no rest with each other; I was always just about to embarrass him, and he sat on my spirit like a stone. Trotter would have understood my refusal to marry him. In a letter to her niece she wrote: "To have a good husband early snatched from us, is indeed a grievous affliction; but to live long with a very bad one, might be much worse, which is the lot of many" (*Works* 2, 302).

But did Trotter ever really love anyone? I wanted her to be like me, a juicy woman of quick and intense passions, flinging herself after one love and then the next. If there is one thing I know about myself, I smiled as I unlocked the door to the rented flat, it is that I'm a lover.

Horribly, however, as I turned on the tea kettle, the image of Harriette came shaking her angry auburn locks in my face. Harriette: Greek, pas-sionate, temperamental, gorgeous, capable of equal portions of sweetness and vengeance. Harriette had a unique gift for always saying what I feared most to hear. Harriette raged at me, "You don't know what love is. You don't know how to love." Is that just what women say when you leave them? I began to have a stomach ache. Maybe I love like a man; that was another of Harriette's accusations. Maybe I don't love. Maybe what I think is love is—what? Liminality? Lust? Codependency? What is love, anyway? Could it be that I . . . ?

I began to need evidence that Trotter loved. It took on desperate importance. While my restless son switched channels, dissatisfied with television, I sifted through note cards, dissatisfied with my research. He came to me whining, needing comfort, disappointed. I put down my notes, met him in that disappointment, and held him in the big armchair by the window. We searched for the North Star in the night sky, escaping ourselves, and I wondered how the course of historical research might have gone through the ages if all the historians had been mothers. Seth. I am sure I love this child. He sets my priorities straight. It shakes my whole being to look at his coltish legs thrown over a chair arm, a bead of sweat on his saddle-nose, the scar on his upper lip. That's reality. He dressed for bed. I read some *Wind in the Willows,* tucked him in, and watched him slip softly into sleep. Then I dug about for my copy of that letter I had read in Texas, in Birch's collection. Catharine Trotter Cockburn loved her children. At the age of sixty-four she wrote to her niece:

> The unexpected loss of my poor child, who was so useful to me, and had been almost all her life with me, was indeed a severe affliction. She was a long time every moment in my thoughts. Whatever I turned my mind to, she mingled with it; all that I found in books, was some way or other applied to her; and still there is not a day but she is frequently the subject of my reflections; nor do I endeavour to divert them from her. . . . I sometimes imagine, that I have now a nearer interest in another state than I had; and please myself with the hopes of joining her spirit there, and finding her rejoicing in her early escape from the evils of this world (*Works* 2, 309).

My throat swelled shut and tasted of sea-water. I looked at Seth's long boy-body in the British bed and hoped I would die before him. The love that Catharine felt for her child, that I feel for mine, is not a conditional thing, a thing that can wither or change with time and the passing of seasons. It's as close to passion as the old woman came, on paper. It's the longest and the deepest love I've known. I began to feel a subtle calming. It wasn't the love Harriette was talking about, but it was a beginning. We did know something about love, Catharine and me.

As an adolescent, Trotter wrote passionately to other girls. All that long night, accompanied by Seth's breathing, I reviewed evidence of her love: the poetry in *Agnes,* the reference to Clarinda in *Olinda's Adventures,* and two languid poems written in 1694, a month before Trotter's sixteenth birthday, to someone named "Mrs. Reresby." The Reresby poems are lovesick teenage excess, skilled imitation of literary convention. But did Trotter know mature, adult love, a love of equals, a love beyond the dreamings, the projections, and the poetry of adolescence? Did I?

Nothing like the passion of her teens appears in her letters to Patrick

Cockburn in the year preceding their marriage. It was clear, by 1707, that she was not going to be able to support herself by writing. After *Agnes de Castro* she managed to get four more plays staged commercially, and two were very successful, but not successful enough. She had tried poetry, plays, and patronage, and she was still living as a guest in one country house after another. Love, by 1707, had become an expensive (perhaps a dangerous) luxury. At the age of twenty-eight, she put away poetry and other childish things and married Patrick Cockburn.

She and I took very different turnings; more choices were available to me. That summer I was thirty-nine and had packed away poetry and certain of my wild ways and was cementing myself to a career in scholarship, careening a little unsteadily through the world with one child at my side and the word "lesbian" written in my stance, my haircut, and my wardrobe. Catharine Trotter would have loved that option. Blessed am I among women, I thought, as morning shone its full face onto the little bed-sitter. There was a glad chorus of birds, the gray sky was clearing to patches of blue, a warm breeze was teasing the windows, Seth was stirring. It was time to make breakfast, to brush and wash and dress ourselves for another day.

Since that summer, the whole era, and the phenomenon in women's history of which Trotter was a part, is coming to light, so that she is considerably less obscure than she was when I first came upon her in 1983 (Cotton, Morgan, Clark, Pearson, Steeves, and Kendall). But what still puzzles me is what Catharine Trotter Cockburn made of it all in her old age and what I can make of it now. History is not so tidy as fiction, and her story will not be rounded off neatly. She married the clergyman, reared her children, and on the other side of menopause she began to write again. Despite asthma, arthritis, poverty, bad weather, and failing eyesight, she wrote.

In 1743, at the age of sixty-four, she published *Remarks upon some Writers in the Controversy concerning the Foundation of Moral Virtue and Moral Obligation, with some thoughts concerning Necessary Existence; the Reality and Infinity of Space; the Extension and Place of Spirits; and on Dr. Watts's Notion of Substance.* It's not to my taste, and it doesn't fit feminist prescriptions of the soul of woman breaking silence, but there is something clean in the way she finished things. She had a good eye for estimating the possible, and she didn't flay her spirit over lost ambitions or vanquished dreams. She educated her children, and then in her last years she laid the sewing aside, she let someone else sweep the hearth, she may even have let the porridge dry out and burn in the pot, and she wrote what it satisfied her to write.

In another letter to her niece, she delivers her recipe for peace of mind, which completely fractures mine: "To hope the best, to submit, and to believe, which I hope I may be as well able to practise, as to preach" (2, 277). "To hope the best." To hope the best, one has to know what the best is, and what woman, trained to believe her best is less and matters less than his best, knows the best when she sees it? "To submit." Submit. I suppose she couldn't have used any other word. Presumably she means submit to the inexorable, in her belief system the will of God; but it might be nothing more almighty than the will of capitalist patriarchy. How does one recognize the inexorable? One woman's inexorable is another woman's failure to envision what is possible, to hope what is really the best. The same precept could keep a battered woman with her batterer, a slave with her master, a prisoner in her cell. And then, "To believe." I raise my eyes from her page to the shelves of rare books preserved for the eyes of the privileged few who have access to them. Believe what, Catharine? Believe in what hierarchy, what great chain of being? Believe in whose power and whose glory, forever?

I wish that she had sat down and written out the whole, bloody truth of her life, which would have helped me sort myself out much better than her commentaries on sermons. I begin to think there is more to life than truth or freedom; that both are spinning through time rather than absolute, that at any moment in time we occupy some moving point on the moving continuum of truth. Of freedom. And of all those other big concepts: beauty, love, peace, wholeness. We all do hold our whole lives in our hands all the time, constantly experimenting to see how much of the pain, how much of the pleasure, how much of the fact of each moment we can recognize. A little denial can be a mechanism, like laughter, that helps us move our leaden feet in a kind of slow dance through the killing days.

"How unhappy some have been, who seem to have deserved much better than ourselves." Perhaps destiny is the sum of one's moment in time, multiplied by one's nationality, race, class, gender, and genes, and divided by the prejudices of the ruling group where one happens to live. I have taken Catharine Trotter Cockburn into myself and merged with her; like an ex-lover, she fuses with my present and gives shape to my ever-mobile identity, which can always use a little help.

References

Ballard, George. *Memoirs of Several Ladies of Great Britain.* Oxford, 1752.

Birch, Thomas. "An Account of the Life of the Author." *The Works of Mrs. Catharine*

Cockburn, Theological, Moral, Dramatic, and Poetical. Ed. Thomas Birch. 2 vols. London, 1751. i–xiviii.

————. Memoirs of Catharine Trotters Cockburn written by various hands, gathered by Thomas Birch for his edition of her collected *Works.* Add. Ms. 4265, various ff. British Library, London.

Clark, Constance. "The Female Wits: Catharine Trotter, Delariviere Manley, and Mary Pix—Three Women Playwrights Who Made Their Debuts in the London Season of 1695–96." Ph.D. diss. City University of New York, 1984.

Cockburn, Catharine Trotter. *Agnes de Castro.* London, 1696.

————. "Calliope's Directions How to Deserve and Distinguish the Muses Inspirations." Add. Ms. 4265, f. 58. British Library, London.

————. *Fatal Friendship.* London, 1698.

————. *Love at a Loss, or Most Votes Carry It.* London, 1701.

————. *Olinda's Adventures: Or, the Amours of a Young Lady.* 1693, 1718. Reprint ed. Robert Adams Day. Los Angeles: William A. Clark Memorial Library, UCLA, 1969.

————. Poems to Reresby, 1695. Add. Ms. 4265, ff. 74–75. British Library, London.

————. *The Revolution of Sweden.* London, 1706.

————. *The Unhappy Penitent.* London, 1701.

————. *The Works of Mrs. Catharine Cockburn, Theological, Moral, Dramatic, and Poetical.* Ed. Thomas Birch. 2 vols. London, 1751.

Cotton, Nancy. *Women Playwrights in England c. 1363–1750.* Lewisburg, Pa.: Bucknell University Press, 1980.

Kendall. *Love and Thunder: Plays by Women in the Age of Queen Anne.* London: Methuen, 1988.

Kendall, Kathryn. "From Lesbian Heroine to Devoted Wife: Or, What the Stage Would Allow." *Journal of Homosexuality* 12 (May 1986): 9–21.

Manley, Delariviere. *The Novels of Mary Delariviere Manley.* Ed. Patricia Koster. 2 vols. Gainesville, Fla.: Scholars' Facsimiles and Reprints, 1971.

Morgan, Fidelis. *The Female Wits: Women Playwrights on the London Stage 1660–1720.* London: Virago, 1981.

Pearson, Jacqueline. *The Prostituted Muse: Images of Women and Women Dramatists 1642–1737.* New York: St. Martins, 1988.

Piers, Lady Sarah. Letters to Catharine Trotter. Add. ms. 4264, ff. 280–341. British Library, London.

Steeves, Edna L., ed. *The Plays of Mary Pix and Catharine Trotter.* 2 vols. New York: Garland, 1982.

Wycherley, William. Letter to Catharine Trotter (undated). Add. ms. 4264, f. 265. British Library, London.

In Between Abject & Object:

The Mourning Sickness of the

Expectant Mother, or, Three

Movements of the Blues

in B Minor

*

Dana Beckelman

A

"This, then, is the terrain," as Jamaica Kincaid opens "At the Bottom of the River." A terrain occupied by a stream that having "at last swelled to a great, fast flowing body of water, falls over a ledge with a roar, a loudness that is more than the opposite of silence, then rushes over dry flat land in imperfect curves" (62). A stream that "awaits the eye, the hand, the foot that shall then give all this meaning." But, as Kincaid asks, "what shall that be" (63)? The "that" of Kincaid's question is the terrain I want to explore, a terrain, like Kincaid's river, that flows between loudness and silence, perpetually fluid. A terrain that empties into evaporation only to fall again, seeping underground only to resurface, meandering in endless imperfection. A terrain I want to explore as mourning.

Somewhere a phone is ringing. Usually, on a weekday, before 7:30 A.M., I expect it to be my mother. What will it be this time, I wonder, wading through the barking dogs and the cat's philosophizing. "Did I wake you?" she always asks. The coffee maker sighs, measuring my life in a slow drip. Why does she think that I cannot wake up all by myself? I stare at the newspaper, still wrapped in plastic wet from the lawn. Maybe she never knows what to expect.

"Hi, Mom," I answer before she speaks sometimes. "So I'm that predictable, am I?" she laughs. "You just wait. Someday someone is going to surprise you and you'll be sorry for making fun of your mother."

Yes, I expect I will. When the dogs haven't barked and the paper is still on the

lawn. When the coffee maker sits silently and I am curled around the cat in the
darkness. When the phone will ring unexpectedly and I will not want to answer it.

In *Inhibitions, Symptoms, and Anxiety* Freud claims, "Anxiety has an unmistakable relation to *expectation;* it is an anxiety *about* something. It has a
quality of *indefiniteness and lack of object.*" (91). In contrast, "Mourning
occurs under the influence of reality-testing," which demands separation
from "the object, since it no longer exists" (98). "At birth," Freud says,
"no object existed and so no object could be missed. Anxiety was the only
reaction that occurred" (96). As Susan Suleiman has pointed out, however, the blindness of psychoanalysis is in formulating birth as if "the only
self worth worrying about in the mother-child relationship were that of
the child" (356). Yet, Jane Gallop believes that is "its great strength; it has
given us access to what is denied by any psychology that assumes that the
child simply becomes an adult, rational, civilized" (137).

For Gallop, the only "blind spot" of psychoanalysis is the child's "inability to have any realistic notion of the mother as an other subjectivity"
(137). If at birth no "object" existed, though, not only has the mother's
"other subjectivity" not been acknowledged, but her "other objectivity"
as well. If anxiety is the reaction of the child, mourning is the reaction of
the mother, for the reality-testing of birth demands that she separate
from an "object" that no longer exists, an object I want to explore as the
"relationship" of pregnancy that has been marginalized by the societal
construction of "expectant motherhood."

In "Mourning and Melancholia," Freud distinguishes mourning, which
he believes ends when the "libidinal object" is replaced, from melancholia, which "pathologically" persists, a distinction Kathleen Woodward
believes has been "cut too sharply." Woodward argues that "we may
point to something *in between* mourning and melancholia, that we may
refer to a grief which is interminable but not melancholic in the psychoanalytic sense" (178). While Freud believes when the work of mourning
"has been accomplished the ego will have succeeded in freeing its libido
from the lost object" (*SE* 14: 252), Woodward claims that in many cases,
"we do not detach ourselves from our losses. Instead we live with them"
(195).

Whereas Freud and Woodward are referring primarily to death, however, birth incarnates *both* the libidinal object and the "loss" of that object,
for what is "lived with" in the child is a physical reminder of the ego
relationship that existed before the separation of birth. That this relationship has been defined as "expectancy" by its supposed "indefiniteness and
lack of object" assumes not only that the object must be physical, but that

the object is yet to come. As Barbara Rothman argues, "The pregnancy is thought of as a time of 'expecting' for the mother—its future the only thing that counts, its present having meaning only in the future" (90). Pregnancy can only anticipate an object and, thus, has no object that can be "lost."

As a result, in the same way Freud expects mourning to end in the replacement of the libidinal object, the relationship of pregnancy has been replaced by the societal "expectancy" of motherhood, an expectation graphically illustrated by Larry Peppers and Ronald Knapp in their study of maternal grief: "For the majority of new, expectant mothers, the pregnancy will be planned, endured, enjoyed, completed, and fulfilled through the birth of a healthy infant. But for approximately one third of these women, conception will not terminate in happiness, smiles, and pleasant anticipation of the future, but in sadness, tears, and painful memories, their babies the victims of perinatal death" (13–14).

Certainly the losses suffered by women due to perinatal death and miscarriage have been tragically misunderstood and maliciously obviated under the pretense that a woman should merely "try again." The more insidious tragedy Peppers and Knapp perpetuate, however, is that pregnancy is assumed to "terminate" in "pleasant anticipation of the future." "Painful memories" are only acknowledged in relation to death. The expectation Peppers and Knapp don't explore is that birth might terminate in a "loss" that is not "death," a "termination" not of the future but of the past.

The term "loss," Woodward claims, "allows us to foreground our role in the story we are telling, to assert a relation, to refer not so much to the event of death [or birth] as to what we have suffered by that death [or separation], to speak of *our* pain, our grief. . . . For by asserting we have lost someone, do we not also mean that we *feel lost* ourselves . . . that we *have been lost*" (177)? In viewing birth as a "gain," we fail to recognize not only the psychic and physical relationship that the mother "has lost" in birth, but that she may "feel lost" herself, that she may "have been lost" in the process. As such, in between conception and birth lies the possibility of a different expectation: a "grief which is interminable but not melancholic," a "painful memory" not only of the past, but incarnated in the future.

Somewhere a phone is ringing. My hand gropes through the darkness. It does not stop to think. "Hello?" Then I remember. I drop the receiver and run to the bathroom, washing my face until the ringing disappears, until I can look in the mirror and see her again. When my thick blonde hair falls across my forehead and turns black with gray streaks as I brush it out of my eyes. Just like she did. When my thin wire-framed glasses slide down my nose and become black and horn-rimmed as I push them back up. Just like she did. When I fiddle with the mole on my chin that is her mole and chin. Just like she did.

I wonder who she saw when she looked in the mirror, who she remembered. Just like I remember her. "You just knew her as Granny," my mother hisses. "She was different as a mother." I try to imagine how Granny must have treated my mother differently, how my mother will treat the child I imagine having someday, what I will see in the mirror then that I don't notice now. I didn't notice the passing years. Granny had always been old to me. I didn't notice the slower walk. She had always walked slowly. After she had a heart attack I offered to live with her, but she said it wasn't necessary. She could take care of herself. I didn't notice when she changed her mind. She had never changed.

Somewhere a phone is ringing. Yes, Granny, I'll come live with you, I scream into the receiver. But the phone line is dead. I never expected her to die. Every summer in San Antonio was the same: the flaming red lipstick oleanders, the cotton-candy azaleas, the chocolate chip cookie afternoons, dancing while they baked. "Que sera, sera. Whatever will be, will be," Granny would sing, swaying me in her arms. "The future's not ours to see. Que sera, sera."

My mother does not want to remember. "Such an unhappy Christmas," she starts to cry. "Such an unhappy way to spend Granny's last Christmas." But I cannot remember Granny without remembering her last Christmas. "Want to come live with your Granny, Dana Ann?"

"But the house is already for sale and Mom expects you to live with her." I did not notice that all I needed to say was yes. But she did. "It's OK, Dana Ann. What will be, will be."

B

At the bottom of Kincaid's river is "a man who lives in a world bereft of its very nature. He lies on his bed as if alone . . . waiting and waiting. . . . He is not yet complete, so he cannot conceive of what it is he waits for" (63). Conceive: to become pregnant; to cause to begin: originate; to take into one's mind; to form a conception of: imagine, image. The classic dualism: women begin in the body; men begin in the mind. Women become pregnant; men imagine. But for Kincaid, imagining is not enough. "He cannot conceive of the fields of wheat," "the union of opposites," "the birds in migratory flight," "the wind that ravages the coastline" (63). He cannot conceive of that which is not his. He cannot imagine an expectation that is not his own.

We do not expect that the "expectant" mother may have already created a relationship with that which cannot be seen. We do not expect that in her psychic differentiation of the child that will be she has become attached to that which already is. We do not expect that in a newborn child a mother may see not only what will be, but all that has already been. We do not expect that she might not want to separate. We do not expect her to remember that which was. We do not expect that the first ego split is not the child's but the mother's. We expect her to forget.

In the short story, "The Vase," Jessamyn West creates a tension between what it is we want to forget and what it is we cannot help remembering. From the beginning she creates a split between Jess and Eliza, a traditional Quaker farming couple. Jess is concerned with the "outside," the farm, the rain, the phenomena of the "natural world," while Eliza is concerned with the "inside," the housework, the home. Jess had planned the day for work, but the rain has forced him to make "use" of his time analyzing the difference between winter and summer rain. Unable to hide "the light of his knowledge" (182), Jess asks Eliza what she thinks. " 'Ain't thee interested in knowing how?' he asked. 'Ain't thy curiosity pricked? Don't natural phenomena mean anything to thee?' Some did, some didn't. The sound rain made was one that didn't. Bread rising, house shining, fire dozing on the hearth, these were phenomena, and natural, too, Eliza supposed, and for the time being quite enough for her" (183).

But the split between the "natural phenomena" of the inside and outside worlds quickly evolves into another (or, perhaps, more appropriately, [an]other) difference between Jess and Eliza. Bored with staring at the rain, Jess picks up what Eliza has set on the secretary among what Jess thinks are "reminders of woman's strangeness" (183). Jess asks what it is. Eliza says it is a vase. It can't be a vase, Jess replies "reasonably," "it's open at both ends" (184). "What'd thee aim making it?" Jess asks. Eliza answers: "I aimed to make a pretty thing" (184–85).

The difference is not merely that Eliza's world is aesthetic while Jess's world is logical, that Jess seems to ask all the questions and Eliza must provide all the answers, that Jess only sees the vase as unfunctional while Eliza sees a symbol of her life. Jess finds as much beauty in the stars and sunsets as Eliza finds in pillow shams and peacock feathers arranged over the fireplace. But the beauty Jess observes is that which is already made, while "the prettiness a woman saw she had to make, she had to build it up from odds and ends" (186). Jess seeks answers from the outside; Eliza finds her own from within. "Prettiness outside, Jess understood, she knew. . . . But prettiness inside? . . . Did Jess even note her handiwork? . . . Did he see how the bareness of timber and stone had been hidden and softened, until the room, to her eye, showed itself prettier than any cloud, and not to be outdone, even, by a rose" (186).

The vase, however, has "come to mean more to her than prettiness" (186). It is not what the vase is now, whether its function is useful or pleasurable, but, rather, what it helps Eliza to remember. Jess remembers temperatures and inches of rain. "Eliza remembered how she had felt and from this determined season and weather" (187).

That the story is told in flashbacks speaks, though, for the greatest difference between Jess and Eliza. Eliza remembers what Jess wants to forget. Years after she had started the vase, Eliza goes back to it after the death of her young daughter, when, even though she had passed through the "first period of grief" and said "God's will be done," she was still left with "a great heaviness" (191). She had saved a broken oil lamp chimney, remembering a neighbor had told her it could be made into an ornament for the parlor. She had envisioned it for a long time, and suddenly one morning, she started it while making breakfast.

Sculpting with putty, around the top, "remembering flowers," she made "petal-sized scallops" (188). She mended the break with a swan, painting it a "dazzling white," surrounding it with blue water and green reeds and thin clouds "all raveling out toward the same direction" (189). She had envisioned making two swans, but she stopped to rest. Then it was time for breakfast, time to raise the children, time to can jellies and answer Jess' questions.

She had never finished it, though there had been times when "its incompletion troubled her mind," making her feel "she had turned away from something . . . that it was more to her than she understood" (190). How strange, she thinks, that she should finally go back to finishing it only after the death of a child. She outlines the second swan, imagining her daughter asking if she was making a bird. "I can never lose her," she thinks (191). But before she can finish, Jess comes in from the snow, crying over his daughter's grave.

> He did a thing he had never done—before or since—he dropped on his knees and laying his head . . . on to her lap, had cried, not quietly, for Jess was not a quiet man.
>
> "Eliza," he asked, "has thee forgotten that the first words Sarah ever spoke were about the snow? There she stood, clapping her little hands together and crying, 'Pretty flowers, pretty flowers.'"

Eliza had not forgotten. The words had been in her mind all afternoon. "No, Jess," she said. "I have not forgotten."

"How can thee be playing then?" Jess cried. "Playing with thy paints? And Sarah's grave there under the snow?"

"I haven't forgotten God, either, Jess," she said. (192)

Eliza comforts Jess by reminding him of God, but she had gone back to the vase because God had not comforted her. Eliza comforts Jess in her arms, but she had sought comfort in remembering the vase. Jess's grief is an outburst, a moment of despair, a memory of his daughter that will pass when the snow melts. In the vase Eliza sustains her mourning permanently. After comforting Jess, when he had grown calm and gone back to work, Eliza decides to leave the vase unfinished, placing it among the other things that she treasured, "reminding her of so much, the dream before sunup, and much beside, that, never dreamed of, had come since that morning" (192).

No, she had never dreamed that a child would die, that what she had started would remain unfinished. She had never dreamed that the second swan would remain a vague outline, or that, in creating a prettiness for the inside, she had depicted a prettiness of the outside. She had never dreamed that the expression of all her expectation would be that to which she returned at the very moment her expectation was shattered. No, the morning she started the vase, she had only dreamed of how wonderful life would be.

> It was earlier than rising time, but she had no sleep left in her and was too happy to lie still any longer. In a moment's musing, she then seventeen, there had come to her such bliss in a sudden picturing of what her life and Jess's might be, that she felt she must be out of bed, and advancing toward it; moving forward into the opening years, toward the children, toward the May mornings and snowy evenings, toward the fine housewifery and loving kindness, toward the old age when she and Jess would say, "Remember, remember," as they lay listening to wind or rain. It all came to her that summer morning on waking and she had to be up out of bed and hastening to meet it. (188).

In the vase, she could record her expectation permanently. In the vase, she could bring the outside world inside. In the vase, she could physically remember how she had felt and all that she had dreamed one summer morning. In returning to the vase, she realizes what she did not expect.

She goes back to the vase thinking, "How different this was, no vision, never misdoubting that there were sorrows ahead." Yet, in seeing the swan take shape, she feels a "tranquil satisfaction," in believing once again "that it was a real wind which moved the frayed clouds across the summer sky" (191). But she does not get to finish. Her moment of comfort is interrupted by Jess's need for comfort.

In leaving the second swan an outline, she depicts the emptiness in the outside world, a swan, that unlike the one she had created with putty to symbolize all that was inside her, cannot begin to express all that she feels inside—the comforting of herself that will always be interrupted, that will never be enough. In leaving the vase unfinished, she realizes that no matter what she expects, no matter how well she now knows that expectations can be shattered, she will never be prepared for their loss. In leaving the vase unfinished, she permanently records a reminder that her loss will always go unfinished. There is no comfort in the outside for what has been lost from within.

The end of the story returns to the present, with Jess handing the vase to Eliza as he decides even in the rain he has to feed the cows. "He clasped Eliza to him before he went out, as warmly as if bound, as in his mind no doubt he was, on a journey, and Eliza felt between his clasping arms and herself, the vase, which she still held, separating them. And yet, she supposed, seen in another way, it was a link. After he left she set it back on the secretary, but she could still feel the pressure of its fluted rim against her breast as she moved about the kitchen busy with her evening work" (193).

In the vase the outside and inside worlds coexist, separated yet linked. In the vase that from which Eliza has been separated can be remembered. In the vase that which remains unfinished is the feeling on Eliza's breast long after she has separated from the object. In the vase that which has been created consciously remains physically felt.

A

Somewhere a phone is ringing. I am waiting at the airport and she is late. So unlike her. I have never gotten past the gate alone, much less to the curb and back to the phone. No answer. I page and wait. I pace between the curb and gate. I try the phone again. One more ring. Still no answer. I settle on the curb, remembering what she told me to do if I ever got lost: "Stay in one place." First, I think she must have gotten stuck in traffic. Then I shrug that maybe she's just had car trouble. But car trouble soon turns into a car wreck and a car wreck suddenly becomes seriously injured, and somewhere between seriously injured and may not last through the night, I expect my mother to have died.

I run back to the phone. Calm down, maybe she's just gotten lost in vacuuming. One more ring. Then I remember. The phone ringing in my dream. I answer it but it just keeps ringing until I wake, groping through the darkness. Jesus, it's 6 a.m. Yes, Mom, you woke me, are you happy now? "Hello?"

"Dana, I want you to be strong." My father's voice. How strange. Only Mom calls in the morning.

"What's wrong, Dad?" I have no idea what to expect.

"Granny died last night."

No, I must have dropped the phone. No, I must have shrieked and screamed and wailed. I cannot forget and yet all I can remember is my roommate rushing into the room, holding the phone out to me. No, I do not want to know any more.

No, I run through the airport. No, I am crying by the time I reach the curb. A car honks and my mother waves, smiling. "Sorry I'm late."

"Where have you been?" I can't decide whether to shake her or hug her.

"I forgot."

She forgot? How could she, at the moment I most felt her loss, forget me?

There is a mourning that you know you'll never get over. You may push it to the back of the cabinet like the cream of mushroom soup that you bought for god knows why, that you just have never gotten into a cream of mushroom mood to eat, but which you keep shuffling around every time you rearrange the cabinet anyway. You may even forget about it at times, like a scar that finally turns so close to flesh color that you rarely notice it. But when you do, it all comes back to you, and you realize that it has never left, that it is all still there buried below the surface, blended in so well with your life that you have no idea how constructed you are by it, how many decisions you make because of it, how many feelings you will never really ever trust completely—all because of this one little subtle reminder.

Somewhere a phone is ringing. The emptiness I do not want to remember and yet the fullness I cannot forget in the silence. I do not want to answer it, and yet I do not want it to quit ringing. Weekdays, before 7:30 A.M., like it has been ringing for years. I never expected to dread the phone not ringing. The dogs will bark endlessly, the cat will have philosophized. I will have made pot after pot of coffee and retrieved every paper on every lawn in the neighborhood. But the phone will not ring.

I will run to the bathroom, but I will not find her face in the mirror. So different she is from me. Her thin brown hair never falls in her face. Her glasses never slide down her nose. Her chin has no moles. I will wash and wash, but there will be no ringing to disappear. Only in the running water will I find her again, the river of loss that anticipates loss, the mourning for my grandmother that shall become the mourning for my mother. The Others from whom I cannot detach and yet still expect to be "I"; the psychic attachment that remains in the Other after the physical separation of the mother.

In the river of the "expectant" mother's mourning, then, is the loudness of creation and the silence of its loss, a sound that is more than its opposite, a sound that is more than the encompassing symbolic can describe. Somewhere a phone is ringing, but in my mourning for my mother mourning her mother mourning her mother, all I can hear is mourning listening to mourning listening to mourning. This, then, shall be the terrain.

References

Freud, Sigmund. *Inhibitions, Symptoms, and Anxiety*. Trans. Alix Strachey. N.Y.: Norton, 1959.

————. "Mourning and Melancholia." *The Standard Edition of the Complete Psychological Works of Sigmund Freud*. Ed. James Strachey. N.Y.: Norton, 1959. Vol. 14: 239–58.

Gallop, Jane. "Reading the Mother Tongue: Psychoanalytic Criticism." *The Trials of Psychoanalysis*. Ed. Francoise Meltzer. Chicago: University of Chicago Press, 1988. 125–40.

Kincaid, Jamaica. "At the Bottom of the River." *At the Bottom of the River*. N.Y.: Vintage, 1985. 62–82.

Peppers, Larry, and Ronald Knapp. *Motherhood and Mourning*. N.Y.: Praeger, 1980.

Rothman, Barbara. *Recreating Motherhood*. N.Y.: Norton, 1989.

Suleiman, Susan. "Writing and Motherhood." *The (M)other Tongue: Essays in Feminist Psychoanalytic Interpretation*. Eds. Shirley Nelson Garner, Claire Kahane, and Madelon Sprengnether. Ithaca: Cornell University Press, 1985. 352–77.

West, Jessamyn. "The Vase." *The Friendly Persuasion*. N.Y.: Avon, 1970. 182–93.

Woodward, Kathleen. *Aging and Its Discontents: Freud and Other Fictions*. (Bloomington: Indiana University Press, 1991.)

LA RONDE

of Children

and Mothers

*

Julia Balén

My navel, that shriveled point of juncture with my mother, feels stretched near bursting, its depth pressed flat against the fullness of my belly. The skin (an amazing organ), gives way to the body of water and foetus within. I press my palms against the sides of the bulge, altering the shape, massaging us both with the same strokes. This garners a response, the pressure of limbs from within against my belly, like a tongue pressing hard along the cheeks. I watch for definition, an elbow, knee, foot. His body stretches, pokes and slides against the inner walls of mine. In the mirror I turn every which way, holding poses. I am me and someone I can adore all at once. I feel more than whole.

Exhausted, I close my eyes as the parasite sucks my fluids. Hooks latched, cell for cell to my womb (that organ that betrays the individuality of all the others) it takes first choice of everything. I get the leftovers. It grows at my expense, strong enough to kick me; heavy enough to spread my hips and make me lumber. I feel shriveled and weakened under the weight.

. . . *my body does not have the same ideas I do.* [1]

She tells me, "You can't hold on forever." My body pushes forward no matter my will. The waters burst on the patio tiles. In the ocean over my head, all I can do is go with the currents. When I think I can take no more, I do. Denial is not possible. Three hours later the person who spent months stretching limbs against my stomach is staring me in the face. What I have gained is amazing. My loss fills the thickness of a cord and the depth of my existence.

His toothless mouth at my breast, tiny fingers tickling everything within their reach, the odor of saliva and warm milk, I once again feel more than full. We explore each other's bodies. Belly to belly, skin to skin, his hands on my breasts, fingers to mouths, eyes, noses, ears. We giggle and hum. The sound vibrates through our bodies, enveloping us together from top to toes.

My breasts swell at the sound of his cry. (Is this what it is like to have a penis grow hard at the sound of a voice?) I can press on them to stop the swelling and the flow of sticky sweet milk, but my body still belongs to him, tied to his needs. The sharing becomes manual rather than automatic: I must hold; he must suck. Immediacy is gone. While our bodies still dance together in the rhythm of his needs, I must move myself to his aid. He grasps and clutches, wriggles and squirms, throwing his body toward me and away again. It is no longer a matter of existing together, as a shared body.

He wriggles away from me, crying to get at something he thinks he wants. Back arched, arms outstretched, hands groping, his body lurches out of my grasp. My hand gropes after him and I want to scream. I draw his body back. His will I gather to me with sounds, vibrating the syllables through my lips, throat, chest and abdomen. It calms me. His attention is once again mine. We share a new music. A new language.

In time we no longer share bodies; we share language and space. Though we touch, the continuity of bodies diminishes. What we shared is only a memory that attempts to recreate itself in language. The initial impulse of language is motherly. The bond of body slips through her fingers and she must quickly fabricate a new one, or the child is lost to her forever.[2]

The writer is someone who plays with his mother's body.[3]

The tragedy for Oedipus, the patriarchal proto-writer, is that he lacked knowledge of his mother's body until it was too late, and then his knowledge was a "*père-version*"[4] of social bonds. Not knowing his father's body, he killed it. This is the *"père-version"* of patriarchy: killing the father to get at the mother, whose power and existence are denied. Yet the father is a fiction until the mother names him. Because the mother "offers" her body as the ground on which father and son meet, two social ills develop: she never owns her own body and the son never comes to know the father's body, nor (more importantly) his own. Without the body bond that is the significance of language, fathers and sons are doomed to battle over the body of the woman who must serve as their ground. Within this social construct, they are violently impotent: she is a powerless corpse.

*

He grabs my breast from under my shirt. Deft hands find their mark, then scrunch the overworked flesh, while his mouth sucks greedily for a diminishing return. He gurgles round my nipple, talking to it, to himself, to me with little sense of difference. His eyes catch my gaze as his tongue presses the deflated flesh from his mouth. He tumbles from my lap and toddles off to play, babbling. Other interests eclipse what my body has left to offer. My body is more often left to me once again.

*

Alice Jardine notes, the "Cartesian orphans of the twentieth century" seem desperately in "the process of internalizing . . . feminine spaces while accounting for those crises [of legitimation]."[5] But we have seen this internalization of the feminine before, and rarely more clearly than in mystical patriarchs, like Augustine, Bernard of Clairvaux, or Meister Eckart, who found their calling in becoming "maternal."[6] It seems that both postmodern writers and mystical patriarchs depend upon the ground of a mythical mother to develop a sense of themselves that must seem forever lost. The cord was cut long ago. Their bodies are their own, yet they do not know their own bodies, not even as well as they think they know their mothers'.

Without the ground of body knowledge, language enters the realm of the "ideal." This schism between body and language, body and constructed self, creates the problem of entropy, loss of meaning. In order to control language, we need a ground to balance this "heady" system. Historically in white western culture, women and ethnic minorities have served as degraded body for the exalted detached soul that constitutes the white, phallic subject of language. Of course, this requires the oppression of the "other" as body in culture and repression of embodied voices in language. It also requires the sacrifice of bodies, both male and female. The process of idealization moves in cycles. As the "ideal" grows progressively static and loses meaning, we search for significance through the imaginary remnants of our mothers' bodies (the only bodies many of us have known) until this becomes too burdensome, bringing us too close to that other side of life: death. Then we work our way back to the "ideal." Lack of body knowledge creates a cycle of misogyny.

*

I am a carpenter building houses, cabinets, furniture. I carry my son on my back as I work, my hair in a tail tickling the back of his neck, the tautness of my muscles pressing through the layers of cotton shirts and carrier against his softness. He sleeps to the sounds of saws, teethes on wood blocks, and bounces to the rhythm of hammers until I can carry him no more. At four years old he returns from school with the wisdom of his peers. Women cannot build houses he insists. He has forgotten my body, though he desires it still.

Descartes' philosophy can be read as a desperate attempt to escape from the body, sexuality, and the wiles of the unconscious. Experientially the first body we escape from (physically, and then emotionally) is that of our mother. [7]

"I think, therefore I am." Emphasis on the "I" idealizes the separation of self from others. Dependence on thought as a proof of existence separates the mind from the body, the self from the be-ing: a double separation.

The subject is merely an effect of language. [8]

When I say "I" it is not the same as a man's asserting the same. Mine is an "I" of minority (except with a child, and then I truly know the powerlessness of my own power). I can never be a true Cartesian self, because Descartes needs my body as the ground for his meaning. I can scream, write, talk, sing, analyze, argue, and yet it seems that my voice is heard as body only, the way a child listens to a mother, for tones and movement rather than symbolic meaning. While I prefer the embodiment inherent in "the feminine" because it allows me more than a bodiless Cartesian "I," I wish he would dis/cover his own body instead of using mine.

Denials of the mother's body, and the limitations it defines,[9] begin before language, but are multiplied with its development. Though she encourages language as a bond between herself and her child, because of the "ideal" realm made possible through language, desire is projected and her body is left behind. Grand historical and theological examples of this include the Bible's claim that the creative power of the world is a male god ("He" creates man first, in his own likeness, and then woman.), and Aristotle's denial of woman's part in procreation which leaves her the role of vessel.

Denial of the mother's body extends to all women, becoming misogyny. The *Malleus Maleficarum,* that compendium of woman-hating cant, claims for example: "All wickedness is but little to the wickedness of a woman. . . . What else is woman but a foe to friendship, an unescapable punishment, a necessary evil, a natural temptation, a desirable calamity, a domestic danger, a delectable detriment, an evil of nature, painted with fair colors!"[10] The vindictive violence of these remarks invites the question of the source of such pervasive anger.

*

At birth, wide-eyed and silent, he embodies the wisdom of a zen master. For weeks his cries are musical calls to fill his needs. He submits to life completely. His body conforms to my breast, my shoulder, the crook of my arm. His skin becomes an extra-sensuous extension of my own. Then suddenly he wants nothing to do with me. Belly down, hands pressed to the floor, he lifts his head, arches his back up from his blanket and screams. My body is no comfort to him. He buries his face in the blanket, stuffs it by fistfuls into his mouth and then throws his body again into a screaming arch. I cannot touch him with body or sound; I can only let him scream.

Misogyny is just one more temper tantrum—anger in the face of embodiment.

*

Given the ways in which gender marking plays upon our own experiences of our bodies, those with bodies that bleed only when injured, those who will never know the growth, movement and expulsion of another from within are, perhaps, more capable of selectively denying the implications of embodiment and, therefore, are potentially more easily caught in the web of language. Unable to know, in the body, how the mother's body is her own; how we can never reconnect to the mother; how language is forever inadequate and all that we have—these other-than-mothers seem more likely to believe in the power of Knowledge and Language; more easily tempted to use this power to deny the "(m)other" that they use for meaning. While selective denial of embodiment is possible for all speaking subjects, if it renders us unable to see that the Word, like God, is the promise of something we cannot have, we will remain easily blinded to our own humanity.

We are scientific because we lack subtlety.[11]

I remind my son of the things I have built. Apartments, houses, book-shelves, magazine racks, cabinets. We touch the wooden stool I built so that he could reach the sink and sit on the toilet. I explain its doweled joints, its simply rounded edges, while fondling the fully inch-thick pine. I remind him of the time I cut the oak for the spice rack. He watched me rout its design. Trying desperately to hide my rage, I ask, "Don't you remember the saws? The blocks of wood you played with?" I plead, "I carried you on my back." His eyes are emotionless. He knows what his friends at school have told him. This is his knowledge.

*

It seems as though the "symbolic," the realm of language and systems of "knowing," imagines a grand self-importance and takes off on a life of its own: as though it were separate from the body. The "ideal," the Platonic version of the symbolic's source, is enthroned above the world in which we live, rendering all those who think or speak its subjects. The worst atrocities have been (and still are) performed in its name.

*

He asks if Kermit the frog is real. I cannot answer simply. He cried when I told him that superman cannot "really" fly. Now he insists on testing the reality of everything. He works intensely to sort it out. He does not give up the dream of flying.

. . . he enjoys the consistency of his selfhood (that is his pleasure) and seeks its loss (that is his bliss). He is a subject split twice over, doubly perverse.[12]

The place he finds his pleasure is not the time in which he claims his self. Does science stretched to its limits reach subtlety? It seems that in search of subtlety, Barthes presses the scientific to its limits, and finds his body.

To break out of the Cartesian self, one must discover one's minority. Barthes' is his homosexuality. This opens the door for his discovery of pleasure and his own body. His perversion of the "*père-version*" creates an opening through which he gains his body. He sheds "subjectivity" to dis-cover his "individuality"; to encounter his "*corps de jouissance* (body of bliss)."[13] Needing the mother's body, or desiring primary narcissism is a far cry from breaking out on one's own; dis-covering one's own body to be something of value.

What is significance? It is meaning, insofar as it is sensually produced.[14]

In desperation and motherly rage I tell my son to stand up for himself, that he must fight back. But he knows that my body is not behind this and he wears my feeling that there must be another way like a badge of courage. I struggle with my body, the tone of my voice, to convince him, for, in spite of myself, I fear for his safety and sense of well-being.

The words of a mother barely count to a child. The child learns from her body, its attitudes, and from the music of her voice. These tell the child far more than words. These are the negatives from which the child develops the print, the imprint of the mother. As children we know her body before we ever come to know her individuality, her words or their meanings. Words function on a different level altogether, usually as manipulation (on both parts) of the bond that belies them. To know the significance of her words, we must come to know our own bodies.

Born of the desire for our initial bond to another, which it replaces, language not only plays metonymically on the memory of the initial bond, but it creates its own metaphorical bonds through repetition. These bonds are important in that they are our connection to life and our connection to each other which makes death more bearable. These bonds are the source of *"a-mort."*[15] The *"père-version"* of these bonds, in their denial of body and woman, is deadly. A language or knowledge based on a system of power that denies its own basis is doomed to loss of significance for it can never find its own ground. It creates a schism between language, the naming of the world, and reality.

I cannot say it all here, I can only imply. This limitation, one of linearity, this inability to say it all, like sensations of overfullness, especially not at the same moment, denies the body full expression. We try to trick language into serving this purpose for us with multiple meanings, layered meanings, layered words, loving words. Some become, like our bodies, servants of time. Slaves. But if we accept the limitations of language as natural and the body as morbid excess, then meaning is lost and expression is dead.

The pleasure of the text is that moment when my body pursues its own ideas—for my body does not have the same ideas I do.[16]

Writing is like combing through tangled hair. I must start with scattered ends and work out the tangles till silky smoothness emerges. I must work my way slowly and in parts, till I clear my way to the roots. There are strands of pleasure and pulls of pain when I catch short a single hair. I play my fingers across the brushlike ends and twirl silky strands between them. It brushes my hands, tickles my palms, slides across my shoulders, face, and back. My arms tire from laboring over my head. I sweat and grow irritated: I rest and return. It is a sensational process. My body recoils from the tension, yet revels in the pleasure, desiring the challenge of this artistic play. I need not kill my father or bury my mother to write; I must merely press my existence through the sieve of language. It can be a brutal process.

Language is a veil and a trap that hides us from ourselves: because it is never possible to say the body completely; because language is born of the attempt to reconnect a severance that it can never reconnect; because, by nature, it can never fulfill; because it is born of a lack, not of the penis, but of a bond. Yet, language is also born of overflow; the abundance of motherhood.

Sapientia: no power, a little knowledge, a bit of wisdom, and as much flavor as possible. [17]

On this note the dance rests until, in time, it resumes. Like dancers, at the end of their exertion, we face each other now with the awkwardness of bodies that are caught in time; arrested; startled by an ending; stopped short. Closure is an artificial construct based on the very egolinguistic assumptions that I here attempt to undermine. And yet, convention, your expectations, demand a sense of ending. Drifting off will not do. Let this be a pause in the dance to catch our breath, for the dance continues.

Notes

1. "*. . . mon corps n'a pas les même idées que moi.*" Roland Barthes, *Le Plaisir du Texte* (Paris: Éditions du Seuil, 1973), 30. Translations of this text are by Richard Miller (New York: Hill & Wang, 1975) 17.

2. Dorothy Dinnerstein, *The Mermaid and the Minotaur: Sexual Arrangements and the Human Malaise,* (New York: Harper & Row, 1976). Dinnerstein suggests that "the baby-tending sex contributed at least equally with the history-making one to the most fundamental of all human inventions: language" (22).

3. "*L'écrivain est quelqu'un qui joue avec le corps de sa mère . . .*" Barthes, *Plaisir* 60 (37).

4. Julia Kristeva, "Héréthique de l'amour" in *Tel Quel,* 74 (Winter 1977) 49. Her play on words emphasizes the importance of point of view (allowing that they are multiple) and thereby challenges the patriarchal assumption of the generic male as subject.

5. Alice Jardine, *Gynesis: Configurations of Woman and Modernity*. (Ithaca: Cornell University Press, 1985), 68–69.

6. Kristeva, "Héréthique" 31. See also Marina Warner's, *Alone of all Her Sex: The Myth and Cult of the Virgin Mary* (New York: Knopf, 1976).

7. Jane Flax, "Mother-Daughter Relationships: Psychodynamics, Politics, and Philosophy," in *The Future of Difference*, ed. Hester Eisenstein and Alice Jardine (New Brunswick: Rutgers University Press, 1980), 26. Translation by Richard Howard as *Roland Barthes by Roland Barthes* (New York: Hill and Wang, 1977).

8. *"Le sujet n'est qu'un effet de langage."* Roland Barthes, *Roland Barthes par Roland Barthes* (Paris: Éditions du Seuil, 1975) 82 (79). Translation by Richard Howard as *Roland Barthes by Roland Barthes* (New York: Hill and Wong, 1977).

9. Dinnerstein notes repeatedly the problems caused by children learning the limitations of human existence at the hands of mothers.

10. Heinrich Kramer and James Sprenger, *The Malleus Maleficarum*, trans. Montague Summers (New York: Dover Publications, 1971), 45.

11. *"Nous serions scientifiques par manque de subtilité."* Barthes, *Plaisir*, 96 (61).

12. *". . . il jouit de la consistance de son moi (c'est son plaisir) et recherche sa perte (c'est sa jouissance). C'est un sujet deux fois clivé, deux fois pervers."* Barthes, *Plaisir* 26 (14).

13. Barthes, *Plaisir* 90 (62).

14. *"Qu'est-ce que la significance? C'est le sens en ce qu'il est produit sensuellement."* Barthes, *Plaisir* 97 (61).

15. Kristeva, "Héréthique" 49 (185). The goal of her "héréthique" is the further development of these bonds.

16. *"Le plaisir du texte, c'est ce moment où mon corps va suivre ses propres idées—car mon corps n'a pas les même idées que moi."* Roland Barthes, *Plaisir* 30 (17).

17. *"Sapientia: nul pouvoir, un peu de savoir, un peu de sagesse, et le plus de saveur possible."* Barthes, *Leçon*, 1978, 46. (My translation.)

SELECTED

BIBLIOGRAPHY

The following list includes essays and books that we have found either exemplary of the kind of writing our contributors have practiced or helpful in exploring theories and practices of autobiographical criticism or both. The journals listed seem especially interested in giving voice to alternative writings.

Articles

Anderson, Linda. "At the Threshold of the Self: Women and Autobiography." *Woman's Writing: A Challenge to Theory.* Ed. Moira Monteith. Sussex: Harvester; New York: St. Martin's, 1986. 54–70.

Annas, Pamela. "Style as Politics: A Feminist Approach to the Teaching of Writing." *College English* 47 (1985): 360–71.

———. "Silences: Women's Language Research and the Teaching of Writing," in *Teaching Writing, Gender, Pedagogy and Equity.* Ed. Cynthia Caywood and Gillian R. Overing. Albany: SUNY Press, 1987. 3–17.

Behar, Ruth. "The Body in the Woman, the Story in the Woman: A Book Review and Personal Essay." *Michigan Quarterly Review* 29.4 (Fall 1990): 695–738.

Cixous, Helene. "Reaching the Point of Wheat, Or, Portrait of the Artist as a Maturing Woman." *New Literary History* 19.1 (Fall 1987): 1–22.

———. "Castration or Decapitation?" Trans. Annette Kuhn. *Signs* 7.11 (Autumn 1981): 41–55.

———. "Sorties: Out and Out: Attacks/Ways Out/Forays." *The Newly Born Woman.* Trans. Betsy Wing. Minneapolis: U of Minnesota P, 1986. 63–132.

Cooper, Jane. "Nothing Has Been Used in the Manufacture of this Poetry That Could Have Been Used in the Manufacture of Bread." *Scaffolding: New and Selected Poems.* London: Anvil, 1984. 19–44.

DeShazer, Mary. "Creation and Relation: Teaching Essays by T. S. Eliot and Adrienne Rich." *Teaching Writing: Gender, Pedagogy, and Equity.* Ed. Cynthia Caywood and Gillian R. Overing. Albany: SUNY Press, 1987. 113–122.

Dillard, Annie. "To Fashion a Text." *Inventing the Truth: The Art and Craft of Memoir.* Ed. William Zinsser. Boston: Houghton, 1987. 53–76.

DuPlessis, Rachel Blau. "For the Etruscans." *The Future of Difference.* Ed. Alice Jardine and Hester Eisenstein. Boston: G. K. Hall, 1981.

Farrell, Thomas J. "The Female and Male Modes of Rhetoric." *College English* 40.8 (April 1979): 909–21.

Fetterley, Judith. Introduction. *Provisions: A Reader from Nineteenth-Century American Women.* Bloomington: Indiana UP, 1985. 1–40.

Flax, Jane. "Postmodernism and Gender Relations in Feminist Theory." *Signs: Journal of Women in Culture and Society* 12 (1987): 621–43.

Flynn, Elizabeth A. "Composing as a Woman." *College Composition and Communication* 39 (1988): 423–35.

Freedman, Diane. "Discourse as Power: Renouncing Denial." *Anxious Power: Reading, Writing, and Ambivalence in Narrative by Women.* Ed. S. J. Sweeney and Carol Singley. Albany: SUNY Press (forthcoming, 1993).

———. "Emily Dickinson: 'Such a Little Figure . . . Visions Vast and Small.'" *The University of Dayton Review* 19.1 (1988): 61–68.

———. "Wide-Sweeping White Whale." *Crazyquilt* 1.2 (December 1986): 25–26.

———. "Wild Apple Associations." *Crazyquilt* 2.1 (March 1987): 46–48.

Frye, Marilyn. "Isms in Collision." *New York Times Book Review,* 30 April 1989: 18.

Gallop, Jane. "Thoughts in a Border State: Feminism and Literary Criticism." *Hurricane Alice.*

Hassan, Ihab. "Parabiography: The Varieties of Critical Experience." *Essays in Feminist Theory.* Ed. Victor A. Kramer. Freedom, Calif.: Crossing, 1983. 421–42.

Heller, Scott. "Experience and Expertise Meet in a New Brand of Scholarship." *The Chronicle of Higher Education,* 6 May 1992: A7–A9.

Holland, Norman. "Transactive Teaching: Cordelia's Death." *College English* 39 (Nov. 1977): 276–85.

———. "Transacting My 'Good Morrow' or, Bring Back the Vanished Critic." *Essays in Feminist Theory.* Ed. Victor A. Kramer. Freedom, Calif.: Crossing, 1983. 211–25.

Jacobus, Mary. Preface. *Reading Woman: Essays in Feminist Criticism.* New York: Columbia UP, 1986. ix–xiv.

Juhasz, Suzanne. "The Journal as Source and Model for Feminist Art: The Example of Kathleen Fraser." *Frontiers* 8.1 (1984): 16–20.

———. "The Critic as Feminist: Reflections on Women's Poetry, Feminism, and the Art of Criticism." *Women's Studies* 5 (197): 113–27.

Juncker, Clara. "Writing (with) Cixous." *College English* 50.4 (April 1988): 424–36.

Kazantis, Judith. "The Errant Unicorn." *On Gender and Writing.* Ed. Micheline Wandor. London: Pandora, 1983. 24–30.

Kennard, Jean. "Personally Speaking: Feminist Critics and the Community of Readers." *College English* 43.2 (Feb. 1981): 140–45.

Lander, Dawn. "Eve Among the Indians." *The Authority of Experience.* Ed. Arlyn Diamond and Lee Edwards. Amherst: U of Massachusetts P, 1977.

Lensink, Judy Nolte. "Expanding the Boundaries of Criticism: The Diary as Female Autobiography." *Women's Studies* 14 (1987): 39–53.

Ling, Amy. "I'm Here: An Asian-American Woman's Response." *New Literary History* 19.1 (Fall 1987): 151–68.

McCleod, Susan. "Some Thoughts About Feelings: The Affective Domain and the Writing Process." *College Composition and Communication* 38 (1987): 426–35.

Messer-Davidow, Ellen. "The Philosophical Bases of Feminist Literary Criticism." *New Literary History* 19 (1987): 65–103.

Mills, Sara, Lynne Pearce, et al. Introduction. *Feminists Reading/Feminist Readings.* Charlottesville: UP of Virginia, 1989. 1–15.

Monteith, Moira. Introduction. *Women's Writing: A Challenge to Theory.* New York: St. Martin's, 1986. 1–9.

Schweickart, Patrocinio. "Reading Ourselves: Toward a Feminist Theory of Reading." *Gender and Reading: Essays on Readers, Texts, and Contexts.* Ed. Elizabeth A. Flynn and Patrocinio Schweickart. Baltimore: Johns Hopkins UP, 1986. 31–62.

Tompkins, Jane. "Criticism and Feeling." *College English* 39.2 (Oct. 1987): 169–78.

———. "Fighting Words: Unlearning to Write the Critical Essay." *Georgia Review* 42 (1988): 585–90.

Torgovnick, Marianna. "Experimental Critical Writing." *Profession 90.* (1990): 27–27.

Wandor, Michelene. "Voices Are Wild." *Woman's Writing: A Challenge to Theory.* Ed. Moira Monteith. Sussex: Harvester; New York: St. Martin's, 1986. 72–89.

Young-Bruehl, Elisabeth. "Pride and Prejudice: Feminist Scholars Reclaim the First Person." *Lingua Franca* 1.3 (Feb. 1991): 15–18.

Zeiger, William. "The Exploratory Essay: Enfranchising the Spirit of Inquiry in College Composition." *College English* 47 (1985): 454–66.

Books

Abel, Elizabeth, ed. *Writing and Sexual Difference.* Chicago: University of Chicago Press, 1982.

Allen, Paula Gunn. *The Sacred Hoop: Recovering the American in American Indian Traditions.* Boston: Beacon, 1986.

Anzaldúa, Gloria. *Borderlands/La Frontera.* San Francisco: Spinsters/Aunt Lute, 1987.

———, ed. *Making Face, Making Soul: Haciendo Caras.* San Francisco: Aunt Lute, 1990.

——— and Cherríe Moraga, eds. *This Bridge Called My Back: Writings by Radical Women of Color.* New York: Kitchen Table, 1983.

Ascher, Carol, Louise DeSalvo, and Sara Ruddick, eds. *Between Women.* Boston: Beacon Press, 1984.

Atheker, Bettina. *Tapestries of Life: Women's Work, Women's Consciousness, and the Meaning of Daily Experience.* Amherst: U Massachusetts P, 1989.

Behar, Ruth. *Translating Woman: Crossing the Border with Esperanza's Story.* Boston: Beacon Press, 1993.

Belenky, Mary Field, et al. *Women's Ways of Knowing: The Development of Self, Voice, and Mind.* New York: Basic, 1986.

Benstock, Shari, ed. *The Private Self: Theory and Practice of Women's Autobiographical Writings.* Chapel Hill: U of North Carolina P, 1988.

Berg, Temma F., Anna Shannon Elfenbein, et al., eds. *Engendering the Word: Feminist Essays in Psychosexual Poetics.* Urbana, Ill.: U of Illinois P, 1989.

Bernikow, Louise. *Among Women.* New York: Harper, 1980.

Bleich, David. *Subjective Criticism.* Baltimore: Johns Hopkins UP, 1978.

Brownstein, Rachel. *Becoming a Heroine.* New York: Viking/Penguin, 1982.

Bulkin, Elly, Minne Bruce Pratt, and Barbara Smith. *Yours in Struggle: Three Perspectives on Anti-Semitism and Racism.* New York: Long Haul, 1984.

Callahan, John. *In the African-American Grain: The Pursuit of Voice in Twentieth-Century Black Fiction.* Urbana and Chicago: U of Illinois P, 1988. 2d ed. Middletown: Wesleyan UP, 1990.

Chester, Gail, and Sigrid Nielsen, eds. *In Other Words: Writing as a Feminist.* London: Hutchinson, 1987. No. 7 in the "Explorations in Feminism" series.

Chodorow, Nancy. *The Reproduction of Mothering: Psychoanalysis and the Sociology of Gender.* Berkeley: U California P, 1978.

Crimshaw, Jean. *Philosophy and Feminist Thinking.* Minneapolis: U of Minnesota P, 1986.

Daly, Mary. *Gyn/Ecology: The Metaethics of Radical Feminism.* Boston: Beacon, 1978.

Duplessis, Rachel. *The Pink Guitar.* New York: Routledge, 1990.

Flynn, Elizabeth A., and Patrocinio Schweickart, eds. *Gender and Reading: Essays on Readers, Texts, and Contexts.* Baltimore, Md.: Johns Hopkins UP, 1986.

Freedman, Diane. *An Alchemy of Genres: Cross-Genre Writing by American Feminist Poet-Critics.* Charlotte: UP of Virginia, 1992.

Frye, Marilyn. *The Politics of Reality: Essays in Feminist Theory.* Freedom, Calif.: Crossing, 1983.

Gallagher, Tess. *A Concert of Tenses: Essays on Poetry.* Ann Arbor: U of Michigan P, 1986.

Gallop, Jane. *Thinking Through the Body.* New York: Columbia UP, 1988.

Gelfant, Blanche. *Women Writing in America: Voices in Collage.* Hanover, N.H.: Dartmouth U and the UP of New England, 1984.

Gilligan, Carol. *In a Different Voice.* Cambridge: Harvard University Press, 1982.

Gould, Karen. *Writing in the Feminine: Feminism and Experimental Writing in Quebec.* Carbondale: Southern Illinois UP, 1990.

Grahn, Judy. *The Highest Apple: Sappho and the Lesbian Poetic Tradition.* San Francisco: Spinsters, 1985.

Griffin, Susan. *Made from this Earth.* New York: Harper, 1982.

————. *Woman and Nature: The Roaring Inside Her.* New York: Harper, 1978.

Hadas, Rachel. *Living in Time.* New Brunswick, N.J.: Rutgers UP, 1990.

Hampl, Patricia. *A Romantic Education.* Boston: Houghton, 1981.

Heilbrun, Carolyn. *Writing a Woman's Life.* New York: Norton, 1988.

Hoffman, Lenore, and Margo Culley, eds. *Women's Personal Narratives: Essays in Criticism and Pedagogy.* New York: Modern Language Association, 1985.

Holloway, Karla, and Stephanie Demetrakopoulos. *New Dimensions of Spirituality: A Biracial and Bicultural Reading of the Novels of Toni Morrison.* Westport, Conn.: Greenwood, 1987.

Howe, Susan. *My Emily Dickinson.* Berkeley: North Atlantic, 1985.

Jackson, David. *Unmasking Masculinity: A Critical Autobiography.* Cambridge, Mass.: Unwin Hyman, 1990.

James, Selma. *The Ladies and the Mammies: Jane Austen and Jean Rhys.* Bristol, England: Falling Wall, 1990.

Jouve, Nicole Ward. *White Woman Speaks with Forked Tongue: Criticism as Autobiography*. New York: Routledge, 1991.

Kaplan, Cora. *Sea Changes: Culture and Feminism*. London: Verso, 1986.

Krieger, Susan. *Social Science and the Self: Personal Essays on an Art Form*. New Brunswick: Rutgers UP, 1991.

Kumin, Maxine. *In Deep: Country Essays*. Boston: Beacon, 1988.

————. *To Make a Prairie: Essays on Poets, Poetry, and Country Living*. Ann Arbor: U of Michigan P, 1979.

Lionnet, Françoise. *Autobiographical Voices: Gender, Race, Self-Portraiture*. Ithaca and London: Cornell UP, 1989.

Lipton, Eunice. *Alias Olympia-A Woman's Search for Manet's Notorious Model and Her Own Desire*. New York: Scribner, 1993.

Lorde, Audre. *Sister Outsider: Essays and Speeches*. Trumansburg, N.Y.: Crossing, 1984.

Mairs, Nancy. *Plaintext: Deciphering a Woman's Life*. New York: Harper, 1986.

————. *Remembering the Bone House*. New York: Harper, 1989.

Miller, Nancy K. *Getting Personal: Feminist Occasions and Other Autobiographical Acts*. New York: Routledge, 1991.

Monteith, Moira, ed. *Woman's Writing: A Challenge to Theory*. Sussex: Harvester; New York: St. Martin's, 1986.

Moraga, Cherrie. *Loving in the War Years*. Boston: South End, 1983.

Oakley, Annie. *Taking It Like a Woman*. New York: Random House, 1984.

Olsen, Tillie. *Silences*. New York: Dell, 1978.

Piercy, Marge. *Parti-Colored Blocks for a Quilt*. Ann Arbor: U of Michigan P, 1986.

Rich, Adrienne. *Blood, Bread, and Poetry: Selected Prose, 1979–1985*. New York: Norton, 1986.

————. *Of Woman Born: Motherhood as Experience and Institution*. New York: Norton, 1976.

————. *On Lies, Secrets, and Silence: Selected Prose, 1966–1978*. New York: Norton, 1978.

Roe, Sue, ed. *Women Reading Women's Writing*. New York: St. Martin's/Harvester, 1987.

Rose, Phyllis. *Writing of Women: Essays in a Renaissance*. Middletown, Conn.: Wesleyan UP, 1986.

Rosen, Norma. *Accidents of Influence-Writing as a Woman and a Jew in America*. Albany, N.Y.: SUNY P, 1992.

Russ, Joanna. *How to Suppress Women's Writing*. Austin: U of Texas P, 1983.

————. *Magic Mommas, Trembling Sisters, Puritans and Powers: Feminist Essays*. Trumansburg, N.Y.: Crossing, 1985.

Ryan, Barbara. "Chrysalis: A Thesis Journal." Diss. U of Washington, 1988.

Showalter, Elaine. *The New Feminist Criticism: Essays on Women, Literature, and Theory*. New York: Pantheon Books, 1985.

Spender, Dale. *The Writing or the Sex? Or Why You Don't Have to Read Women's Writing to Know It's No Good*. New York: Pergamon, 1989.

Steedman, Carolyn. *Landscape for a Good Woman: A Story of Two Lives*. New Brunswick, N.J.: Rutgers, 1987.

Stimpson, Catherine. *Where the Meanings Are: Feminism and Cultural Spaces*. New York: Methuen, 1988.

Trinh, T. Minh-ha. *Woman, Native, Other*. Bloomington and Indianapolis: Indiana UP, 1989.

Walker, Alice. *In Search of Our Mother's Gardens*. New York: Harcourt, 1983.

————. *Living by the Word: Selected Writings.* New York: Harcourt, 1988.

Williams, Patricia. *An Alchemy of Race and Rights.* Cambridge, Mass.: Harvard UP, 1991.

Journals

The American Voice. Sallie Bingham and Frederick Smock, editors, 332 West Broadway, Suite 1215, Louisville, Ky. 40202.

Belles Lettres: A Review of Books by Women. Dept. AL, 11151 Captain's Walk, North Potomac, Md. 20878.

Calyx. P.O. Box B, Corvallis, Oreg. 97339.

Conditions. P.O. Box 159046, Brooklyn, N.Y. 11215-9046.

Diversity: The Lesbian Rag. Box 66106, Station F, Vancouver, B.C., Canada V5N 5L4.

(f.) Lip. Sandy (Frances) Duncan, et al., editors, 2533 W. 5th Avenue, Vancouver, B.C., Canada V6K I59.

Frontiers. c/o Women's Studies. University of Colorado, Boulder, Colo. 80309.

Hurricane Alice. 207 Lind Hall, 207 Church Street, SE, Minneapolis, Minn. 55455.

Ms. P.O. Box 57132, Boulder, Colo. 80322-7132.

Sinister Wisdom. P.O. Box 3252, Berkeley, Calif. 94703.

Sojourner. 143 Albany Street, Cambridge, Mass. 02139.

Sonora Review. Editorial Offices, University of Arizona, Department of English, Tucson, Ariz. 85721.

Trivia. Linda Nelson and Lise Weil, editors, P.O. Box 606, N. Amherst, Mass. 01059.

Women's Diaries: A Quarterly Newsletter. P.O. Box 18, Pound Ridge, N.Y. 10576.

Woman of Power. Char McKee, editor, P.O. Box 827, Cambridge, Mass. 02238.

CONTRIBUTORS

Julia Balén is the author of "Constitutionally (W)hole: A Psychosexual Meditation" in *Engender* (1990); "Truth Tramples Chastity, Modesty and Purity or the Tongue on Virginia's Cheek" in *Ticklish Proceedings,* edited by Kayann Short; and "Duras' Laughing Cure for Lacan's Hysterical Lack," forthcoming in *Marguerite Duras: The Unspeakable,* edited by Mechthild Cranston. Mother of a son of fifteen, Balén is currently doing research for Annette Kolodny and the Arizona Board of Regents Commission on the Status of Women while finishing a Ph.D. in Comparative Literature at the University of Arizona. Her dissertation explores that point of connection between literature, language, and bodily existence.

Dana Beckelman is completing a Ph.D. in Rhetoric and Composition at the University of Wisconsin/Milwaukee. She is interested in psychoanalytic and feminist rhetorical theory and has published in *Canadian Women Studies/les cahiers de la femme* and *Freshman English News.*

Ellen Brown, a survivor of United Methodist parsonages scattered across Louisiana, is currently completing a book-length feminist reading of Henry James's New York Edition. Her next project involves a series of essays employing narrative criticism to investigate women's literature, language, madness, and space.

Sandra M. Brown received an M.F.A. in fiction writing from the University of Pittsburgh, class of '90, the year her son graduated from high school and her daughter from college. Her long-suffering husband notes that her becoming a writer is a fitting destiny for the 1958 winner of the Betty Crocker Homemaker of Tomorrow Award—a cleverly disguised writing contest.

Rosanne Kanhai-Brunton, from Trinidad, received her Ph.D. from Pennsylvania State University in 1990. She is Assistant Professor of English at Western Washington University. She is active in CAFRA, Caribbean Association for Feminist Research and Action. She lives in Bellingham, Washington with her two sons.

Suzanne L. Bunkers is Professor of English and Women's Studies at Mankato State University. For the past ten years she has been doing research on unpublished diaries and journals by nineteenth-century Midwestern American women. Her books, *The Diary of Caroline Seabury* (1991) and *"Faithful Friends": 19th Century Midwestern Women's Diaries* (forthcoming), are part of the University of Wisconsin Press's series on American autobiography. At present, Suzanne is completing an edition of *The Diary of Sarah Gillespie Huftalen,* and she is writing *In Search of Susanna: An Auto/Biography* (both forthcoming from the University of Iowa Press). She lives in Mankato, Minnesota with her daughter Rachel and their feline friends, Dani, Emily, Mitzi, and Kitty.

Peter Carlton used to teach English at St. John's University in Minnesota. He now does freelance writing and editing and lives in Minneapolis.

Brenda Daly, Associate Professor of English and Women's Studies, Iowa State University, is currently writing a book called *Changing Lives: Father Daughter Incest in Twentieth-Century Fiction and Film.* Her book, *Dialogic Daughters in the Fiction of Joyce Carol Oates,* is now under review by Sandra M. Gilbert's Ad Feminam series with Southern Illinois Press. She has co-edited the collection *Narrating Mothers: Theorizing Maternal Subjectivities* (1991).

Victoria Ekanger is Acting Instructor at the University of Washington, where she earned an M.A., M.F.A., and Ph.D., and now teaches Women's Studies, Creative Writing, and American Literature. She is completing a novel about the ins and outs of Catholic guilt.

Diane P. Freedman, Assistant Professor of English at the University of New Hampshire, teaches courses in U.S. American literature and literary criticism. "Border-Crossing as Method and Motif" is part of a chapter of her book, *An Alchemy of Genres: Cross-Genre Writing by American Women Poet-Critics* (University Press of Virginia, 1992). Her essays also appear in the *Bucknell Review, College Literature,* and *Women and Language* and in two books by SUNY Press, *Constructing and Reconstructing Gender* and *Anxious Power: Reading, Writing, and Ambivalence in Narrative by Women.* Her poems have been published in *Sou'wester, Crazyquilt, Ascent,* and *Wind.* She is editor of *Millay at 100: A Critical Reappraisal* and co-editor, with Olivia Frey, of *Nexus: Writings on Location* (both forthcoming).

Olivia Frey is Associate Professor of English and Director of Women's Studies at St. Olaf College, where she teaches in the Paracollege—an alternative program within the college. She teaches and has published on feminist studies, peace studies, and educational studies. She is presently working on a book, *The Face of Critical Discourse: Autobiographical Criticism* and a second anthology, *Nexus: Writings on Location,* with Diane P. Freedman.

Shirley Nelson Garner is Professor of English at the University of Minnesota, Twin Cities. She is co-editor, with Madelon Sprengnether and Claire Kahane, of *The (M)other Tongue: Essays in Feminist Psychoanalytic Interpretation* (Cornell University Press, 1985) and a co-editor, with the Personal Narratives Collective, of *Interpreting Women's Lives: Personal Narratives and Feminist Theory* (Indiana University Press, 1989). She is a founder of *Hurricane Alice: A Feminist Quarterly* and on its editorial board; she currently directs the University of Minnesota's Center for Advanced Feminist Studies.

Henry Louis Gates, Jr., the W. E. B. Du Bois Professor of the Humanities at Harvard, is the author of *The Signifying Monkey, Figures in Black,* and *Loose Canons: Notes on the Culture Wars.*

Melody Graulich teaches American Literature at the University of New Hampshire. She has published a number of essays on American women writers and feminist criticism. She also edited *Western Trails: A Collection of Stories by Mary Austin* and a previously unpublished Austin novel, *Cactus Thorn,* and she wrote essays on Austin included in each volume as well as in the recent reprint of Austin's autobiography, *Earth Horizon.* For some time she has been struggling to find an autobiographical voice to use in a book-length study of Western women writers, *Liberating Traditions: Women Writers and the American West.* "Somebody Must Say These Things" is dedicated to Melody's mother, Gloria Graulich.

Gail B. Griffin is Associate Professor of English and Director of Women's Studies at Kalamazoo College in Michigan. In addition to poetry, criticism, and essays on the history of women's education, she is the author of *Calling: Essays on Teaching in the Mother Tongue* (Trilogy Books, 1992).

Dolan Hubbard, a 1986–1988 Carolina Minority Postdoctoral Scholar, is Assistant Professor in the Department of English at the University of Tennessee at Knoxville. He has published in *Black American Literature Forum, CLA Journal, The Centennial Review, The Langston Hughes Review* and *Obsidian II.*

Kendall entered academia late in life, after a long struggle to make ends meet as an actress and writer. She holds B.A. and M.A. degrees in English from the University of New Orleans and a Ph.D. in drama from the University of Texas at Austin. Her anthology of eighteenth-century women's plays, *Love and Thunder* (Methuen, U.K.), is available from Heinemann Educational Books. She is currently in Nigeria as a Fulbright Scholar, studying Nigerian women in theater.

Susan Koppelman, an independent scholar, lives in St. Louis and is the editor of numerous collections of short fiction by women, including *May Your Days Be Merry and Bright and other Christmas Stories by Women* (New American Library, 1990), and, with Dorothy Abbott, *The Signet Classic Book of Southern Short Stories* (Signet, 1991). Her most recent collection is *Women's Friendships: A Collection of Short Stories* (University of Oklahoma, 1991). She edited the original collection of feminist literary criticism *Images of Women in Fiction: Feminist Perspectives* (Popular Press, 1972). She keeps an extensive correspondence going with her many writer friends.

Shirley Geok-lin Lim is Professor of Asian American Studies at the University of California, Santa Barbara. She has edited *Approaches to Teaching Kingston's The Woman Warrior* (MLA Press) and co-edited *Reading Asian American Literatures* (Temple University Press, 1992) and *The Forbidden Stitch: An Asian American Woman's Anthology* (Calyx, 1989). Her critical book, *Literature and Nationalisms: Selected English-Language Writers from the Philippines and Singapore,* is forthcoming (New Day, Quezon City). Author of three books of poetry and a collection of short stories, she has received the Commonwealth Poetry Prize, Asiaweek Short Story Prize, and the Before Columbus American Book Award.

Linda Robertson teaches writing and chairs the Rhetoric Department at Hobart and William Smith Colleges.

Carol Taylor teaches folkore, black literature, multi-ethnic literature, and composition at Ohio State University–Mansfield, in the Department of English. She has done extensive fieldwork among the Sea Island blacks (commonly referred to as "Gullahs" or "Geeches") off the coast of South Carolina and Georgia. Her work examines the context in which their traditions and customs are manifested and is concerned with the people's historical vision of themselves, their land, and their respective islands.

Jane Tompkins, Professor of English at Duke University, has published articles and books on nineteenth-century American literature, literary theory and pedagogy, reader-response theory, and the rhetoric of contemporary criticism. Her most recent book is *West of Everything: The Inner Life of Westerns* (Oxford, 1992).

Cheryl B. Torsney, Associate Professor of English at West Virginia University, teaches American literature, women's writing, and literary theory. The author of a number of essays on Henry James and a critical study *Constance Fenimore Woolson: The Grief of Artistry*, she is also the editor of *Critical Essays on Constance Fenimore Woolson* and, with Judy Elsley, *Quilt Culture: Essays on the Quilt as Metaphor*.

Traise Yamamoto is a poet and a graduate student at the University of Washington, where she is writing her dissertation on the construction of Japanese-American female subjectivity.

Frances Murphy Zauhar is Assistant Professor of English at St. Vincent College. She is currently working on a book of early American women writers and the literary profession.